The
Bumper Book
Of
Babies' Names

The Bumper Book Of Babies' Names

by

Jacqueline Harrod and André Page

Contents

	PAGE
Introduction	7
Glossary	8
Boys' Names A–Z	9
Girls' Names A–Z	165

Illustrations by Robert Day.

Introduction

Until the time of William the Conqueror, surnames were not used in Britain and so the only way to define any particular person was by their Christian name. In the early days the list of Christian names was very short. But, over the years, as each new influx of foreigners settled in Britain, the list gradually lengthened; the Anglo-Saxons, Norsemen, Danes, Normans, Huguenots and Flemish weavers, to name just a few, all introduced interesting, new names to Britain, many of which are still in use today.

In the Middle Ages most boys were given the following names: John, Richard, Thomas and William; while the choice for girls was similarly limited to Joan, Alice, Agnes, Cicely and Matilda.

The Puritans of the seventeenth century abandoned the names of saints and instead gave their children obscure names they found in the Bible. They also introduced names based on the abstract virtues of Faith, Hope and Patience.

Poets and playwrights of the sixteenth and seventeenth centuries coined many names favoured by modern parents, among them Marina and Vanessa.

And through it all, as now, royal names were consistently adopted; while aristocratic surnames began to be used as Christian names by those who had no family connection.

Victorians, for some unknown reason, began the craze for botanical names – Poppy, Heather, Lily, Daisy – and extended this to the names of minerals and precious stones.

But it is the twentieth century which unleashed the vast number of names in common use today. Russia, Germany, Italy, Ireland, France and Spain have all had an influence. As have, of course, the numerous American and Australian films and television programmes we see daily on our screens. The list of possible names is now so long that expectant parents are naturally often overwhelmed by the choice available to them.

We hope this collection will help you to choose the right name for your child. But please remember: the name has got to last a lifetime so don't select a name in haste that your child will regret at length!

Glossary

b. = born
c. = circa (about)
d. = died
q.v. = quod vide (which see)

Boys' Names

AARON
From the Hebrew, meaning 'high mountain'. In the Bible, the name of Moses' older brother (by three years) and the first High Priest of Israel. Aaron had a rod which transformed into a snake, devouring the rods of Pharaoh's sorcerers, proving his divine calling.

Two notable possessors of the name are Aaron Hill the poet (1685–1750), and the American composer Aaron Copland, most famous for his orchestral suite, *Appalachian Spring*.

ABEL
From the Hebrew, meaning 'breath', or the Assyrian, meaning 'son'. The second son of Adam and Eve, a shepherd, murdered in a fit of jealousy by his brother, Cain.

The Puritans made the name popular as they scrutinised the Bible for names to replace those of non-Biblical saints.

Abel was King of Denmark 1250–1252.

ABELARD
From the Teutonic Adelhard, meaning 'resolute'.

ABIEL
This name means 'father of strength'.

ABNER
From the Hebrew Abhner, meaning 'father of light'. In the Bible, Abner was a cousin of Saul. This is a first name which is mainly used in the United States today.

ABRAHAM

From the Hebrew, meaning 'father of a multitude'. The Old Testament Abraham was father of the Hebrew nation: his son, Isaac, was born when the patriarch was one hundred years old. (In the Koran Abraham is entitled El Khalil, 'the friend of God'.)

Although borne by several early Christian saints, and mentioned in the Domesday Book, the name was only made popular in Britain by the Puritans of the seventeenth century.

ADALBERT

German for Albert, q.v.

ADAM

From the Hebrew, meaning 'red'. Perhaps this denotes the colour of the earth used by the Almighty to form the Biblical first man.

The name was most popular in the north of England in the thirteenth century because of an outlaw, Adam Bell, a Robin Hood type hero.

Adam de la Hale was the author of the first known opera, *The Play of Robin and Marion,* performed in Naples in 1275.

ADAMO

Italian for Adam, q.v.

ADAN

Spanish for Adam, q.v.

ADAO

Portuguese for Adam, q.v.

ADDA

A Welsh form of Adam, q.v.

ADLAI

From the Hebrew Adlai, meaning 'witness'. Little used today.

ADOLF

German for Adolph, q.v.

ADOLPH

From the Germanic, meaning 'noble warrior'.

ADOLPHE
French for Adolph, q.v.

ADOLPHO
Italian and Spanish for Adolph, q.v.

ADOLPHUS
Swedish for Adolph, q.v.

ADRIAN
From the Latin, meaning 'man from the Adriatic'. The only Englishman to become Pope, Nicholas Brakespear, took the name Adrian IV and was head of the church from 1154–1159.

AENEAS
From the Greek, meaning 'one who is praised'.

AGOSTO
Italian for Augustus, q.v.

AIDAN
Gaelic diminutive, meaning 'little fiery one'. St. Aidan was a seventh century Irish monk who founded a monastery on Lindisfarne, where English boys were educated. He was known as the Apostle of Northumberland. He died at Bamburgh in 651. His emblem in art is a stag.

AILMER
Mentioned in the Curia Regis. A possible variant of Aylmer, q.v.

AINSLEY
Originally a surname, meaning 'my meadow', which has become a popular first name.

AINSLIE
A variant of Ainsley, q.v.

AL
A diminutive of Albert (q.v.) and of Alan (q.v.).

ALAIN
A French form of Alan, q.v.

11

ALAN
A Celtic name, meaning 'harmony'. It was introduced into England at the time of the Norman Conquest. Two companions of William the Conqueror, Alain, Count of Brittany and Alain le Roux, 1st Earl of Richmond, popularised the name but not the spelling, which was speedily altered by the English.

ALARIC
From the Old German, meaning 'ruler of all'. The Visigoth King, Alaric I, was responsible for the sacking of Rome in A.D. 410.
    The Victorians revived the name in the mid-nineteenth century.

ALARICO
Spanish for Alaric, q.v.

ALASDAIR
The Gaelic form of Alexander (q.v.), Alastair and Alistair are popular phonetic spellings of this name.

ALASTAIR
A variant of Alasdair, q.v.

ALBAN
From the Latin, meaning 'white'. St. Alban was the first British martyr. A Romano-Briton, he lived in Verulamium, now the city of St. Albans. During Diocletian's persecution, he gave shelter to a fleeing Christian and was beheaded for this act of charity in A.D. 209. St. Alban's Abbey stands on the site.

ALBERIC
Swedish for Aubrey, q.v.

ALBERT
From the Old German, meaning 'noble knight'. St. Albert the Great (1206–1280) is called 'The Universal Teacher' because he wrote on many topics from theology to physics and botany.
    Prince Albert of Saxe-Coburg-Gotha married Queen Victoria in 1840 and made the name very popular.

ALBERTO
Italian for Albert, q.v.

ALBIN
From the Latin, meaning 'one who is fair'.

ALBRECHT
German for Albert, q.v.

ALDO
From the Teutonic, meaning 'old'.

ALDOUS
From the Teutonic, meaning 'old'. This name is mentioned in the Hundred Rolls of A.D. 1273.

ALDRED
From the Teutonic Aethelred, meaning 'mighty'. This name is mentioned in the Domesday Book.

ALDUS
A variant of Aldous, q.v.

ALEC
A diminutive of Alexander, q.v.

ALESSANDRO
Italian for Alexander, q.v.

ALEX
A diminutive of Alexander, q.v.

ALEXANDER
From the Greek, meaning 'defending man'. Bestowed upon many saints, martyrs and kings, it has been a popular name for over three thousand years.

Alexander the Great (356–323 B.C.), conqueror of most of the known world, was admired for his courage and acts of humanity and became the hero of numerous English and French medieval romances.

The inventor, Alexander Graham Bell (1847–1922) and Sir Alexander Fleming (1881–1955), discoverer of penicillin, are worthy of note.

ALEXANDRE
French for Alexander, q.v.

ALEXIO
Portuguese for Alexander, q.v.

ALEXIS
See the entry in the girls' section.

ALF
A diminutive of Alfred, q.v.

ALFIE
A diminutive of Alfred, q.v.

ALFRED
From the Old English, meaning 'elf counsel'. King Alfred the Great (849–899) was responsible for England's first navy and was the first English king to have his face on a coin.

Other famous men to bear the name include the poet Alfred, Lord Tennyson (1809–1892), and the Swedish inventor, Alfred Nobel (1833–1896) founder of the annual Nobel prizes.

ALFREDO
Italian and Spanish for Alfred, q.v.

ALGERNON
From the French, meaning 'with whiskers'. Supposedly a nickname given to an eleventh century Count of Boulogne, named Eustace, to avoid confusion with his father, who had the same name.

Algernon Moncrieff is the debonair friend of Jack Worthing, hero of Oscar Wilde's masterpiece, *The Importance of Being Earnest.*

ALGIE
A diminutive of Algernon, q.v.

ALGY
A diminutive of Algernon, q.v.

ALICK
A variant of Alexander, q.v.

ALISDAIR
A variant of Alexander, q.v.

ALISTAIR
A variant of Alexander, q.v.

ALISTER
A variant of Alexander, q.v.

ALLAN
A variant of Alan, q.v.

ALLARDE
From this surname, from Picardy in France, meaning 'brave and noble'.

ALLEN
A variant of Alan, q.v.

ALLYN
A variant of Alan, q.v.

ALMAR
A name mentioned in the Domesday Book and from the Ango-Saxon Aethelmar, meaning 'noble'.

ALMARIC
From the Anglo-Saxon Aethelmar, meaning 'noble'. This name is mentioned in some thirteenth century records in Berkshire.

ALMERIC
From the Teutonic, meaning 'energetic'.

ALNOD
The name of a landholder mentioned in the Domesday Book. Little used today.

ALOISIUS
A variant of Aloysius, q.v.

ALONSO
Spanish for Alphonso, q.v.

ALONZO
A variant of Alphonso, q.v.

ALOYSIUS
From the Latin, meaning 'warrior'. St. Aloysius lived in Italy in the sixteenth century.

ALPHONSE
French for Alphonso, q.v.

ALPHONSO
From the Teutonic, meaning 'ready noble'.

ALRIC
Little used today as a first name but it was the name of a bishop mentioned in the Domesday Book. It possibly comes from the Germanic Almaric, q.v.

ALSTON
From the Anglo-Saxon Aethelston, meaning 'of noble estate'.

ALUN
A variant of Alan, q.v.

ALURIC
A name mentioned in the Domesday Book, meaning 'elf's counsel'.

ALVA
From the Latin, meaning 'blond'. This was the second name of Thomas Edison, the American inventor.

ALVIN
From the Old German Alhwin, meaning 'great friend'.

ALVIS
From the Norse Alviss, meaning 'full of wisdom'.

ALWIN
From the Anglo-Saxon Aethelwin, meaning 'friendly'. This name is mentioned in the Domesday Book.

ALWYN
A variant of Alwin, q.v.

AMADEUS
From the Latin, meaning 'lover of God'. Amadeus was the second

name of the composer Mozart.

AMBROISE
French for Ambrose, q.v.

AMBROSE
From the Greek, meaning 'pertaining to the Immortals'. Ambrosia was the food of the gods, as nectar was their drink.
St. Ambrose (c. 334–397), Bishop of Milan, is numbered among the four great Latin Doctors of the Church and the first to make extensive use of hymns for both teaching and divine praise.

AMBROSI
Italian for Ambrose, q.v.

AMBROSIO
Spanish for Ambrose, q.v.

AMBROSIUS
Dutch and Swedish for Ambrose, q.v.

AMERIGO
Italian for Emery, q.v.

AMERY
From the Old German Almaric, meaning 'noted ruler'.

AMIAS
A variant of Amyas, q.v.

AMORY
From the Old German Almaric, meaning 'noted ruler'.

AMOS
From the Hebrew, meaning 'bearer of a burden'. Amos was a prophet mentioned in the Bible.

AMYAS
From this surname and meaning 'coming from Amiens'.

ANASTASIUS
From the Greek, meaning 'risen again'.

17

ANATOLE
From the Greek, meaning 'man from the east'.

ANATOLIO
Spanish for Anatole, q.v.

ANDERS
Swedish for Andrew, q.v.

ANDRÉ
French for Andrew, q.v.

ANDREA
Italian for Andrew, q.v.

ANDREAS
Dutch and Swedish for Andrew, q.v.

ANDRES
Spanish for Andrew, q.v.

ANDREW
From the Greek, meaning 'manly'. The first apostle called by Jesus, brother to St. Peter and patron saint of both Scotland and Russia. Over six hundred churches are dedicated to St. Andrew in England alone.
  Prince Andrew, Duke of York (b. 1960), is the bearer of this enduringly popular name.

ANDY
A diminutive of Andrew, q.v.

ANEURIN
From the Welsh, meaning 'gold'. The Welsh Labour politician, Aneurin Bevan (1897–1960) made this name famous in modern times. He introduced the National Health Service in 1948.

ANGELO
From the Italian, meaning 'angel'.

ANGUS
From the Gaelic, meaning 'one choice'. The legendary Aonghus Turimleach was one of three Irish brothers who invaded Scotland.

They brought with them the 'Stone of Scone', which used to reside beneath the Coronation Chair in Westminster Abbey and has now been returned to Scotland.

The Clan MacDonell have used the name Angus since the fifteenth century.

ANSELM
From the Teutonic, meaning 'divine helmet'.

ANSELME
French for Anselm, q.v.

ANSELMI
Italian for Anselm, q.v.

ANSELMO
Portuguese and Spanish for Anselm, q.v.

ANTHONY
The name of an ancient Roman family, the most famous of whom was Mark Antony (83–30 B.C.), the lover of Queen Cleopatra.

Many saints have this name, including St. Anthony of Egypt (251–356), the founder of monasticism, and St. Anthony of Padua (1195–1231), a famous preacher and patron of lost property.

The abbreviation Tony first appeared in the seventeenth century.

ANTON
Swedish and German for Anthony, q.v.

ANTONIO
Italian, Spanish and Portuguese for Anthony, q.v.

ANTONY
A variant of Anthony, q.v.

ARALDO
Italian for Harold, q.v.

ARCHAMBAULT
French for Archibald, q.v.

ARCHIBALD
From the Old German, meaning 'very bold'. Another of the names

brought to England at the Norman Conquest. The clans Campbell and Douglas particularly favour this name.

Archie Armstrong was court jester to James I of England. Archie Rice is the anti-hero of John Osborne's play, *The Entertainer.* And an Archibald of renown was the teddy bear loved by Sir John Betjeman, mentioned in his poetic autobiography, *Summoned by Bells.*

ARCHIE
A diminutive of Archibald, q.v.

ARCHIMBALD
German for Archibald, q.v.

ARISTIDE
From the French, meaning 'best son'.

ARMAND
French for Herman, q.v.

ARMANDO
Spanish for Herman, q.v.

ARMITAGE
From this surname, meaning 'one who lived by the hermitage'.

ARNALDO
Spanish for Arnold, q.v.

ARNAUD
French for Arnold, q.v.

ARNOLD
From the Old German, meaning 'eagle power'. This name evolved from the Norman version, Arnaud. It was rare until the 1870s; revived in honour of Thomas Arnold, reforming headmaster of Rugby and his poet son, Matthew Arnold, perhaps?

ARNOLDO
Italian for Arnold, q.v.

ART
A diminutive of Arthur, q.v.

ARTHUR
From the Gaelic, meaning 'stone' or the Celtic, meaning 'a bear'. King Arthur, who supposedly flourished in the fifth to sixth centuries, is the most famous bearer of the name.

Prince Arthur (1486–1502) was the eldest son of Henry VII. The name became popular in the nineteenth century due to Arthur Wellesley, Duke of Wellington (1769–1852), the conqueror of Napoleon.

Tennyson's poem, *In Memoriam,* was written to commemorate his friend, Arthur Hallam.

ARTURO
Italian and Spanish for Arthur, q.v.

ARTUS
French for Arthur, q.v.

ASA
From the Hebrew, meaning 'physician'.

ASHER
From the Hebrew, meaning 'fortunate'. In Genesis in the Old Testament, Asher was a son of Jacob.

ASHLEY
From the Old English, meaning 'ash wood'. Originally a place and surname, it may have been used as a first name in honour of Anthony Ashley Cooper, Earl of Shaftesbury (1801–1885), the social reformer. The statue of Eros at Piccadilly Circus in London was erected in his honour.

ASTLEY
From the Old English, meaning 'eastern wood'. Originally a place name and the family name of the barons Hastings.

AUBERT
French for Albert, q.v.

AUBIN
French for Albin, q.v.

AUBREY
From the Old German, meaning 'elf counsel'. It was brought from

Normandy to Britain by the de Veres, who became Earls of Oxford.

The artist Aubrey Beardsley (1872–1898) is well-known for his art-nouveau book illustrations, particularly for *The Yellow Book.*

AUGUSTINE
A Latin diminutive, meaning 'venerable'. The African St. Augustine of Hippo (354–430) wrote two books which are still in print: his auto-biography, *The Confessions of St. Augustine,* and the *City of God.*

Another St. Augustine arrived in Kent in 597 and became the first Archbishop of Canterbury.

AUGUSTUS
From the Latin, meaning 'venerable'. This was taken as a title by Roman emperors, beginning with Octavian, the adopted son of Julius Caesar. The month of August is named after him.

The German royal family, the Hanoverians, brought the name to Britain in the eighteenth century and it has been the name of two Polish kings.

AUSTEN
A variant of Austin, q.v.

AUSTIN
The medieval form of Augustine.

AVEARY
A variant of Avery, q.v.

AVERY
This name means 'ruler of elves'.

AYLMER
From the Teutonic, meaning 'famous noble'.

AYLWARD
Fom the Old English Agilward, meaning 'guardian'.

AYLWYN
From the Old English Aethelwin, meaning 'noble friend'.

BALDOVIN
Italian for Baldwin, q.v.

BALDWIN
From the Germanic Baldavin, meaning 'bold friend'. Baldwin was the Count of Flanders in the ninth century, and this name is mentioned in the Domesday Book.

BALTHASAR
From the Semitic, meaning 'king's protector'. This was the name of one of the Three Wise Men.

BARCLAY
From this surname, meaning 'one who lived by the birch meadow'.

BARNABA
Italian for Barnabas, q.v.

BARNABAS
From the Aramaic, meaning 'son of consolation'. In the New Testament, Barnabas was a companion to St. Paul and is believed to have urged St. Mark to write his gospel.
    Later, St. Barnabas went as a missionary to Cyprus, being martyred there at the Port of Salamis.

BARNABE
French for Barnabas, q.v.

BARNABY
This is the anglicised version of Barnabas. The unfortunate Barnaby Fitzpatrick was whipping boy to the Tudor king, Edward VI.

Dickens' novel about the Gordon Riots, *Barnaby Rudge,* first published in 1841, must always spring to mind.

BARNARD
French for Bernard, q.v.

BARNEBAS
Spanish for Barnabas, q.v.

BARNETT
A variant of Bernard, q.v.

BARNEY
A variant of Barnaby, q.v.

BARON
From the Old English, meaning 'noble'.

BARRIE
A variant of Barry, q.v.

BARRINGTON
A common English place name and aristocratic surname, now often used as a first name.

The Barrington family motto – 'Honesta quam splendida' – translates as 'Honourable acquisitions rather than splendid'.

BARRY
From the Celtic, meaning 'spear'. Barry is a place name in both Scotland and Wales, while Barry Island is named after an early Irish hermit.

W. M. Thackeray wrote a novel entitled *The Memoirs of Barry Lyndon,* which first appeared in 1844.

BART
A diminutive of Bartholomew, q.v.

BARTHEL
German for Bartholomew, q.v.

BARTHELEMY
French for Bartholomew, q.v.

BARTHOLOMEUS
Dutch and Swedish for Bartholomew, q.v.

BARTHOLOMEW
From the Aramaic, meaning 'son of Talmai'. He was one of the twelve apostles, but little is known about him. Tradition states that he spread the Gospel in India and Armenia, where he was martyred by being flayed alive.

Ben Jonson's comedy, *Bartholomew Fair,* first performed in 1614, commemorates an annual fair begun on St. Bartholomew's Day, 24th August 1133. This raised funds for St. Bartholomew's Hospital in London.

The fair took place every year until 1855, by which time the rowdiness and nuisance caused had become intolerable.

BARTLEMY
A variant of Bartholomew, q.v.

BARTOLOME
Spanish for Bartholomew, q.v.

BARTOLOMEO
Italian for Bartholomew, q.v.

BASIL
From the Greek, meaning 'kingly'. Always a very popular name in Eastern Europe, the Crusaders brought it back with them to England.

St. Basil the Great, Doctor of the Church (c.330–379), had a remarkable family: his grandmother, father and mother, his elder sister and two younger brothers are *all* canonised saints! Surely unique.

Basilica originally meant a royal palace before it acquired its modern meaning of church.

BASILE
French for Basil, q.v.

BASILIO
Spanish and Italian for Basil, q.v.

BASILIUS
Dutch and Swedish for Basil, q.v.

BASSETT
From the French *le bas*, meaning 'small in stature'.

BAUDOIN
French for Baldwin, q.v.

BAXTER
From this surname, meaning 'baker'.

BEAU
From the French, meaning 'handsome'. A best-selling novel by P.C. Wren about life in the French Foreign Legion, first published in 1924, has a hero named 'Beau Geste' (which is also the title of the book).

Earlier than this a 'beau' was a man obsessed with fashion: 'Beau' Nash of Bath and George 'Beau' Brummell, friend of George IV, are two examples.

BEDE
Old English for 'prayer'. An English historian, the Venerable Bede (c.673–735) was a monk in a monastery at Jarrow.

His most famous work is the *Ecclesiastical History of the English People*, written to cover the period of the Roman Invasion to A.D. 731. He was the first English Doctor of the Church and the only Englishman named in Dante's *Paradiso*.

BELTRAN
Spanish for Bertram, q.v.

BEN
A diminutive of Benedict (q.v.) and of Benjamin (q.v.)

BENEDETTO
Italian for Benedict, q.v.

BENEDICT
From the Latin, meaning 'blessed'. There are at least five canonised saints named Benedict; the most famous of whom was the founder of the Benedictine Order, dying at the first Benedictine Monastery on Monte Cassino in 547.

Another, St. Benedict Labre, is the patron saint of tramps. Bennett is a medieval diminutive of the name.

BENGT
Swedish for Benedict, q.v.

BENITO
Spanish and Italian for Benedict, q.v.

BENJAMIN
From the Hebrew, meaning 'son of my right hand'. In the Old Testament, Benjamin was the youngest and favourite son of Jacob and Rachel.

Benjamin Disraeli, Earl of Beaconsfield (1804–1881), novelist and prime minister, was the most famous bearer of the name in Victorian times.

'Big Ben', nickname of the clock and tower of the Houses of Parliament, was reputedly named after Big Ben Caunt, the seventeen stone, bare-knuckle boxing champion of England in the 1840s and 1850s. Another, more dignified, theory proposed that it was named in honour of a portly Welshman, Sir Benjamin Hall. He was First Commissioner of Public Works from 1855 to 1858, when the bell was ordered.

BENJAMINO
Italian for Benjamin, q.v.

BENJIE
A diminutive of Benjamin, q.v.

BENNY
A diminutive of Benjamin, q.v.

BENOIT
French for Benedict, q.v.

BERKELEY
An English place name and surname, meaning 'birch wood', now used as a first name.

BERNARD
From the Old German, meaning 'brave as a bear'. As with many names, this was brought to England at the Norman Conquest and is mentioned several times in the Domesday Book.

St. Bernard of Clairvaux (1090–1153) founded the very austere Cistercian Order.

St. Bernard of Montjoux (c.996–1081) had built two rest houses for travellers at the top of two Alpine passes, now known as the Great and Little St. Bernard. He is the patron saint of mountaineers.

BERNARDO
Spanish and Italian for Bernard, q.v.

BERNHARD
Swedish and German for Bernard, q.v.

BERNIE
A diminutive of Bernard, q.v.

BERT
A diminutive of Albert (q.v.) and of Bertram (q.v.)

BERTIE
A pet form of the names Albert and Bertram, now used independently. The most famous Bertie in Britain is Bertie Wooster, the delightful, upper class hero of a series of books by P.G. Wodehouse.

BERTRAM
From the Teutonic, meaning 'bright raven'.

BERTRAND
French for Bertram, q.v.

BEVERLEY
See the entry in the girls' section.

BEVIS
From the Old French, meaning a 'bull'.

BILL
A diminutive of William, q.v.

BILLY
A diminutive of William, q.v.

BING
From the Old German, meaning 'from the hollow'.

BLAIR
From the Gaelic, meaning 'battleground'. A Scottish surname, now used as a first name.

BLAISE
From the Latin, meaning 'stuttering'. Little is known about St. Blaise, a bishop martyred in the fourth century, whose feast day is 3rd February. He is the patron saint of diseases of the throat. The *Pensées* of Blaise Pascal (1623–1662), a French philosopher, scientist and writer, are still read.

BLAKE
From the Old Norse, meaning 'pale' or 'shining'. A place name and surname, now used as a first name. It was originally given as a nickname to someone with extremely fair hair or complexion.

BLAKELEY
From this surname, meaning 'one who dwells by the black meadow'.

BOAZ
From the Hebrew, meaning 'in him is strength'. The Old Testament Ruth married the wealthy Boaz. The name was popular with Puritans in the seventeenth century.

BOB
A diminutive of Robert, q.v.

BOBBY
A diminutive of Robert, q.v.

BONAR
From the Old French, meaning 'gentle'.

BONIFACE
From the Latin, meaning 'good man'.

BONIFACIO
Spanish and Italian for Boniface, q.v.

BONIFACIUS
Dutch, Swedish and German for Boniface, q.v.

BORIS

From the Slavonic, meaning 'to fight'. This popular Russian name came into use in Britain in the twentieth century. Saints Boris (d.1015) and his brother Gleb, the sons of Russia's first Christian prince, are venerated in the Orthodox calendar on 24th July.

Boris Leonidovich Pasternak (1890–1960), Russian poet and author of the famous novel, *Dr. Zhivago*, was awarded the Nobel Prize for literature in 1958. (The Ashmolean Museum, Oxford, possesses a fine portrait of the young Boris and his brother Alexander, painted by their father, Leonid.)

BOYD

From the Celtic, meaning 'yellow haired'.

BOYLE

This name means 'born in the time of danger'.

BRAD

A diminutive of Bradley, q.v.

BRADLEY

An Old English place name, meaning 'broad clearing', and surname, now used as a first name.

Bradley Headstone is a character in the Dickens' novel, *Our Mutual Friend*, first published in 1865.

BRAMWELL

An Old English place name, meaning 'bramble well', and surname, now used as a first name.

William Bramwell Booth (1856–1929), the son of the founder of the Salvation Army, appears to have popularised the name.

BRANDON

An English place name, meaning 'hill covered with broom', and surname, now used as a first name.

Duke of Brandon is one of the many titles of the Duke of Hamilton.

BRANWELL

A variant of Bramwell. The unfortunate (Patrick) Branwell Brontë (1817–1848), brother to the writers Charlotte, Emily, and Anne, is the most famous bearer of the name.

BREE

This is a most unusual modern name, seemingly taken from the book *The Lord of the Rings* by J.R.R. Tolkien. The village of Bree, under Bree-Hill, was the chief village of Bree-land. The men of Bree had brown hair and were short and stocky with a cheerful disposition.

BRENDAN

From the Old Irish, meaning 'stinking hair'. St. Brendan (c.486–578) founded the monastery of Clonfert in Galway, which existed until the sixteenth century.

A tenth century tale, *Brendan's Voyage,* in which he sailed to the beautiful land of Promise in the Atlantic, spread his fame far and wide.

BRETT

From the Old French, meaning 'man from Brittany'. Brett is the surname of the viscounts Esher.

BRIAN

From the Irish, meaning 'hill'. The name was popular in both Brittany and Ireland. Brian Boru (941-1014) drove the Danish armies out of Ireland in 1014 at the decisive battle of Clontarf. He was murdered in his tent after the battle.

The Normans brought the name to England at the Norman Conquest and it is mentioned in the Domesday Book.

BRIANO

Italian for Brian, q.v.

BRIANT

From the Celtic, meaning 'strong'.

BRICE

From the Welsh Brys, meaning 'fast one'.

BRIGHAM

From the Old English, meaning 'dweller by the bridge'.

BRINDLEY

From the Anglo-Saxon, meaning 'one who lives on the brow of the hill'.

BRINTON
This name, which was featured on a birth certificate in 1901, means 'one who lives by the burnt town'.

BRODERICK
From the Norse, meaning 'brother'. It was traditionally given to a second son.

BRUCE
Originally a French place name, which became a Scottish surname. Many boys were named after the Scottish king Robert the Bruce (1274–1329), who was inspired by a spider to persevere after his defeat at Methven. He went on to defeat the English at the Battle of Bannockburn in 1314: one hundred thousand English soldiers, led by Edward II, were defeated by thirty thousand Scots headed by Robert the Bruce.

BRUNO
From the German, meaning 'brown'. St. Bruno (1033–1101), a nobleman from Cologne, founded the Carthusian Order at the Grande Chartreuse, near Grenoble, in 1084.

Lewis Carroll wrote a book for children entitled *Sylvie and Bruno,* first published in 1889.

BRYAN
A variant of Brian, q.v.

BRYANT
From the Celtic, meaning 'strong'.

BRYCE
An English variant of Brice, q.v.

BRYN
A Welsh first name, meaning 'hill'.

BUCHAN
A Scottish place name, meaning 'little hut', and surname, now used as a first name. It is the surname of the barons Tweedsmuir.

BURL
From the Old English, meaning 'cup bearer'.

BYRON
From the Old English, meaning 'at the cattlesheds'. The poet Lord Byron (George Gordon, 6th Baron Byron, 1788–1824) became the most famous Englishman of his time after the publication of *Childe Harold's Pilgrimage* in 1812. He died of fever at Missolonghi while leading the fight for Greek independence.

CAESAR
From the Latin, meaning 'longhaired', and later 'emperor'.

CAIN
This name, which means 'possessed', derives from the Bible and the French town of Caen. It is not a popular first name because of Cain's murder of his brother Abel.

CAL
A diminutive of Caleb, q.v., and of Callum, q.v.

CALDER
From this surname and from the Gaelic, meaning 'one who lived by the oak wood'.

CALEB
From the Hebrew, meaning 'bold'. The Old Testament Caleb set out with Moses from Egypt and was, with Joshua, one of the two original migrants to enter the Promised Land. A popular name with seventeenth century Puritans.

CALEY
From the Irish Gaelic, meaning 'slender'.

CALHOUN
From the Irish surname, meaning 'from the forest'.

CALLUM
The Gaelic form of the name Columba, meaning 'dove'. St. Columba (c.521–597) left Ireland with twelve companions to found a monastery on the island of Iona, off the west coast of Scotland.

CALUM
A variant of Callum, q.v.

CALVERT
From the Old English, meaning 'calf herder'. An English surname, now used as a first name. It was very popular in Victorian times.

CALVIN
From the Latin, meaning 'bald'. It was first used as a Christian name to honour John Calvin (1509–1564), the French Protestant theologian and reformer.
  Calvin Coolidge was the President of the U.S.A. from 1923–1929.

CALVINO
Spanish and Italian for Calvin, q.v.

CAMERON
From the Gaelic, meaning 'crooked nose'. A Scottish clan name and surname, now used as a first name.
  The Clan Cameron were among the first supporters of Charles Stuart, the Young Pretender, better known as 'Bonnie Prince Charlie', crushed so decisively at the Battle of Culloden (1746).

CAMPBELL
From the Gaelic, meaning 'crooked mouth'. A Scottish clan name and surname, now used as a first name.
  The Clan Campbell became infamous in Scottish history for their part in the Massacre at Glencoe on 13th February 1692 when thirty-eight members of the Clan MacDonald were treacherously murdered.

CAREY
From this Welsh surname, meaning 'castle dweller'.

CARL
German and Swedish for Charles, q.v.

CARLETON
From the surname Carlton, meaning 'from the farmer's place'.

CARLISLE
From this surname, meaning 'of the castle tower'.

CARLO
Italian for Charles, q.v.

CARLOS
Spanish for Charles, q.v.

CARMICHAEL
From the Gaelic, meaning 'loved of St. Michael'.

CARR
From this surname, meaning 'marsh dweller'.

CARSON
From this surname, meaning 'son of a marsh dweller'.

CARTER
From this surname, meaning 'driver'.

CARTHEW
From the Cornish, meaning 'rock or large stone'.

CARVER
From the Cornish Car-veor, meaning 'great rock'.

CARY
From the Old Welsh, meaning 'castle dweller'.

CASEY
An Irish surname, now given as a first name to both boys and girls. The American engine driver folk-hero from Kentucky, 'Casey' Jones (1864–1900), saved the lives of his passengers on the 'Cannonball Express' by sacrificing his own.

CASHEL
A name given to a boy born in this part of Ireland.

CASPAR
A variant of Casper, q.v.

CASPER
From the German, meaning 'imperial'. According to tradition, Casper was one of the three kings or wise men who came to Bethlehem to worship the Infant Jesus, bringing gifts of gold, frankincense and myrrh.

CASSIDY
From this Irish surname, meaning 'clever'.

CAVAN
From the Irish Gaelic, meaning 'handsome'.

CECIL
From the Latin, meaning 'blind'. The surname of a great English family, favoured by Elizabeth I, now used as a first name.

Cecil Rhodes (1853–1902), the British statesman, gave his name to Rhodesia, now Zimbabwe.

CÉCILE
French for Cecil, q.v.

CECILIUS
Dutch for Cecil, q.v.

CEDRIC
This seems to have been coined by Sir Walter Scott for a character in his novel, *Ivanhoe* (1819). Cedric is the father of the hero, Wilfred of Ivanhoe.

The name became hugely fashionable in the late nineteenth century after the publication of *Little Lord Fauntleroy* (1886) by Frances Hodgson Burnett. The young American hero, Cedric Errol, won all hearts despite wearing black velvet suits with lace collars and sporting long yellow curls!

CHAD
From the Old English, meaning 'warlike'.

CHARLES

From the Old High German, meaning 'man'. This is the most regal of names, beginning with Charles the Great or Charlemagne (742–814). He was crowned Emperor of the Holy Roman Empire on Christmas Day, 800.

Ten French kings were named Charles, including Charles the Fat and Charles the Bald; as were sixteen Swedish sovereigns and four Spanish kings.

Great Britain had Charles I (1600–1649), executed for treason and his son, Charles II, nicknamed 'The Merry Monarch'.

The classic writer Charles Dickens and the film star Charlie Chaplin are known worldwide.

CHARLIE

A variant of Charles, q.v.

CHARLTON

Originally an English place name, meaning 'settlement of peasants', and a surname. Its use as a first name seems to have begun in the 1870s.

The actor Charlton Heston (b. 1924) is a well-known bearer of the name.

CHESTER

From the Old English Caester, meaning 'camp dweller'.

CHRÉTIEN

French for Christian, q.v.

CHRIS

A diminutive of Christopher (q.v.) and of Christian (q.v.).

CHRISTIAN

From the Greek, meaning 'anointed'. The first use of the name to indicate a 'follower of Christ' occurred at Antioch (Acts II v.26).

John Bunyan's allegory, *Pilgrim's Progress,* first published in 1684, charts the adventures of Christian as he travels from the City of Destruction to the Celestial City.

Ten Danish kings have borne the name.

CHRISTIANO

Spanish and Italian for Christian, q.v.

CHRISTIE
A variant of Christopher, q.v.

CHRISTOFFER
Danish for Christopher, q.v.

CHRISTOPHE
French for Christopher, q.v.

CHRISTOPHER
From the Greek, meaning 'one who carries Christ'. The legendary St. Christopher carried the Infant Jesus across a ford. A church was built in his honour as early as 450. He is the patron saint of all travellers.

Sir Christopher Wren (1632-1723), the great British architect and Professor of Astronomy, designed St. Paul's Cathedral and many other London churches to replace those destroyed in the Great Fire of London, 1666.

CHRISTOPHORUS
German for Christopher, q.v.

CHUCK
A variant of Charles, q.v.

CIPRIANO
Spanish for Cyprian, meaning 'native of Cyprus'.

CIRILLO
Italian for Cyril, q.v.

CIRILO
Spanish for Cyril, q.v.

CIRO
Spanish for Cyrus, q.v.

CLARENCE
From the Latin, meaning 'of Clare'. Edward III created the title Duke of Clarence for his son Lionel on his marriage to a young lady of the de Clare family in 1362.

Clarence Harvey was the hero of a Maria Edgeworth novel entitled *Helen,* published in 1834.

CLARIDGE
This name means 'son of Clarice'.

CLARK
From the surname, meaning a person who was able to read and write. Clark Gable (1901–1960), the American actor who played Rhett Butler in the film *Gone With The Wind*, popularised the name in modern times.

CLARRY
A variant of Clarence, q.v.

CLAUDE
From the Latin, meaning 'lame'. It came into use in Britain in the nineteenth century.

Claude Lorraine (1600–1682), the French landscape painter, and Claude Debussy (1862–1918), the French composer notable for the opera *Pelléas and Mélisande* (1902) and the sea symphony *La Mer* (1905), are just two of those who add lustre to the name.

CLAUDIO
Spanish and Italian for Claude, q.v.

CLAUDIUS
Dutch and German for Claude, q.v.

CLAUS
A variant of Nicholas, q.v.

CLAYTON
A British place name, meaning 'settlement on a clay-bed', and surname. It has been used as a first name for over two hundred years.

CLEGG
From the Cornish, meaning 'rock'.

CLEM
A diminutive of Clement, q.v.

CLEMENS
Danish for Clement, q.v.

CLEMENT

From the Latin, meaning 'merciful'. A name popular with the early Christians and used by fourteen Popes.

St. Clement Slovensky (d.916) is honoured in Bulgaria as one of the evangelisers of the country.

Clement Attlee (1883–1967), the British Labour politician, became Prime Minister in 1945.

CLEMENTE

Spanish and Italian for Clement, q.v.

CLEMENTIUS

Dutch for Clement, q.v.

CLIFF

A diminutive of Clifford, q.v.

CLIFFORD

An English place name, meaning 'ford near a cliff' and aristocratic surname, now used as a first name.

The Clifford family motto is 'Semper paratus', meaning 'Always ready'. The shortened version of the name has been popularised by the singer Cliff Richard.

CLINT

A diminutive of Clinton, q.v.

CLINTON

A place name, meaning 'settlement near a hill', and surname, now used as a first name.

Sir Henry Clinton (1738?–1795) was commander-in-chief of all British forces in America during the American Revolution.

Clint Eastwood (b.1930), the American actor, has made popular the shortened version of the name.

CLIVE

A place name, meaning 'cliff' and surname, now used as a first name.

Robert Clive (1725–1774), known as 'Clive of India', founded the empire of British India and was governor of Bengal. Employees of the East India Company gave the name to their sons in his honour.

COLBERT

From the German, meaning 'bright one'.

COLIN
A medieval pet form of Nicholas and enduringly popular. Edmund Spenser (1552?-1599) wrote a long allegorical poem about a shepherd, *Colin Clouts Come Home Againe.*

Colin Craven was a main character in the children's classic, *The Secret Garden,* first published in 1911.

CONAN
From the Gaelic, meaning 'high exalted'.

CONNEL
From the Gaelic, meaning 'courageous'.

CONNOR
From the Old Irish, meaning 'lofty desires'. An Irish name now popular all over Great Britain.

CONRAD
From the German, 'brave counsel'. Conrad was the romantic and mysterious hero of Lord Byron's poem, *The Corsair,* published in 1814.

CONRADE
French for Conrad, q.v.

CONRADO
Spanish and Italian for Conrad, q.v.

CONSTANTIN
French, German and Dutch for Constantine, q.v.

CONSTANTINE
From the Latin, meaning 'constant'. Constantine the Great (280?–337) was the first Christian Emperor of Rome. He built the city of Constantinople on the site of ancient Byzantium, now called Istanbul.

There were three early Scottish kings named Constantine, the first of whom was killed in battle by the Vikings in 877.

CONSTANTINO
Spanish and Italian for Constantine, q.v.

COREY
An Irish surname, now used as a first name.

CORNELIO
Spanish and Italian for Cornelius, q.v.

CORNELIUS
From the Latin, meaning 'a hero'. It was the name of a great Roman family and a martyred pope of the third century.
Shakespeare gave the name to a courtier in his tragedy, *Hamlet*.

COSIMO
Spanish and Italian for Cosmo, q.v.

COSME
French for Cosmo, q.v.

COSMO
From the Greek, meaning 'world harmony'.

COURTENAY
An aristocratic surname, now used as a first name for both boys and girls. The family of de Courtenay, earls of Devon, came originally from Courtenay in France.

COURTNEY
A variant of Courtenay, q.v.

CRAIG
A surname, from the Gaelic meaning 'rock', now used as a first name.
It is the surname of the viscounts Craigavon. *Craig's Wife,* a play by George Kelly, was awarded a Pulitzer Prize in 1926.

CRAWFORD
A Scottish place name, meaning 'ford where the crows gather', and a surname, now used as a first name.
Mary and Henry Crawford play a vital part in Jane Austen's novel, *Mansfield Park.*

CRÉPIN
French for Crispin, q.v.

CRISPIN
From the Latin, meaning 'curly'. Saints Crispin and Crispinian were brother shoemakers of Soissons, martyred c.285. It was a very popular name in the Middle Ages.

Henry V defeated the French at the Battle of Agincourt on St. Crispin's Day, 25th October 1415.

CRISPINO
Italian for Crispin, q.v.

CRISPO
Spanish for Crispin, q.v.

CRISPUS
German for Crispin, q.v.

CRISTOBAL
Spanish for Christopher, q.v.

CRISTOFORO
Italian for Christopher, q.v.

CURTIS
From the Old French, meaning 'courteous'. A surname, now used as a first name. This was given as a nickname to Robert, Duke of Normandy, the eldest son of William the Conqueror.

CUTHBERT
From the Anglo-Saxon Cuthbeort, meaning 'bright'.

CYPRIAN
This name means 'native of Cyprus'.

CYRIL
From the Greek, meaning 'lordly'. St. Cyril (c.827–869) and his brother St. Methodius are revered as the 'Apostles to the Slavs'. He invented the Cyrillic alphabet now used by the Russians and Bulgarians.

The name came into use in Britain in the nineteenth century, revived by the Tractarians.

CYRILL
German for Cyril, q.v.

CYRILLE
French for Cyril, q.v.

CYRILLUS
Swedish, Dutch and Danish for Cyril, q.v.

CYRUS
From the Persian, meaning 'of the throne'.

DACRE
A Cumberland place name, meaning 'trickling stream', and an aristocratic surname, now used as a first name. The first baron Dacre was created in 1321 by Edward II.

DAGMAR
From the Teutonic, meaning 'bright day'.

DAI
The Welsh pet-form of David, q.v.

DALE
A surname, meaning 'dweller in the valley', now used as a first name. In Victorian times this was given to both girls and boys, but now seems to be restricted to the male sex.

DAMIAN
From the Greek, meaning 'to tame'. Damian and Cosmas were twin brothers who practised medicine and charged no fees to the poor. They were martyred for their Christian faith at Cyrrhus in Syria: the year is unknown, but their feast day is 27th September. They are the

patron saints of physicians. Damian was first used in England in 1205.

DAMIEN
A variant of Damian, q.v.

DAMON
From the Greek, meaning 'divine power'. Damon and Pythias of Syracuse were close friends. Pythias was sentenced to death, but begged to be allowed to go home to order his affairs. Damon took his place, prepared to die for his friend if he was late in returning. Pythias returned in good time, so impressing the king, Dionysius I, that he both freed and befriended the pair.

DAN
A diminutive of Daniel, q.v.

DANDIE
A name sometimes given to boys in Scotland named Andrew, q.v.

DANE
Dutch for Daniel, q.v. It also means 'one who comes from Denmark'.

DANIEL
From the Hebrew, meaning 'God has judged', Daniel is found in England before the Norman Conquest, but only as a name for monks and bishops. It became most popular for the ordinary people in the Middle Ages; perhaps to honour the Old Testament Daniel, who stepped unscathed from the lions' den. Daniel Defoe (1660–1731) wrote *Robinson Crusoe* and *Journal of the Plague Year.*

DANIELLE
Italian for Daniel, q.v.

DANNY
A variant of Daniel, q.v.

DARBY
From the Gaelic, meaning a 'freeman'.

DARCY
A French place name and surname, now used as a first name. A companion to William the Conqueror, Norman D'Arcy, was granted

much land in Lincolnshire.

The arrogant Darcy, beloved by Elizabeth Bennet in Jane Austen's novel, *Pride and Prejudice,* must be the archetypal romantic hero.

DARIUS
From the Persian, meaning 'good man'. Darius was a king of Persia.

DARRELL
A variant of Darryl, q.v.

DARREN
The origin of this name is uncertain, perhaps taken from an Irish surname or from Darius, q.v. Its popularity seems to date from the early 1950s.

DARRYL
A French place name and surname, carried to England at the time of the Norman Conquest by a family who came from Airelle.

The most prominent bearer of the name in modern times was Darryl F. Zanuck, the American film producer and founder of Twentieth Century Fox.

DAVE
A diminutive of David, q.v.

DAVID
From the Hebrew, meaning 'darling'. The shepherd-boy David slew the giant Goliath with his slingshot: he became King of Judah and, eventually, of all Israel. He was a poet; many of the psalms are attributed to him. (Strangely, though David was one of the greatest Biblical heroes, no-one else in the Bible is named after him.)

Two Scottish kings have been called David. David I (1084–1153) established a form of central government and issued the first royal coinage. David II (1324–1371) invaded England, suffered defeat and was imprisoned for eleven years.

DAVIDDE
Italian for David, q.v.

DAVIDE
French for David, q.v,

DAVIE
A variant of David, q.v.

DAVY
A variant of David, q.v.

DEAN
An Old English place name, meaning 'valley', and surname, now used as a first name.

James Dean (1931–1955), the American actor whose early and tragic death turned him into an enduring cult figure, has done much to popularise the name.

DECIMUS
From the Latin, meaning 'tenth'.

DECLAN
An ancient Gaelic name. Declan was an associate of St. Colman of Lindisfarne in the seventh century. Little else is known about him. This name has become hugely popular in recent years.

DEMETRE
French for Demetrius, q.v.

DEMETRIO
Italian for Demetrius, q.v.

DEMETRIUS
From Demeter, the Greek goddess of the harvest, meaning 'belonging to Demeter'. Demetrius was a silversmith mentioned in the Bible.

DENIS
A variant of Dennis, q.v.

DENNIS
A medieval form of the Greek name, Dionysos, the god of wine. St. Denis, the patron saint of France, was a missionary sent into Gaul in the year 250. He was beheaded in 258 at a place in Paris called Montmarte, or 'Martyr's Hill'. The Normans introduced the name into England.

DENZIL
From the Cornish place name, meaning 'stronghold', and surname. It

has been used as a first name since the sixteenth century.

In 1629, the Speaker of the House of Commons refused to put forward for consideration by the MPs a proposition opposed by Charles I. Denzil Holles responded to this by holding Speaker Finch down in his chair until he changed his mind. After floods of tears, he did!

DEREK
A shortened version of Theodoric, meaning 'people's ruler'. It was brought to England from Holland in the fifteenth century and became popular in the 1890s.

Sir Derek Jacobi (b.1939), the actor, is a famous modern bearer of the name.

DERMOT
From the Irish, meaning 'free from envy'. Dermot was the lover of Grainne, the wife of Finn MacCool of Irish legend.

DERRICK
A variant of Derek, q.v.

DERRY
A variant of Derek, q.v.

DESMOND
Originally an Irish surname, meaning 'man from South Munster', it has been popular as a first name all over Great Britain from the early 1900s.

DEXTER
From the Latin, meaning 'skilful'.

DICK
A variant of Richard, q.v.

DICKON
A pet-name for Richard (q.v.), dating back to the thirteenth century. Dickon was the animal-loving boy in the children's classic, *The Secret Garden,* first published in 1911.

DIGBY
An English place name, meaning 'a settlement by a ditch', and surname, used as a first name since the late 1800s.

The naval commander and writer, Sir Kenelm Digby (1603–

1665), was the first to discover how vital oxygen is for plant life.

DIONISIO
Spanish and Italian for Dennis, q.v.

DIONYSUS
German for Dennis, q.v.

DIRK
The Dutch version of Derek, now generally used. The actor and writer Dirk Bogarde (born Derek Van Den Bogaerde) has done much to popularise the name.

And no Scottish highlander in full ceremonial dress would be without his dirk, or fighting knife.

DMITRI
Russian for Demetrius, q.v.

DOMENICO
Italian for Dominic, q.v.

DOMINGO
Spanish for Dominic, q.v.

DOMINIC
From the Latin, meaning 'of the Lord'. It was popular with the early Christians and often given to children born on a Sunday.

St. Dominic (1170–1221), a Spaniard, founded the Order of Preachers or 'Dominicans' in 1216. One of his last undertakings was to send thirteen friars to Oxford.

DOMINIQUE
French for Dominic, q.v.

DOMINY
A variant of Dominic, q.v.

DON
A diminutive of Donald, q.v.

DONALD
From the Gaelic, meaning 'proud ruler'. A Scottish clan name and surname, now used as a first name.

Three Scottish kings have borne the name. Donald III (c. 1031–1097) was twice deposed, and blinded. He was the last king to be buried on Iona.

DONNY
A variant of Donald, q.v.

DONOVAN
From an Irish surname, meaning 'dark brown', now popular as a first name.

DORAN
There are two meanings possible for this name:
a) From the Greek, meaning 'gift' or
b) From an Irish surname, meaning 'descendent of the exile'.

DORIAN
From the Greek, meaning 'a man from Doris', which is a place in central Greece.

Oscar Wilde appears to have invented this name for the hero of his moral novel, *The Picture of Dorian Gray,* first published in 1891.

DOUG
A diminutive of Douglas, q.v.

DOUGAL
From the Gaelic, meaning 'dark stranger'. This was originally the name given by the Irish to Danish settlers. It later became a nickname given by the Lowland Scots to Highlanders.

DOUGIE
A variant of Dougal (q.v.) and of Douglas (q.v.)

DOUGLAS
A Scottish place name, meaning 'dark water', and a surname, now used as a first name.

The Douglases were the greatest noble family of medieval Scotland. Their founder, James Douglas (1286–1330), called 'Black Douglas', invaded England and plundered many towns and villages in the North. He died fighting the Moors in Spain, having stopped off there for a battle on his way to the Crusades.

The Douglases also acquired the French dukedom of Tourain, when a Scots army led by the Earl of Douglas defeated the English at

Beauge in 1421.

The botanist David Douglas (1798–1834) gave his name to the Douglas Fir, bringing the seeds from America to Scotland.

DREW
Now considered the diminutive form of Andrew (q.v.), it has a long history. The German name Drogo, meaning 'to carry', was brought to England by followers of William the Conqueror in its French form, Dru. It became popular and was anglicised into Drew.

DUANE
From an Irish surname, meaning 'little dark one'. It was made popular by the American singer and guitarist Duane Eddy in the 1950s.

DUDLEY
A place name, meaning 'Dudda's clearing', and aristocratic surname, now used as a first name.

Robert Dudley, Earl of Leicester (1532–1588) was the favourite of Elizabeth I and the main character in Sir Walter Scott's novel, *Kenilworth*.

The pianist and actor Dudley Moore has made the name popular in recent times.

DUFFY
From the Irish Duff, meaning 'dark skinned'.

DUGALD
From the Gaelic, meaning 'dark stranger'.

DUGGIE
A variant of Douglas, q.v.

DUGUID
A Scottish Christian name, meaning 'one who does good'.

DUKE
From the French *duc*, meaning 'leader'.

DUNCAN
From the Gaelic, meaning 'dark skinned warrior'. The Scottish king Duncan I (1010–1040) was murdered by his cousin, Macbeth (who is immortalised in the Shakespeare play of the same name). Duncan II

(1060–1094) ruled for approximately six months and was murdered by his uncle, Donald III. (Perhaps this explains why no other Scottish rulers have chosen to bear the name.)

DUNSTAN
From the Old English, meaning 'stony hill'.

St. Dunstan (c.909-988) revived monasticism in England after the ravages wrought by Scandinavian invasions. He became Archbishop of Canterbury in 959. The present Coronation rite is derived from the one compiled and used by Dunstan in crowning Edgar I King of all England in Bath Abbey in 973. Dunstan also loved playing the harp, working in metal and calligraphy!

Dunstan Cass is a character in the novel *Silas Marner* by George Eliot.

DWIGHT
This name means 'white haired'.

DYLAN
From the Welsh, meaning 'flood'. In Celtic myth, Dylan was the son of a sea god. As soon as he was born, he plunged into the sea and swam like a fish.

The Welsh poet Dylan Thomas (1914–1953) and the American singer Bob Dylan (b. 1941), real name Robert Zimmerman, have made the name popular.

EACHAN
From the Gaelic, meaning 'horse'.

EAMON
A variant of Eamonn, q.v.

52

EAMONN
The Irish version of Edmund (q.v.), used generally in Britain since the mid-twentieth century.

Eamon de Valera (1882–1975) was twice president of the Republic of Ireland, only retiring from politics at the age of ninety.

EARL
A variant of Earle, q.v.

EARLE
From the Old English, meaning 'warrior' or 'nobleman'. One of the five ranks of the peerage and a surname, now used as a first name.

John Earle (1601–1665) wrote *Microcosmography* (1628), considered one of the finest prose works of the seventeenth century.

EBENEZER
From the Hebrew, meaning 'stone of help'.

ED
A diminutive of the following (q.v.): Edward, Edmund, Edwin and Edgar.

EDDIE
A diminutive of the following (q.v.): Edward, Edmund, Edwin and Edgar.

EDEN
From the Hebrew, meaning 'delight'. The name of the Biblical Paradise, the country and garden in which Adam and Eve dwelt.

EDGAR
From the Anglo-Saxon, meaning 'fortunate spear'. This is one of the royal Anglo-Saxon names to survive the Norman Conquest.

King Edgar (944–975) was the first king of all England. The American writer, Edgar Allan Poe (1809–1849), wrote haunting poems and horror stories, including *The Pit and the Pendulum*.

EDGARD
French for Edgar, q.v.

EDGARDO
Italian for Edgar, q.v.

EDMOND
Dutch and French for Edmund, q.v.

EDMUND
From the Old English, meaning 'happy protection'. St. Edmund, king and martyr (841–869), the ruler of East Anglia, was murdered by the Danes. His body was enshrined at Bury St. Edmunds.

The Astronomer Royal, Edmund Halley (1656–1742), predicted the return of the comet which bears his name.

Edmund was a favourite name of Jane Austen. She wrote 'There is a nobleness in the name of Edmund. It is a name of heroism and renown'.

EDMUNDO
Spanish for Edmund, q.v.

EDOUARDO
French for Edward, q.v.

EDRIC
From the Old English, meaning 'happy ruler'. A baptismal name of the Anglo-Saxons, revived by the Victorians.

EDUARD
Dutch and German for Edward, q.v.

EDUARDO
Spanish and Italian for Edward, q.v.

EDUINO
Italian for Edwin, q.v.

EDVARD
Danish and Swedish for Edward, q.v.

EDWARD
From the Anglo-Saxon, meaning 'prosperous protector'. A very popular name, used since Anglo-Saxon times. King Edward the Elder (870–924) had three sons who became kings, and six daughters who married kings or dukes in England, France and Germany.

King Edward the Confessor (1003–1066) founded Westminster Abbey and was canonised in 1161.

Eight post-Conquest rulers have borne this name: Edward V

(1470–1483) was one of the two tragic Princes in the Tower, supposedly murdered on the orders of their uncle Richard III.

EDWIN
From the Anglo-Saxon, meaning 'fortunate friend'. King Edwin (d.633) was the first Christian King of Northumberland. The name was revived by the Victorians. *Edwin Drood* was the last, unfinished novel of Charles Dickens (1812–1870).

EGBERT
From the Anglo-Saxon, meaning 'shining sword'.

EGIDIO
Italian for Giles, q.v.

EGMOND
A variant of Egmont, q.v.

EGMONT
From the Anglo-Saxon, meaning 'sword's protection'.

ELBERT
A variant of Albert, q.v.

ELDRED
From the Old English, meaning 'old counsel'. An Anglo-Saxon Christian name, one of many revived by the Victorians.

ELI
A diminutive of Elias (q.v.) and of Elijah (q.v.). From the Hebrew, meaning 'high'. Eli was a high priest in the Old Testament.

ELIA
Italian for Elijah, q.v.

ELIAS
Dutch and German for Elijah. Elias Howe was the inventor of the sewing machine.

ELIE
French for Elijah, q.v.

ELIJAH
From the Hebrew, meaning 'Jehovah is God'. Elijah was a prophet in the Old Testament.

ELIOT
A variant of Elliot, q.v.

ELISHA
This name means 'God is my salvation'. Elisha was a prophet in the Old Testament.

ELLERIE
A variant of Ellery.

ELLERY
A surname, now used as a first name by both girls and boys. Frederic Dannay and Manfred Lee were American cousins who invented the fictional detective, Ellery Queen, hero of many magazine stories and novels.

ELLIOT
A medieval diminutive of Elias, meaning 'The Lord is my God'. A surname, now used as a first name.
    Thomas Stearns Eliot (1888–1965), the American-born poet, became a British subject in 1927. He is recognised as one of the major influences in the twentieth century. Elliot is the surname of the earls of Minto.

ELLIOTT
A variant of Elliot, q.v.

ELLIS
A variant of Elijah, q.v.

ELMER
From the Anglo-Saxon Aethelmaer, meaning 'famous noble'. A name mainly used in the United States.

ELMO
From the Greek, meaning 'amiable'.

ELROY
From *le roi*, meaning 'the king'.

ELVIN
A variant of Elwin, q.v.

ELWIN
From the Anglo-Saxon, meaning 'old friend'. A surname, now used as a first name.

ELY
A variant of Eli, q.v.

EMERI
French for Emery, q.v.

EMERSON
A medieval surname, meaning 'descendent of a man called Emery', now used as a first name.
    The American, Ralph Waldo Emerson (1803–1882), was a famous poet, essayist and philosopher.

EMERY
From the Old German, meaning 'power'. It was brought to England by the Normans and given to both sexes until the eighteenth century, when it became exclusively male.

EMIL
From the Teutonic, meaning 'industrious'.

EMILE
French for Emil, q.v.

EMILIO
Spanish for Emil, q.v.

EMLYN
From a Welsh place name, now used as a first name. Emlyn Williams (1905–1987), actor and playwright, wrote several memorable plays including *The Corn is Green* and *Night Must Fall.*

EMMANUEL
From the Hebrew, meaning 'God with us'. A variant is Manny.

EMMANUELE
Italian for Emmanuel, q.v.

EMMERICH
German for Emery, q.v.

EMMETT
From the Teutonic, meaning 'industrious'.

EMMOT
A variant of Emmett, q.v.

EMORY
A variant of Emery, q.v.

ENGELBERT
From the Teutonic, meaning 'bright angel'.

ENNIS
From the Gaelic, meaning 'chief one'.

ENOCH
From the Hebrew, meaning 'consecrated'. In the Bible, Enoch was the father of Methuselah.

ENRICO
Italian for Henry, q.v.

ENRIQUE
Spanish for Henry, q.v.

EPHRAIM
From the Hebrew, meaning 'fruitful'. Ephraim was a son of Joseph in the Old Testament.

ERASME
French for Erasmus, q.v.

ERASMO
Spanish and Italian for Erasmus, q.v.

ERASMUS
From the Greek, meaning 'beloved'.

ERASTE
French for Erastus, q.v.

ERASTUS
From the Greek, meaning 'beloved'. Variants are Ras and Rastus.

ERIC
From the Norse, meaning 'ruler of all'. The name was brought to England by the Danes. King Eric Bloodaxe fled from Norway to England in 934 and captured Northumberland from King Edred.

Dean Farrar wrote the popular Victorian children's story *Eric, or Little by Little* in 1858, which popularised the name.

Eric Blair was the real name of the novelist George Orwell (1903–1950).

ERMIN
A Welsh name, meaning 'lordly'.

ERNALD
A variant of Arnold, q.v. This name is mentioned in the Domesday Book.

ERNEST
From the German, meaning 'determined'. The name was brought to Britain in the eighteenth century by the Hanoverians.

The first Duke of Saxe-Gotha, Ernest the Pious (1601–1675), insisted on compulsory education for all children in his domain. A wise man.

Ernest Pontifex was the unwise hero of Samuel Butler's classic novel, *The Way of All Flesh* (1903).

ERNESTO
Spanish and Italian for Ernest, q.v.

ERNESTUS
Dutch for Ernest, q.v.

ERNIE
A variant of Ernest, q.v.

ERNST
German for Ernest, q.v.

ERROL
A Scottish place name and surname, now used as a first name. The Tasmanian-born, swashbuckling film star, Errol Flynn (1909–1959),

made the name very popular.

ERWIN
From the Anglo-Saxon Eoforwine, meaning 'the sea's friend'.

ESAU
From the Hebrew, meaning 'hairy'. Esau was the son of Jacob in the Old Testament.

ESMOND
From the Old English, meaning 'divine protection'. It was revived in Victorian times; perhaps influenced by the popularity of the novel by William Thackeray, *The History of Henry Esmond,* published in 1852.

ESTEBAN
Spanish for Stephen, q.v.

ETHAN
From the Hebrew, meaning 'strong'. The Old Testament mentions four men named Ethan. One was renowned for his wisdom, only King Solomon was wiser. Another was a priest who sang as the Ark of the Covenant was brought to Jerusalem by King David.
   Ethan Frome is the title of one of the shorter novels of Edith Wharton (1862–1937).

ETHELBERT
From the Anglo-Saxon, meaning 'bright and noble'.

ETHELRED
From the Anglo-Saxon, meaning 'bright and noble'.

ETIENNE
French for Stephen, q.v.

ETTORE
Italian for Hector, q.v.

EUGEN
German for Eugene, q.v.

EUGENE
From the Greek, meaning 'noble'. Four Popes and several obscure

saints have borne this name

The American playwright Eugene O'Neill (1888–1953), who wrote *The Iceman Cometh* and *Long Day's Journey Into Night* among others, won the Nobel Prize for Literature in 1936.

EUGENIO
Spanish and Italian for Eugene, q.v.

EUGENIUS
Dutch for Eugene, q.v.

EURAUD
French for Everard, q.v.

EUSEBIUS
From the Greek, meaning 'reverent'.

EUSTACE
From the Greek, meaning 'good harvest'.

EUSTACHE
French for Eustace, q.v.

EUSTASIUS
German for Eustace, q.v.

EUSTATIUS
Dutch for Eustace, q.v.

EUSTAZIO
Italian for Eustace, q.v.

EUSTQUIO
Spanish for Eustace. q.v.

EVAN
The Welsh version of John. A very popular first name.

EVELYN
See the entry in the girls' section.

EVERARD
From the Teutonic, meaning 'with the strength of a boar'.

EVERARDO
Italian for Everard, q.v.

EVERHART
Dutch for Everard, q.v.

EVERLEY
From this surname, meaning 'one who dwelt in the boar meadow'.

EWAN
From the Gaelic, Eoghan, a name of great antiquity. There is dispute over its derivation. Some claim it to be a version of Eugene, q.v.; while others claim it is a Celtic name, meaning 'born of the yew'. Ewan is the Scottish version, now popular all over Britain.

EWART
The Scottish form of Everard, q.v.

EWING
A Scottish name, meaning 'fiery'.

EZRA
From the Hebrew, meaning 'help'.

FABIAN
From the Latin, meaning 'bean'. The name of an ancient and illustrious Roman family, who listed among their members a historian; and a general whose tactics against Hannibal inspired the naming of the Fabian Society. This intellectual society of non-revolutionary socialists was founded in London in 1884.

Pope Fabian was martyred in 250 under Emperor Decius. The name was brought to England by the Normans.

FABIANO
Italian for Fabian, q.v.

FABIEN
French for Fabian, q.v.

FANCOURT
This is derived from the place-name of Fovecourt, near Beauvais in France.

FANE
From the surname, meaning 'joyful'.

FARRELL
From the Gaelic, meaning 'warrior'.

FEDERICO
Spanish for Frederick, q.v.

FEDERIGO
Italian for Frederick, q.v.

FELICE
Italian for Felix, q.v.

FELIPE
Spanish for Philip, q.v.

FELIX
From the Latin, meaning 'happy'. There are many saints named Felix, including sixty-seven martyrs. The Burgundian bishop, St. Felix of Dunwich (d.648) came to preach the gospel in East Anglia. He gave his name to the town of Felixstowe.

FERDINAND
From the German, meaning 'bold life'. Many kings of Castile have borne this name, the most famous of whom was Ferdinand V of Aragon (1452–1516), who with his wife Isabella gave financial backing to the explorer, Christopher Columbus.

Shakespeare gave this name to the King of Navarre in *Love's*

Labour's Lost and to Miranda's beloved in *The Tempest*.

FERGIE
A diminutive of Fergus, q.v.

FERGUS
From the Gaelic, meaning 'man's strength'. Fergus is one of the heroes of Ulster in ancient Gaelic legend.

FFION
A variant of Finn, q.v.

FIDEL
From the Latin *fidelis,* meaning 'faithful'.

FIDELE
French for Fidel, q.v.

FIDELIO
Italian for Fidel, q.v.

FILIP
Swedish for Philip, q.v.

FILIPPO
Italian for Philip, q.v.

FINDLAY
A variant of Finlay, q.v.

FINGAL
From the Celtic, meaning 'white stranger'.

FINLAY
From the Gaelic, meaning 'fair warrior'. A Scottish surname, now used as a first name. Finlay was the father of the infamous Macbeth, King of Scotland.

FINN
From the Gaelic, meaning 'fair'. Finn MacCool is a great hero in Irish folklore, the subject of tales and ballads innumerable. From his headquarters in County Kildare, Finn led a band of warriors, called the Fenians, who gave help to all who required it.

FINNIAN
A variant of Finn, q.v. St. Finnian (d.549) was the founder of Irish monasticism.

FLEMING
A Scottish name, meaning 'refugee'.

FLETCHER
From this surname, meaning 'arrowmaker'.

FLINT
From the Anglo-Saxon, meaning 'brook'.

FLOYD
From the Welsh, meaning 'grey haired'.

FORBES
From the Gaelic, meaning 'prosperous'.

FORD
From this surname, meaning 'one who lived at the ford'.

FORDYCE
A Scottish name, meaning 'man of wisdom'.

FORREST
From this surname, meaning 'one who dwells in the forest'.

FOSTER
From the same surname as Forrester, meaning 'one who looked after the forest'.

FRANCESCO
Italian for Francis, q.v.

FRANCHOT
French for Francis, q.v.

FRANCIS
From the Latin, meaning 'a Frenchman'. The name of two French kings and two emperors of the Holy Roman Empire: the most famous bearer of the name is St. Francis of Assisi (1182–1226), renowned for preaching to the birds, taming a wolf and beginning the tradition of

the Christmas Crib.

In reality, his name was Giovanni; but he became so proficient in French that he was called 'il Francesco' (the Frenchman), and his baptismal name was forgotten, even among his followers.

Two sailors, Sir Francis Drake (1540–1596), the first English circumnavigator of the globe, and Sir Francis Chichester (1901–1972) who sailed alone around the world in *Gipsy Moth IV* in 1966–1967, add lustre to the name.

FRANCISCO
Spanish for Francis, q.v.

FRANCOIS
French for Francis, q.v.

FRANE
A name meaning 'foreigner'. Mentioned in the Domesday Book.

FRANK
This is now considered a diminutive of Francis (q.v.), but originally the name referred to the Teutonic tribe of Franks, led by King Clovis, who invaded Gaul in the fifth century A.D. and gave their name to the whole country of France. It came to England with the Normans.

FRANKLIN
From the Old French, meaning 'free citizen'. A surname, now used as a first name. The franklin was a landowner in the England of the thirteenth and fourteenth centuries who was not of noble birth.

Geoffrey Chaucer (1343–1400) included *The Franklin's Tale* in his *Canterbury Tales*.

Sir John Franklin (1786–1847), the English Arctic explorer, was lost in the attempt to discover a North-West passage to the Pacific.

FRANS
Swedish for Francis, q.v.

FRANTS
Danish for Francis, q.v.

FRANZ
German for Francis, q.v.

FRASER
A French place name and a Scottish surname, now used as a first name. It is the surname of barons Lovat, Saltoun and Strathalmond.

FRAZER
A variant of Fraser, q.v.

FRED
A diminutive of Frederick, q.v.

FREDDIE
A diminutive of Frederick, q.v.

FREDERIC
French for Frederick, q.v.

FREDERICK
From the Old German, meaning 'peaceful ruler'. This has been a popular name in Britain since the eighteenth century. Frederick, Prince of Wales (1707–1751), son of George II and father of George III, was killed by a blow from a cricket ball.

The most famous bearer of the name was Frederick II (1712–1786), King of Prussia, called 'The Great'. He was a very far from 'peaceful ruler', being renowned as a soldier and a totally unscrupulous politician. (He played the flute well, too!)

FREDRIK
Swedish for Frederick, q.v.

FREEMAN
From the Anglo-Saxon, meaning 'freeholder'.

FRITZ
A German variant of Frederick, q.v.

FULK
From the Norman Folkard, meaning 'the strong people'.

FYFE
This name means 'native of Fife'.

GABRIEL
From the Hebrew, meaning 'man of God'. Gabriel the Archangel announced the birth of Jesus to the Blessed Virgin Mary in St. Luke's Gospel and is also mentioned in the Old Testament Book of Daniel.

Gabriel Fahrenheit (1686–1736) was a German physicist who introduced improvements to the construction of thermometers by the use of mercury. He gave his name to a temperature scale in which the melting point of ice is 32°F and boiling point is 212°F.

GAD
From the Hebrew, meaning 'good fortune'.

GALE
From the Anglo-Saxon, meaning 'gay'.

GALLOWAY
A Scottish name, meaning 'a man from Galloway'.

GARETH
From the Welsh, meaning 'gentle'. The name of one of the knights of King Arthur's Round Table, unwittingly killed by Sir Lancelot. Alfred, Lord Tennyson (1809–1892) told the story of *Gareth and Lynette* in his hugely popular epic poem, *Idylls of the King*.

GARFIELD
From this surname, meaning 'one who lives by the battlefield'.

GARNET
From the stone of this name.

GARRARD

A variant of Gerard, q.v.

GARTH

From the Old Norse, meaning 'enclosure' or 'garden'. A surname, now used as a first name.

GARY

A diminutive form of Gareth, q.v. It was made very popular in the twentieth century by the American actor Gary Cooper (1901–1961), really Frank J. Cooper, who starred in the classic Western, *High Noon.*

GASTON

From the French, meaning 'a man from Gascony'.

GAVIN

From the Welsh, meaning 'white hawk'. The Scottish form of Gawain, a knight of the Round Table and a nephew to King Arthur.

Gavin Maxwell (1914–1969) wrote the popular autobiographical book, *Ring of Bright Water.*

GAYLORD

From the French Gaillard, meaning 'brisk'.

GAYNOR

This name means 'son of the fair head'.

GENE

A diminutive of Eugene, q.v. Gene Kelly is famous for his singing and dancing in the classic musical, *Singin' In The Rain.*

GEOFF

A diminutive of Geoffrey, q.v.

GEOFFREY

From the Old German, meaning 'peace'. Brought to England by the Normans in the eleventh century.

The name was made famous by Geoffrey Chaucer (1343–1400), considered the father of English poetry, who was a secret agent, diplomat and controller of customs in addition. His *Canterbury Tales* and *Troilus and Cressida* remain in print to torment the school-children of Britain. He was the first poet to be buried in Westminster

Abbey, in the portion known as 'Poets' Corner'.

GEORG
Danish, German and Swedish for George, q.v.

GEORGDIE
A northern English and Scottish variant of George, q.v.

GEORGE
From the Greek, meaning 'farmer'. St. George, a soldier saint and martyr of whom little is known, was deeply revered in the East. The Emperor Constantine had a church erected in his honour. The Crusaders chose St. George as their champion and spread his cult across Europe. Edward III made St. George the patron saint of England: by 1415, his feast day was a public holiday.

The first four royal Georges, ruling from 1714 until 1830, made the name very popular and this has continued to the present day.

George Washington became first President of the United States in 1789.

GEORGES
French for George, q.v.

GERAINT
From the Celtic, meaning 'ruler with a spear'. Geraint was the name of a Cornish saint.

GERALD
From the Old German, meaning 'spear rule'. This was introduced by the Normans and popular in the Middle Ages. It was revived in the late nineteenth century.

Saint Gerald of Aurillac (855–909) was a considerable landowner, famous for his justice. St. Odo of Cluny wrote a 'Life' of St. Gerald which made him very popular in medieval France.

GERARD
A variant of Gerald, q.v. There have been several saints with this name. St. Gerard Majella (1726–1755), an Italian Redemptorist lay-brother, is still invoked by mothers in labour for the safe delivery of their child.

Gerard Manley Hopkins (1844–1889), the English poet and Jesuit priest, wrote *The Wreck of the Deutschland* and *Pied Beauty* among others. Not one of his poems was published in his lifetime.

GERARDO
Italian for Gerard, q.v.

GERHARD
Swedish and Danish for Gerard, q.v.

GERHARDT
German for Gerard, q.v.

GEROLD
A variant of Gerald (q.v.), mentioned in the Domesday Book.

GERVASE
This name means 'spearman'. Gervase was the name of a monk in the Middle Ages.

GERWEN
A variant of Gerwyn, q.v.

GERWYN
From the Welsh, meaning 'fair love'.

GIACOMO
Italian for Jacob, q.v.

GIBSON
From this surname, meaning 'son of Gilbert'.

GIDEON
From the Hebrew, meaning 'one who cuts down'. The name of an Israelite ruler of the Old Testament, who delivered his people from the Midianites at the instigation of an angel. Popular with the Puritans of the seventeenth century and taken by them to America.

GIFF
A diminutive of Gifford, q.v.

GIFFORD
From the Anglo-Saxon, meaning 'brave gift'.

GIL
Spanish for Giles (q.v.) and a diminutive of Gilbert (q.v.)

GILBERT

From the German, meaning 'bright pledge'. Brought to England at the Norman Conquest, the name became very popular.

St. Gilbert of Sempringham (c.1085–1189) was the founder of the only specifically English religious order for both men and women. The Gilbertine Order was suppressed by King Henry VIII and all its houses appropriated.

The English writer, Gilbert Keith Chesterton (1874–1936), is best remembered for creating the Roman Catholic priest and sleuth Father Brown.

GILBERTO

Italian for Gilbert, q.v.

GILBEY

From the Teutonic, meaning 'by a pledge'.

GILCHRIST

From the Celtic, meaning 'servant of Christ'.

GILES

From the Latin, meaning 'young goat'. St. Giles (d.c.712) was one of the most popular saints of Western Europe. The most famous incident told about him concerns his protection of a pet deer, hunted by the Visigoth King Wamba, who loosed an arrow after it. He found St. Giles, himself holding the deer, wounded in the arm. St. Giles Cripplegate in London and the High Kirk in Edinburgh are dedicated to him. He is the patron of the poor and of the crippled.

GILLESPIE

From this Celtic surname, meaning 'bishop's servant'.

GILROY

From the Gaelic, meaning 'servant of a red head'.

GIORGIO

Italian for George, q.v.

GIOVANNI

Italian for John, q.v.

GIRALDO

Italian for Gerald, q.v.

GIRAUD
French for Gerald, q.v.

GIULIO
Italian for Julius, q.v.

GLANVILLE
From the French, meaning 'one who lives by the oaks'.

GLEN
From the Gaelic, meaning 'narrow mountain valley'. A place name and surname, now used as a first name.

The American bandleader, Glenn Miller (1904–1944), who died mysteriously over the English Channel during the Second World War, and several film stars and singers have made this name popular in modern times.

GLENN
A variant of Glen, q.v.

GLYN
A variant of Glen, q.v.

GLYNN
A variant of Glen, q.v.

GODARD
French for Goddard, q.v.

GODDARD
From the German, meaning 'strong in God'.

GODEFROI
French for Godfrey, q.v.

GODFREY
From the Old German, meaning 'God's peace'. This was brought to England by the Normans.

Godfrey de Bouillon was the hero of *Jerusalem Delivered,* the epic masterpiece of the Italian poet, Torquato Tasso (1544–1595).

GODWIN
From the Anglo-Saxon, meaning 'friend of God'. The name appears

in the Domesday Book.

GOFFREDO
Italian for Godfrey, q.v.

GOLDING
From the Anglo-Saxon, meaning 'son of the golden'.

GORDON
A place name, Scottish clan name and surname, now used as a first name. Sir Gordon Richards (1904–1986) was one of the most successful flat-racing jockeys.

General Gordon (1833–1885), who was besieged by the Mahdi at Khartoum and died so dramatically when the city was stormed, made the name very popular in late Victorian England.

GORMAN
From the Celtic, meaning 'of the blue eyes'.

GOTTFRID
Swedish for Godrey, q.v.

GOTTFRIED
Dutch and German for Godfrey, q.v.

GOTTHARD
Dutch for Goddard, q.v.

GOTTHART
German for Goddard, q.v.

GOWER
From the Gaelic, meaning 'pure'.

GRAEME
A variant of Graham, q.v.

GRAHAM
From the Old English, meaning 'homestead belonging to Granta'. A place name, Scottish clan name and surname, now used as a first name. The name was introduced into Scotland by the Norman William de Graham in the early twelfth century.

GRAHAME
A variant of Graham, q.v.

GRAINGER
From the Anglo-Saxon, meaning 'farmer'.

GRANT
From the French, meaning 'tall'. A surname, now used as a first name. Ulysses S. Grant (1822–1885) was a Union General in the American Civil War and became eighteenth president of the U.S.A.

GRANVILLE
A place name in Normandy, meaning 'large settlement', and surname, now used as a first name. The motto of the earls of Granville is 'Frangas non flectes', translated as 'You may break, not bend'.

GRAY
A variant of Grey, q.v.

GREG
A diminutive and variant of Gregory, q.v.

GREGOIRE
French for Gregory, q.v.

GREGOOR
Dutch for Gregory, q.v.

GREGOR
German for Gregory, q.v.

GREGORIO
Spanish and Italian for Gregory, q.v.

GREGORY
From the Greek, meaning 'watchful'. A popular name in the early Christian church, sixteen popes and many saints have borne the name. The name was introduced into England at the Norman Conquest and is the name of a Scottish clan.

St. Gregory the Great (c.540–604) was the first monk to be elected pope. He sent missionaries to England under the charge of St. Augustine in 597, and was responsible for the development of the Gregorian chant, or plainsong.

Pope Gregory XIII (1502-1585) introduced the reformed Gregorian calendar on 24th February 1582.

Gregory de Rokesley (d. 1291) was eight times Lord Mayor of London.

GREVILLE
An aristocratic surname, now used as a first name. Charles Cavendish Fulke Greville (1794–1865), English diarist, was the clerk of the Council in Ordinary. His journals, the *Greville Memoirs,* are necessary to any student of the nineteenth century.

GREY
From the Anglo-Saxon, meaning 'grey haired'.

GRIFFITH
From the Celtic, meaning 'red chief'.

GROVER
From this surname, meaning 'one who lived in the grove'.

GRUFFYDD
Welsh for Griffith, q.v.

GUGLIELMO
Italian for William, q.v.

GUIDO
Swedish, German, Italian and Spanish for Guy, q.v.

GUILBERT
French for Gilbert, q.v.

GUILLAUME
French for William, q.v.

GUILLERMO
Spanish for William, q.v.

GUISEPPE
Italian for Joseph, q.v.

GUISTINO
Italian for Justin, q.v.

GUNTER
A variant of Gunther, q.v.

GUNTHER
From the Norse, meaning 'battle warrior'.

GUS
A diminutive of Gustave (q.v.) and of Augustus (q.v.).

GUSTAFF
Dutch for Gustave, q.v.

GUSTAV
German for Gustave, q.v.

GUSTAVE
From the Swedish, meaning 'Goth's staff'.

GUY
From the German, meaning 'wood'. A saint's name, it was introduced by the Normans and popular, until Guy Fawkes and others made the attempt to blow up the Houses of Parliament on 5th November 1605.

Sir Walter Scott's novel, *Guy Mannering* (1815), and the hero of the very popular *Heir of Redcliffe* (1853) by C.M. Yonge, revitalised the name.

GWILYM
Welsh for William, q.v.

GWYN
From the Celtic, meaning 'blond'.

GYLES
A variant of Giles, q.v.

HADLEY
From this surname, meaning 'one who lives by the heath meadow'.

HADRIAN
From the Latin, meaning 'one who is dark'.

HAKON
From the Norse, meaning 'one of the exalted race'.

HAL
A diminutive of Henry, q.v.; used most famously by Shakespeare as the pet-name of the future Henry V in the plays *Henry IV: Part I* and *Part II*.

HAMAR
From the Norse, meaning 'strong man'.

HAMILTON
A place name and aristocratic surname, used as a first name for nearly two hundred years. It is the surname of the dukes of Abercorn and five other peers.

HAMISH
The Gaelic version of James, q.v.

HAMMOND
From this surname and from the Teutonic, meaning 'belonging to Hamon'.

HAMON
An Anglo-Saxon name from Heahmund, meaning 'great protection'.

HANK
A variant of Henry (q.v.), mainly used in the United States.

HANNIBAL
From the Phoenician, meaning 'by Baal's grace'. Hannibal was a general of Carthage.

HANS
From the Teutonic Johannes (the German for John, q.v.).

HARALD
Danish and Swedish for Harold, q.v.

HARBEN
From the Gaelic, meaning 'warrior'.

HARCOURT
From the French, meaning 'of the fort farm'. This name is mentioned in the eleventh century Battle Abbey Rolls.

HARDING
From the Teutonic, meaning 'bold friend'.

HARDY
From the Teutonic, meaning 'bold'.

HARLEY
A place name and surname, meaning 'wood with hares', now used as a first name. Robert Harley, 1st Earl of Oxford (1661–1724), and his son Edward, collected the thousands of rare manuscripts and papers bought by the Government in 1754 to be preserved for the nation at the British Museum.

HAROLD
From the Old English, meaning 'army rule'. A royal name, particularly associated with Harold II (1022–1066), son of Godwin of Wessex, killed at the Battle of Hastings.

(King Harold I of Norway (850–933) unwisely vowed not to cut or comb his hair until he became sole king of that country: to achieve this took ten years! He cannot have been a wholesome companion.)

The name fell from favour until Byron's verse epic, *Childe Harold's Pilgrimage,* took Britain by storm in the early nineteenth century.

HARRIS
From this surname, meaning 'Harry's son'.

HARRISON
A surname, used as a first name since Victorian times.

HARRY
A variant of Henry, q.v.

HARTLEY
A place name, meaning 'stag wood', and surname, now used as a first name. The poet Coleridge named his son Hartley in 1796 as a compliment to the philosopher, David Hartley (1705–1757), who was famous for his book *Observations on Man.*

HARVEY
This name was brought to England at the time of the Norman Conquest. St. Herve, anglicised to Harvey, was venerated all over Brittany. He was born blind in the sixth century, and was a wandering minstrel before becoming a hermit.

This name is mentioned eleven times in the Domesday Book.

HAYDEN
From this surname, meaning 'one who lives by the cliff heath'.

HECTOR
From the Greek, meaning 'holding fast'. In Greek legend, he was the son of Priam and Hecuba, the noblest of all the Trojan heroes. He was slain by Achilles and his body was dragged around Troy three times, lashed to Achilles' chariot.

Hector Munro (1870–1916) was the real name of the writer, 'Saki'.

HEINRICH
German for Henry, q.v.

HENDRIK
Danish and Dutch for Henry, q.v.

HENRI
French for Henry, q.v.

HENRIK
Swedish for Henry, q.v.

HENRY
From the Old German, meaning 'home ruler'. A solidly regal name, borne by eight English kings. Henry V (1387–1422) is renowned for an outstanding victory at Agincourt in 1415. His son, Henry VI (1421–1471), came to the throne at eight months and is remembered for founding Eton College and King's College, Cambridge.

Henry FitzAilwyn was the first Lord Mayor of London in 1189: his first duty was to organise the ransom of Richard the Lionheart, captured on his way home from the Third Crusade.

Sir Henry Irving (1838–1905) received a knighthood in 1895, the first actor to be so honoured.

HERBERT
From the Old German, meaning 'army bright'. St. Herbert (d.687) lived a hermit's life on the island in Lake Derwentwater. The name died out in England after this, to be reintroduced at the Norman Conquest. Herbert FitzHerbert was treasurer to Henry I (1068–1135).

Herbert Farjeon (1887–1945), the English writer and playwright, wrote *Nine Sharp* and the delightfully named *An Elephant in Arcady,* among others.

HERMAN
From the Old High German, meaning 'soldier'. This is another of the names introduced into England by the Normans. The American writer Herman Melville (1819–1891) wrote *Moby Dick: or, The Whale,* as well as dwelling with cannibals and becoming involved in a mutiny!

HERNANDO
Spanish for Ferdinand, q.v.

HEROLD
Dutch for Harold, q.v.

HEW
A Welsh variant of Hugh, q.v.

HILAIRE
From the Latin, meaning 'cheerful'. A bearer of this name was Hilaire Belloc, the writer.

HILARIO
Spanish for Hilary, q.v.

HILARIUS
Danish, Dutch, German and Swedish for Hilary, q.v.

HILARY
See the entry in the girls' section.

HIRAM
From the Hebrew, meaning 'most noble'.

HOGAN
From the Irish, meaning 'youthful'.

HOLMAN
This name means 'one who lives by a holm', 'holm' being the Scandinavian for a 'river island'. A bearer of this name was William Holman Hunt, the painter.

HOMER
From the Greek, meaning 'security'. Homer was the name of a Greek poet believed to have lived around 700 B.C. It is used as a first name mainly in the United States.

HORACE
From the Latin, meaning 'time'. The name of an ancient Roman family and a renowned lyric poet, it was first used in England during the sixteenth century.

Horace Walpole (1717–1797), son of the first British Prime Minister, is famous for his prolific letters which provide an unrivalled view of the eighteenth century. He also wrote the earliest Gothic novel, *The Castle of Otranto* (1764).

HORACIO
Spanish for Horace, q.v.

HORATIO
From the Latin, meaning 'keeper of the hours'. One famous bearer of

the name was Horatio, Lord Nelson.

HORATIUS
German for Horace, q.v.

HORATS
Dutch for Horace, q.v.

HOWARD
An aristocratic surname, most notably of the Duke of Norfolk, Earl Marshal of England, used as a first name from Victorian times.

John Howard (1726–1790) became famous for his efforts to secure prison reforms; he died in Russia, having gone there to investigate conditions in the Russian army. The Howard League for Penal Reform is named after him.

HOWELL
From the Welsh, meaning 'one who is alert'.

HUBERT
From the Old German, meaning 'bright heart'. St. Hubert (656–727), Bishop of Liège and patron of huntsmen, made the name popular in the Middle Ages. It was revived by the Victorians.

Hubert Lane was the perpetual enemy of the hero of the many *William* books for children, written by Richmal Crompton.

HUDSON
A surname, meaning 'son of Hudd' or 'Hugh', now used as a first name. Henry Hudson (d.1611), an English explorer, made four voyages in search of the North-East and North-West Passages. Hudson Bay, Hudson Strait and the Hudson River are named after him. On his last voyage, he was set adrift by mutineers and never seen again.

HUGH
From the Old German, meaning 'bright spirit'. There are several saints bearing this name. St. Hugh of Lincoln (c. 1135–1200) was a Carthusian monk, later a bishop. He is famous for having a pet swan and being responsible for the rebuilding of Lincoln Cathedral.

Huw and Hew are Welsh variants of the name.

HUGHIE
A variant of Hugh, q.v.

HUGIBERT
German for Hubert, q.v.

HUGO
The Latin form of Hugh, revived by the Victorians. It is mentioned in the Domesday Book. Also Dutch, Swedish, Spanish, Danish and German for Hugh, q.v.

HUGUES
French for Hugh, q.v.

HUMFRID
Swedish for Humphrey, q.v.

HUMFRIED
Dutch and German for Humphrey, q.v.

HUMPHREY
From the Old German, meaning 'peaceful giant'. The name was introduced by the Normans. Humphrey, Duke of Gloucester (1391–1447) was the youngest son of Henry IV and brother of Henry V, with whom he fought at Agincourt. He was a great patron of literature.

The American actor Humphrey Bogart (1899–1957) played the private detective, Sam Spade, in the classic film *The Maltese Falcon*.

HUNFREDO
Spanish for Humphrey, q.v.

HUW
A Welsh variant of Hugh, q.v.

HUXLEY
From the Anglo-Saxon, meaning 'of Hugh's lea'.

HYDE
From the Anglo-Saxon, meaning 'from the hide', a 'hide' being a land measure.

HYMAN
From the Hebrew, meaning 'man of life'.

IACOVO
Italian for Jacob, q.v.

IAIN
A variant of Ian, q.v.

IAN
The Scottish form of John, q.v. The writer Ian Fleming (1908–1964) created James Bond, a secret agent for British Intelligence.

IDRIS
From the Welsh, meaning 'fiery Lord'.

IFOR
A variant of Ivor, q.v.

IGNACE
French for Ignatius, q.v.

IGNACIO
Spanish for Ignatius, q.v.

IGNATIUS
From the Latin, meaning 'fiery one'.

IGNAZ
German for Ignatius, q.v.

IGNAZIO
Italian for Ignatius, q.v.

IKE
A variant of Isaac, q.v.

ILARIO
Italian for Hilary, q.v.

ING
A variant of Ingram, q.v.

INGRAM
From the Scandinavian, meaning 'of the meadow'.

INIGO
A Spanish version of the name Ignatius, regularly used in Great Britain. The English architect Inigo Jones (1573–1652) was responsible for introducing the proscenium arch to the theatre and designed the Banqueting Hall in Whitehall and the Queen's House at Greenwich, among others.

INNIS
From the Gaelic, meaning 'of the river island'.

IRA
From the Hebrew, meaning 'watchful'.

IRVINE
A variant of Irving, q.v.

IRVING
From the Anglo-Saxon, meaning 'friend of the sea'.

ISAAC
From the Hebrew, meaning 'God be kind'. The Old Testament Isaac was the son of Abraham and Sarah, born when his father was one hundred years old.

Mentioned in the Domesday Book, it became generally popular in Britain after the Reformation.

Sir Isaac Newton (1642–1727), mathematician and discoverer of the law of gravity, whose magnificent tomb can be seen in Westminster Abbey, is the most famous bearer of the name.

IVAN
The Russian form of John, used steadily in Great Britain since the

late nineteenth century. Ivan III (1440–1505) was the first Russian ruler to use the title of Tsar (Caesar).

IVES
A variant of Ivo, q.v.

IVO
From the German, meaning 'yew wood'. A popular name in Normandy, it was brought to England at the Norman Conquest. An Englishwoman, sister of Edwin, Earl of Mercia and Morcar, Earl of Northumbria, married an Ivo Taillebois shortly afterwards.

IVOR
From the Welsh, meaning 'lord'. (David) Ivor Novello (1893–1951), the composer and actor-manager, was a well-known bearer of the name.

IZAAK
A variant of Isaac, q.v. Fishermen will never forget the writer and ironmonger Izaak Walton (1593–1683), best known for his book *The Compleat Angler*, still in print today.

JABEZ
An Old Testament reference, 1 Chronicles, ch.4 v9 – 'His mother called him Jabez, saying "Because I bore him in pain"' – explains the use of this from the seventeenth century onwards, when Puritans rejected non-Biblical names.

JACK
A popular diminutive of John; the name of many heroes in tales and

songs for children, including *Jack the Giant-Killer* and *Jack and Jill* (which demonstrate its age).

JACKSON
From this surname, meaning 'son of Jack'.

JACOB
From the Hebrew, meaning 'supplanter'. In the Bible, Jacob was twin brother to Esau and the son of Isaac and Rebecca. He had twelve sons, who became the fathers of the twelve tribes of Israel.

Always a favourite in the Jewish community, it attained general popularity at the Reformation.

Jacob Flanders was the hero of the first memorable novel by Virginia Woolf, entitled *Jacob's Room* (1922).

JACOBO
Spanish for Jacob, q.v.

JACQUES
French for Jacob, q.v.

JAGO
The Cornish version of James (q.v.), now popular all over Britain.

JAIME
Spanish for James, q.v.

JAKE
A variant of Jacob, q.v.

JAKOB
German for Jacob, q.v.

JAMES
The English form of Jacob. The apostle, St. James the Great, son of Zebedee, was one of the most popular saints of the Middle Ages. His shrine at Compostella in Spain had its first pilgrimage from England in 1148.

James VI of Scotland (1566–1625) became James I of England in 1603 and the name has remained popular ever since. The English explorer Captain James Cook (1728–1779) discovered New Caledonia and the Sandwich Islands, now known as Hawaii. He was murdered there by the natives, after an altercation over a stolen boat.

JAMIE
A diminutive of James, q.v.

JAN
Dutch and Swedish for John, q.v.

JARED
From the Hebrew, meaning 'descent'. The Old Testament Jared is the father of Enoch and the grandfather of Methuselah. The name was revitalised by Puritans in the seventeenth century.

JARROD
An old surname derived from Gerald (q.v.), now used as a first name.

JARROLD
From the Old English, meaning 'of the weald'.

JARVIS
A surname derived from Gervase, now used as a first name. Mr. Jarvis Lorry, clerk at Tellson's Bank in London, is a character in *A Tale of Two Cities* by Charles Dickens. He helps Lucy Manette and Charles Darnay to escape from France during the French Revolution.

JASON
The English version of Joshua, q.v. In Greek mythology, Jason led his band of Argonauts in the quest for the Golden Fleece. There are two men of this name mentioned in the New Testament: the first sheltered St. Paul and his followers in his home at Thessalonica, suffering persecution for this. It seems to have been used as a first name in Britain since the seventeenth century.

JASPER
The English form of the name Casper, q.v. One of Mrs Jarley's wax-work exhibits in *The Old Curiosity Shop* by Charles Dickens (1812–1870) is Jasper Packlemerton 'of atrocious memory, who courted and married fourteen wives, and destroyed them all by tickling the soles of their feet when they was sleeping in the consciousness of innocence and virtue'. (Unforgettable!!)

JAY
Now an independent name, originally used as a pet-form for names beginning with the letter 'J'.

JEAN
French for John, q.v.

JED
From the Hebrew, meaning 'beloved of the Lord'. The shortened form of Jedidiah; bestowed on King Solomon as an additional name by the prophet Nathan. It was used by seventeenth century Puritans and taken by them to America.

JEFF
A diminutive of Jeffery or Jeffrey, variants of Geoffrey, q.v.

JEFFERSON
From the Old English, meaning 'son of Jeffrey'.

JEFFERY
A variant spelling of Geoffrey (q.v.).

JEFFREY
A variant spelling of Geoffrey, q.v.

JEMMY
A variant of James, q.v.

JENKIN
A Welsh variant of John, q.v.

JÉRÉME
French for Jeremy, q.v.

JEREMIAH
From the Hebrew, meaning 'Jehovah's appointed'.

JEREMIAS
Spanish for Jeremy, q.v.

JEREMY
The English version of Jeremiah, the great Hebrew prophet, used in Britain from the thirteenth century.

The Engiish philosopher Jeremy Bentham (1748–1832) is now best known for bequeathing his body to University College, London, where it is preserved in a cupboard, sitting fully clothed on a chair.

JEROME

From the Greek, meaning 'sacred name'. St. Jerome (c.342–420) was a rarity among saints in being known for his bad temper. The greatest of Biblical scholars, he was responsible for translating the Bible into Latin from its original tongue. His popularity was great in the Middle Ages.

Jerome Klapka Jerome (1859–1927) wrote the incomparable *Three Men in a Boat* (1889).

JERRY

A variant of Jeremy, q.v.

JERVIS

A variant of Jarvis, q.v.

JESS

A variant of Jesse, q.v.

JESSE

From the Hebrew, meaning 'Jehovah is God'. Jesse was the father of David in the Old Testament.

JETHRO

From the Hebrew, meaning 'excellence'. In the Old Testament Jethro was a father-in-law to Moses. It came into use as a baptismal name in Britain after the Reformation.

Jethro Tull (1674–1741), the agriculturalist, invented the seed drill, among other things.

JIM

A variant of James, q.v.

JIMMY

A variant of James, q.v.

JOACHIM

From the Hebrew, meaning 'may Jehovah exult'. Legend gives this name to the father of the Blessed Virgin Mary. It has been used in England since the thirteenth century.

JOB

From the Hebrew, meaning 'persecuted'. In the Old Testament, he endured great suffering with exemplary patience. His story was a favourite of the medieval miracle plays. *Job* is the title of a masque composed by Ralph Vaughan Williams.

JOCELYN
Another of the names brought to England in the eleventh century by the Normans, and mentioned in the Domesday Book. Originally a masculine name only, it is now bestowed on both boys and girls.

Joscelin of Furness, an English Cistercian monk of the twelfth century, wrote several 'Lives' of the saints, including *The Life and Miracles of St. Patrick.*

Jocelyn is the title of a novel by John Galsworthy (1898).

JOE
A variant of Joseph, q.v.

JOEL
From the Hebrew, meaning 'the Lord is God'. The Bible contains fourteen men with this name: the most famous of these was a prophet whose *Book of Joel* was written c.500 B.C. The name has been used in Britain since the sixteenth century.

The American Joel Chandler Harris (1848–1908) wrote *Uncle Remus: His Songs and Sayings,* introducing us to Brer Rabbit.

JOEY
A variant of Joseph, q.v.

JOHAN
Swedish for John, q.v.

JOHANN
German for John, q.v.

JOHANNES
German for John, q.v.

JOHN
From the Hebrew, meaning 'God is merciful'. The name of many saints and twenty-five popes, this has been one of the most popular names in Western Europe since the twelfth century. Both St. John the Baptist and St. John the Divine, writer of the fourth gospel, have two feast days each in the church calendar.

The unpopular King John (1167–1216) was forced by the barons to sign the Magna Carta at Runnymede on 15th June 1215, outlining royal powers and the rights of free men.

The first English novel, *Euphues: the Anatomy of Wit,* was written by John Lyly in 1578.

The Scottish writer and physician to Queen Anne, John Arbuthnot (1667–1735), wrote *The History of John Bull*; a name which personifies the 'typical' Englishman.

JOHNNY
A variant of Jonathan, q.v.

JOLYON
A medieval version of the name Julian (q.v.), made popular by the hero of the *The Forsyte Saga,* written by John Galsworthy (1867–1933), and later televised.

JON
A variant of John, q.v.

JONAH
From the Hebrew, meaning 'dove'. The Old Testament Jonah had been told by God to preach repentance in the wicked city of Nineveh. He refused and boarded a ship going in the opposite direction. When storms arose, the sailors threw Jonah into the sea to avert catastrophe.

Being swallowed by a whale, he lived in its belly for three days until deposited on dry land. Wisely, he then went to Nineveh and caused the city to repent. The story was very popular in the Middle Ages.

JONAS
Greek and Swedish for Jonah, q.v. St. Jonas was martyred in Iran in 327.

JONATHAN
From the Hebrew, meaning 'God's gift'. The Biblical Jonathan is best remembered as a friend to King David. It has been used in Britain since the thirteenth century.

The clergyman Jonathan Swift (1667–1745), satirist and political writer, is best remembered for his novel *Gulliver's Travels.*

JORDAN
The name of the principal river in Israel, where Christ was baptised by John the Baptist. Twelfth century Crusaders brought back a flask of Jordan water to be used in the baptism of their children and

bestowed the name on both boys and girls, as now.

JORGE
Spanish for George, q.v.

JOSÉ
Spanish for Joseph, q.v.

JOSEPH
From the Hebrew, meaning 'may Jehovah add'. The Old Testament Joseph was the favourite son of Jacob and famed for his 'coat of many colours', before being sold into slavery in Egypt by his jealous brothers. The most renowned Joseph in the New Testament was husband to the Blessed Virgin Mary.

And heartfelt thanks to Joseph Lister (1827–1912), the founder of antiseptic surgery; and to the civil engineer Sir Joseph Bazalgette (1819–1891), who designed London's main drainage system.

JOSH
A variant of Joshua, q.v.

JOSHUA
From the Hebrew, meaning 'Jehovah saves'. The Biblical Joshua led the Israelites into the Promised Land after the death of Moses. It came into general use after the Reformation.

Sir Joshua Reynolds (1723–1792), the English portrait painter, was a founding member of the Royal Academy and its first president.

JOSIAH
From the Hebrew, meaning 'God heals'. The Old Testament Josiah (c.639–609 B.C.), King of Judah, came to the throne at the age of eight and was killed at Megiddo, fighting the Egyptians. The name came into use in Britain after the Reformation.

Josiah Wedgwood (1730–1795), the founder of the pottery company, is the most well-known bearer of the name.

JOSS
A variant of Jocelyn, q.v.

JUAN
Spanish for John, q.v.

JUDE
From the Hebrew, meaning 'praised'.

JULES
French for Julius, q.v.

JULIAN
Derived from Julius, the name of an ancient Roman family, the most famous member of which was Julius Caesar (100–44 B.C.).

There are many saints named Julian: St. Julian the Hospitaller is the patron of ferrymen and innkeepers. The name has been used in Britain since the thirteenth century.

JULIO
Spanish for Julius, q.v.

JULIUS
From the Latin, meaning 'bearded'.

JUSTIN
From the Latin, meaning 'just'. A name popular among the early Christians in Rome. St. Justin (100–165) was beheaded for refusing to sacrifice to idols. His *Dialogues* and *Apologies* survived and have been translated into English.

KANE
A French place name, meaning 'field of combat' and surname, now used as a first name.

KAREL
Dutch for Charles, q.v.

KARL

Karl is the popular German version of Charles, q.v.

KAVAN

From the Gaelic, meaning 'handsome'.

KEANE

From the Irish, meaning 'long' or 'tall'.

KEIR

From the Gaelic, meaning 'swarthy'. A surname, now used as a first name. (James) Keir Hardie (1856–1915), who did not go to school and began work in the coalmines at the age of ten, is renowned as the first Labour Member of Parliament.

KEITH

From the Gaelic, meaning 'forest'. A Scottish place name and surname, used as a first name all over Britain from the late nineteenth century.

KELLY

See the entry in the girls' section.

KELSEY

An English place name and surname, used as a first name since the 1870s.

KELVIN

From the Gaelic, meaning 'one who lives by a narrow stream'.

KEN

A variant of Kenneth, q.v.

KENDALL

A place name, meaning 'valley of the River Kent', and surname. It has been used as a first name from mid-Victorian times.

KENDRICK

From the Gaelic, meaning 'Henry's son'.

KENNETH

From the Gaelic, meaning 'handsome'. A Scottish royal name, it has been used all over Britain since the late nineteenth century.

Kenneth I MacAlpin was the first king of Scotland, and invaded England six times. Kenneth Grahame (1859–1932), Governor of the Bank of England, is more famous for writing *The Wind in the Willows*.

KENNY
A variant of Kenneth, q.v.

KENRICK
From the Gaelic, meaning 'son of Henry'.

KENT
From the Celtic, meaning 'bright'.

KENYON
From the Gaelic, meaning 'white haired'.

KERN
From the Gaelic, meaning 'dark'.

KERR
From the Gaelic, meaning 'spear'.

KESTER
An abbreviation of Christopher popular in the seventeenth century and now enjoying a revival.

KEVIN
From the Irish, meaning 'handsome at birth'. St. Kevin (d.618) was the founder of the monastery at Glendalough, County Wicklow. Always a popular name in Ireland, it became generally used in the 1920s.

KIERAN
From the Irish, meaning 'dark-haired'. Over twenty Irish saints have borne this name. St. Kieran of Clonmacnois (516–549) was once dismissed from a monastery for too great a generosity to the poor. There was nothing left for the monks to eat. This name has been generally popular since the 1950s.

KIM
See the entry in the girls' section.

KINGSLEY

An Old English place name, meaning 'king's wood', and surname, now used as a first name. The novelist Charles Kingsley (1819–1875) wrote *Westward Ho!* and *The Water Babies.* Kingsley Amis wrote, among other novels, the very funny *Lucky Jim* which has been filmed and televised.

KIRK

From the Old Norse, meaning 'church'. A place name and surname, now used as a first name. Sir John Kirk (1832–1922), the Scottish administrator and naturalist, distinguished himself by helping to abolish slavery in Zanzibar (now Tanzania) and was one of the first white men to see Lake Nyasa.

KIT

A variant of Christopher, q.v.

KLEMENS

German for Clement, q.v.

KOENRAAD

Dutch for Conrad, q.v.

KONRAD

Swedish for Conrad, q.v.

KRISPIJN

Dutch for Crispin, q.v.

KRISTIAN

Swedish for Christian, q.v.

KRISTOFOR

Swedish for Christopher, q.v.

KURT

German for Conrad, q.v.

KYLE

From the Gaelic, meaning 'channel between islands'. A place name and a surname, now used as a first name for both boys and girls.

The Kyles of Bute, very narrow straits between the Scottish coast and the island of Bute, are noted for their beautiful surroundings.

LACHLAN
From the Gaelic, meaning 'warlike'.

LAMBERT
From the Teutonic, meaning 'of the bright land'. This name is mentioned in the Domesday Book.

LAMBERTO
Italian for Lambert, q.v.

LANCE
A diminutive of Lancelot, the hero of Arthurian legend, whose affair with Queen Guinevere brought disaster.

Lance has been used as a first name in England since the thirteenth century.

LANCELOT
From the Teutonic, meaning 'land'.

LARRY
A variant of Laurence, q.v.

LARS
A diminutive of Larson, q.v.

LARSON
From the Scandinavian, meaning 'son of Lars'.

LAURENCE
From the Greek, meaning 'laurel'. This was a popular name among

the early Christians and the name of a saint much revered in the Middle Ages. St. Laurence (d.258) was martyred in Rome by being roasted on a gridiron. The Saxon church of St. Laurence in Bradford-Upon-Avon, Wiltshire, dates from 700 and is the most complete example to survive.

The actor Laurence Olivier (Lord Olivier) was the best-known bearer of the name in modern times.

LAURENS
Dutch for Laurence, q.v.

LAURENT
French for Laurence, q.v.

LAURIE
A variant of Laurence, q.v.

LAURITZ
Danish for Laurence, q.v.

LAWRENCE
A variant of Laurence, q.v.

LAWRY
A variant of Laurence, q.v.

LAWSON
From the Anglo-Irish, meaning 'son of Lawrence'.

LEANDER
From the Greek, meaning 'lion man'.

LEANDRE
French for Leander, q.v.

LEE
From the Old English, meaning 'field' or 'pasture'. A place name and surname, now used as a first name.

LEIF
From the Norse, meaning 'beloved'.

LEIGH
A variant of Lee, q.v.

LEIGHTON
From the Old English, meaning 'herb garden'. A place name and surname, used as a first name since the late 1800s.

The British painter and sculptor Frederic Leighton (1830–1896) is the only English painter to be raised to the peerage: unfortunately, this happened only a few days before his death. His home in Holland Park Road, London, is open to the public as the Leighton House Museum.

LEMAR
This name, which is mentioned in the Domesday Book, means 'famous'.

LEMUEL
From the Hebrew, meaning 'devoted to the Lord'.

LEN
A variant of Leonard, q.v.

LENNY
A variant of Leonard, q.v.

LEO
From the Latin, meaning 'lion'. The name of thirteen popes, of which five are saints. Saint Leo I (390–461), known as 'the Great', induced Attila the Hun and his army to withdraw beyond the River Danube, after confronting them in person.

Leo is a northern constellation of stars (as in Leo Minor) and the fifth sign of the zodiac. The name has been used in Britain since the thirteenth century.

LEON
A variant of Leo, q.v.

LEONARD
From the Old German, meaning 'bold as a lion'. St. Leonard was a French hermit in the sixth century. Many miracles were attributed to him and he became very popular during the Middle Ages in France and England. Crusaders revered him as the patron saint of prisoners.

LEONARDO
Italian for Leonard, q.v. Leonardo da Vinci (1452–1519), artist and sculptor, also designed a flying-machine and parachute, a fore-runner of the tank, and nearly discovered the circulation of blood!

LEONHARD
German for Leonard, q.v.

LEOPOLD
From the German, meaning 'people bold'. The name became popular in Britain in the nineteenth century. Leopold, the King of the Belgians, was Queen Victoria's favourite uncle: she named her fourth son in his honour.

LEOPOLDO
Spanish and Italian for Leopold, q.v.

LEROY
From the French, meaning 'the king'. A surname originally bestowed on servants of a king, it has been used in Britain as a first name since the beginning of the twentieth century.

The French horologist, Pierre LeRoy (1717–1785), did much work on the chronometer and made many fine clocks and watches.

LEUPOLD
German for Leopold, q.v.

LEVI
From the Hebrew, meaning 'joined'. Levi was a son of Jacob in the Old Testament.

LESLIE
A Scottish place name (in Aberdeenshire) and a surname, used as a first name since the end of the nineteenth century. It is the surname of the earls of Rothes.

LESTER
A contraction of Leicester (the English place name) and a surname, now used as a first name.

Whether or not you follow the sport of kings, the jockey Lester Piggot is the best-known bearer of this name.

LEW
A dimunitive of Lewis which is a variant of Louis, q.v.

LEWIS
The anglicised version of the French name Louis (q.v.), used since the thirteenth century.

LIAM
The Irish form of William, now generally popular.

LINCOLN
From this surname, meaning 'one who came from Lincoln'.

LINDSAY
A place name and surname, now given as a first name to both boys and girls. It is the surname of the earls of Crawford, whose motto - 'Astra castra, numen lumen munimen' – translates as 'The stars my camp, God my light and protection'.

LINDSEY
A variant of Lindsay, q.v.

LINTON
A variant of Lynton, q.v.

LIONEL
From the Greek, meaning 'little lion'. Edward III (reigned 1327–1377) named his third son Lionel in honour of the gallant Sir Lionel, one of King Arthur's legendary knights of the Round Table. The name was very popular in the Middle Ages. The composer Lionel Bart wrote the musical *Oliver.*

LLEWELLYN
From the Welsh, meaning 'leader' or 'lion'. Llywelyn ap Gruffyd, or Llwelyn the Last, died in 1282 fighting Edward I of England, and Welsh independence was lost.

LLEWELYN
A variant of Llewellyn, q.v.

LLOYD
From the Welsh, meaning 'grey'. A Welsh surname and first name, now used all over Britain. David Lloyd George (1863–1945) was

Prime Minister from 1916–1922.

LODEWIJK
Dutch for Louis, q.v.

LOGAN
From the Gaelic, meaning 'small hollow'. A Scottish place name and surname, now used as a first name. Mount Logan is the highest mountain in Canada.

LON
Variant of Laurence, q.v.

LONNIE
Variant of Laurence, q.v.

LORENZE
German for Laurence, q.v.

LORENZO
Spanish and Italian for Laurence, q.v.

LORN
A variant of Lorne, q.v.

LORNE
From the Gaelic, meaning 'warrior'.

LOTARIO
Italian for Luther, q.v.

LOTHAIRE
French for Luther, q.v.

LOU
A diminutive of Louis, q.v.

LOUIS
From the Old German, meaning 'renowned warrior'. The name of eighteen French kings (the first of whom, Louis the Fair (778–840), was the son of Charlemagne), it was brought to Britain at the Norman Conquest.

The French-born sculptor Louis Roubiliac (1702?–1762) spent all his working life in England. He is most famous for funeral monuments erected in Westminster Abbey.

LUC
French for Luke, q.v.

LUCA
Italian for Luke, q.v.

LUCAN
A variant of Luke, q.v.

LUCAS
A variant of Luke, q.v.

LUCIAN
From the Latin, meaning 'light'. Two early Christian martyrs bore this name. The Greek writer Lucian (A.D. 125–180) is best remembered for his entertaining satirical dialogues.

LUCIANO
Italian for Lucian, q.v.

LUCIEN
French for Lucian, q.v.

LUCIO
Spanish for Luke, q.v.

LUCIUS
A variant of Luke, q.v.

LUCRETIUS
From the Latin, meaning 'light'.

LUDOVIC
The Latin version of Louis, q.v.

LUDVIG
Swedish for Louis, q.v.

LUDWIG
German for Louis, q.v.

LUIGI
Italian for Louis, q.v.

LUKAS
Swedish for Luke, q.v.

LUKE
From the Greek, meaning 'coming from Lucania', a place in southern Italy. St. Luke was the author of the third gospel and the Acts of the Apostles. A Greek physician from Antioch, he was a constant companion to St. Paul. The name was brought to England at the Norman Conquest.

LUTERO
Spanish for Luther, q.v.

LUTHER
From the Teutonic, meaning 'noted warrior'.

LYLE
From the French, meaning 'of the isle'.

LYNDON
From the Old English, meaning 'lime-tree hill'. A place name and surname, now used as a first name.

LYNN
From the Celtic, meaning 'of the pool'.

LYNTON
From the Old English, meaning 'place on the torrent'. A place and surname, now used as a first name.

MADOC
From the Welsh, meaning 'fortunate'.

MAGNUS
From the Latin, meaning 'great'. A royal name in Norway and Denmark: Magnus II, King of Norway (d.1265), sold the Isle of Man to Scotland. A popular first name in Scotland, it is now used all over Britain.

MAKEPEACE
This name means 'man of peace'. A bearer of this name was the novelist William Makepeace Thackeray.

MALACHI
From the Hebrew, meaning 'messenger'.

MALCOLM
From the Gaelic, meaning 'disciple of Columb'. There have been four Scottish kings with this name: Malcolm IV (1141–1165) was the last Gaelic-speaking monarch. Sir Malcolm Sargent (1895–1967) was the conductor-in-chief at the Promenade concerts at the Royal Albert Hall from 1957 until his death.

MANFRED
From the Old English, meaning 'peaceful'.

MANNY
A diminutive of Emmanuel, q.v.

MANUEL
Spanish for Emmanuel, q.v.

MARC
French for Mark, q.v.

MARCEL
A French name, meaning 'warlike'.

MARCELLO
Italian for Marcel, q.v.

MARCELLUS
From the Latin, meaning 'warlike'.

MARCELO
Spanish for Marcel, q.v.

MARCO
Italian for Mark, q.v.

MARCOS
Spanish for Mark, q.v.

MARCUS
The Latin form of Mark (q.v.), which came into use in Britain in the nineteenth century.
   The Roman Emperor Marcus Aurelius (A.D. 121–180) wrote his famous *Meditations* in Greek as he rested between battles.

MARIO
From the Latin, meaning 'warlike'.

MARIUS
From the Latin, meaning 'warlike'.

MARK
Derived from the name of Mars, the Roman god of war. The Biblical St. Mark was the writer of the second gospel. A martyr, his body was enshrined in the original church of San Marco, in Venice.
   In Arthurian legend, Mark was the King of Cornwall. The name was popular throughout the Middle Ages.

MARKUS
German and Swedish for Mark, q.v.

MARLEY
From the Old English, meaning 'pleasant wood'. A place name and surname, now used as a first name.

The reggae musician Bob Marley (1945–1981) made his surname a popular choice for music-loving parents.

MARLON
From the French, meaning 'hawk-like'.

MARMADUKE
From the Celtic, meaning 'servant of Madoc'. This name is mentioned in the Domesday Book.

MARSHALL
From the Anglo-Saxon, meaning 'steward or chief horseman'.

MARTIJN
Dutch for Martin, q.v.

MARTIN
From the Latin, meaning 'belonging to Mars'. St. Martin of Tours (c.315–397) was one of the first holy men not martyred to be venerated as a saint. The story of his dividing his cloak with a beggar was a favourite subject with medieval artists and many churches are dedicated to him.

MARTINO
Spanish and Italian for Martin, q.v.

MARTY
A variant of Martin, q.v.

MARTYN
A variant of Martin, q.v.

MASON
An old occupational surname, now used as a first name. The Mason-Dixon Line, the boundary line popularly used to distinguish the northern from the southern states of America, is named after two British astronomers. Charles Mason and Jeremiah Dixon surveyed it between 1763 and 1767 to put an end to land disputes.

MATEO
Spanish for Matthew, q.v.

MATHESON
From this surname, meaning 'Matthew's son'.

MATHIEU
French for Matthew, q.v.

MATT
A diminutive of Matthew, q.v.

MATTAEUS
Danish for Matthew, q.v.

MATTEO
Italian for Matthew, q.v.

MATTHAUS
German for Matthew, q.v.

MATTHEUS
Dutch and Swedish for Matthew, q.v.

MATTHEW
From the Hebrew, meaning 'gift of the Lord'. In the New Testament, St. Matthew was the writer of the first gospel. He was a tax-collector until called to be an apostle. The name was brought to England at the Norman Conquest.

MATTHIAS
The Latin form of Matthew, q.v. In the New Testament, the name of the disciple chosen to replace Judas Iscariot.

MAURICE
From the Latin, meaning 'a Moor' or 'dark skinned'. St. Maurice was a member of a Roman Legion serving in Gaul in the third century, all of whom were martyred for refusing to take part in heathen sacrifices. The name was brought to England at the time of the Norman Conquest.

MAURICIO
Spanish for Maurice, q.v.

MAURITS
Dutch for Maurice, q.v.

MAURIZIO
Italian for Maurice, q.v.

MAX
A diminutive of Maximilian, q.v.

MAXIM
A variant of Maximilian, q.v.

MAXIMILIAN
From the Latin, meaning 'greatest'. A European royal name, popular in Germany, now used worldwide. The Viennese born Maximilian, Emperor of Mexico (1832–1867) caused a civil war and was executed by firing squad.

Maxim De Winter is the romantic hero of the novel *Rebecca* (1938), written by Daphne du Maurier.

MAXIMILIANO
Spanish for Maximilian, q.v.

MAXIMILIANUS
Dutch for Maximilian, q.v.

MAXIMILIEN
French for Maximilian, q.v.

MAXIMO
Spanish for Maximilian, q.v.

MAXWELL
A Scottish place name, meaning 'Magnus's stream', and surname, now used as a first name.

MAYNARD
From the Teutonic, meaning 'strong and mighty'.

MAYNE
A variant of Maynard, q.v.

MELVILLE

A French place name and surname, used as a first name from the late nineteenth century.

Melville Island is situated off the coast of Northern Australia.

MELVIN

From the Anglo-Saxon, meaning 'friend'.

MENARD

French for Maynard, q.v.

MEREDITH

See the entry in the girls' section.

MERLIN

From the Welsh, a contraction of Carmarthen, meaning 'sea-hill fort'. A great figure of Arthurian Legend, Merlin had charge of the infant Arthur and ensured his future greatness as a king. A seer and magician, he transported Stonehenge from Ireland to Salisbury Plain in one night. Nothing now remains of him but his voice, thanks to the enchantments of the Lady of the Lake.

MERVIN

A variant of Mervyn and Merlin, q.v.

MERVYN

The English form of Merlin, q.v.

MICAH

From the Hebrew, meaning 'who is God-like'.

MICHA

A form of Micah, q.v.

MICHAEL

From the Hebrew, meaning 'Who is like God?'. The Bible speaks of the Archangel Michael as leader of the heavenly hosts. Tradition states that he drove the rebel angels from heaven: St. Michael and all Angels is the most popular church dedication in Britain. The name has been a favourite since the twelfth century.

Michael Faraday (1791–1867), a blacksmith's son, became a famous chemist and a pioneer in the science of electricity.

MICHEL
French for Michael, q.v.

MICHELE
Italian for Michael, q.v.

MICK
A variant of Michael, q.v.

MICKY
A variant of Michael, q.v.

MIGUEL
Spanish for Michael, q.v.

MIKAEL
Swedish for Michael, q.v.

MIKE
A diminutive of Michael, q.v.

MILES
From the Old German, meaning 'merciful'. The name was brought to Britain by the Normans and became popular. It was revived by the Victorians.

Miles is a character in the famous Coventry Mystery Plays of the fifteenth century.

MILNE
From this surname, meaning 'one who lives by a mill'.

MILO
From the Greek, meaning 'strong'.

MILTON
An Old English place name, meaning 'mill farm' and surname, used as a first name from the nineteenth century.

The poet and writer John Milton (1608–1674) is famous for the epic poem *Paradise Lost* (1667) and for *Samson Agonistes*. Latin secretary to Oliver Cromwell, the strain of the work caused him to lose his sight.

MISCHA
Slav for Michael, q.v.

MITCH
A diminutive of Mitchell, q.v.

MITCHELL
A surname derived from the medieval French version of Michael, now used as a first name. Reginald Mitchell (1895–1937), a leading designer in the history of aviation, was responsible for the Spitfire.

MONTAGUE
A French place name, meaning 'pointed hill', and surname, now used as a first name. Drogo de Montaigu accompanied William the Conqueror to England.

Montague Rhodes James (1862–1936), Provost of Eton, was the writer of the finest ghost stories in English literature, notably *Casting the Runes* and *The Tractate Middoth*.

MONTGOMERY
From the French, meaning 'from the castle hill'.

MONTY
A variant of Montague, q.v., and of Montgomery, q.v.

MOORE
From the French, meaning 'like a Moor'.

MORAY
A variant of Murray, q.v.

MORGAN
From the Welsh, meaning 'sea-bright'. A surname, now used as a first name for both boys and girls.

MORITZ
German for Maurice, q.v.

MORLEY
From this surname, meaning 'one who dwells by the moor meadow'.

MORRICE
A variant of Maurice, q.v.

MORRIS
A variant of Maurice, q.v.

MORTIMER
A French place name and surname, now used as a first name. The archaeologist Sir Mortimer Wheeler, who fought long and hard to establish archaeology as an academic subject in the University of London, is the best-known bearer of the name.

MORTON
An Old English place name, meaning 'farm on the fen', and surname, used as a first name since the mid nineteenth century.

MUNGO
This is the Celtic nickname meaning 'most dear' for St. Kentigern, founder of the church in Glasgow. The Scottish explorer Mungo Park (1771–1806) navigated the river Niger in West Africa, finally dying in the rapids at Bussa after great hardships.

MUNRO
A Scottish surname, now used as a first name.

MURDO
A variant of Murdoch, q.v.

MURDOCH
From the Gaelic, meaning 'sailor'. A surname, now used as a first name.

MURRAY
A Scottish place name, meaning 'settlement beside the sea', and surname, now used as a first name. It is the surname of the dukes of Atholl, the only family in Britain permitted to keep a private army.

NAHUM
From the Hebrew, meaning 'comforter'.

NAPIER
From the surname Napier, meaning 'cloth-worker'.

NASH
From the surname, meaning 'one who lives by the ash tree'.

NAT
A diminutive of Nathaniel, q.v.

NATAL
Spanish for Noel, q.v.

NATALE
Italian for Noel, q.v.

NATHAN
From the Hebrew, meaning 'gift'. In the Old Testament, the prophet Nathan rebuked King David for sending Uriah to his death in battle so that David could marry his widow, Bathsheba.

The name came into general use in the seventeenth century when Puritan parents rejected non-Biblical names.

NATHANIEL
From the Hebrew, meaning 'God has given'. In the New Testament, the personal name of the apostle Bartholomew (which means 'son of Talmai'), who tradition states was martyred by being flayed alive in

Armenia. The name became common after the Reformation.

The Scarlet Letter is the best-known work of the American writer Nathaniel Hawthorne (1804–1864). He also wrote the delightful *Our Old Home* while American consul in Liverpool.

NEAL
A variant of Neil, q.v.

NED
A pet-form of Edward, q.v. Common in the Middle Ages, it is now enjoying a revival.

NEIL
From the Gaelic, meaning 'champion'. Well known before the Norman Conquest, the name travelled from Ireland to Scandinavia and on to Britain.

In 1969 Neil Armstrong was the first man to step upon the moon.

NELSON
Originally a surname, meaning 'son of Neil' or 'Nell'. Its use as a first name was in honour of Admiral Lord Nelson (1758–1805), who defeated the French and Spanish at the Battle of Trafalgar and died in action. He was given a state funeral and lies buried in the crypt of St. Paul's Cathedral in London.

NEVILLE
A French place name and aristocratic surname, used regularly as a first name from the mid-nineteenth century. Gilbert de Nevil came to England as a companion to William the Conqueror. (Arthur) Neville Chamberlain, Prime Minister of Great Britain 1937–1940, had the melancholy task of taking the country into the Second World War.

NEWTON
From this surname, meaning 'one who lives by the new town'.

NIAL
A variant of Neil, q.v.

NIALL
A variant of Neil, q.v.

NICHOLAS
From the Greek, meaning 'people's victory'. The patron saint of chil-

dren, sailors, merchants and pawnbrokers; venerated in both East and West; St. Nicholas, fourth century bishop of Myra, is best known as the original 'Father Christmas', taken from the Dutch Sinte Claus. It has been a favourite name in Britain since the twelfth century.

Nicholas of Cusa (1401–1464), a German theologian, suggested the earth rotated around the sun approximately fifty years before the theory was formulated by Copernicus.

NICK
A diminutive of Nicholas, q.v.

NICKLAS
Swedish for Nicholas, q.v.

NICKY
A diminutive of Nicholas, q.v.

NICOL
The medieval version of Nicholas, (q.v.), now used in its own right.

NICOLA
Italian for Nicholas, q.v.

NICOLAS
Spanish for Nicholas and also a British variant of Nicholas, q.v.

NIGEL
The Latin version of Neil (q.v.), introduced to England by the Normans and mentioned in the Domesday Book. It was revived by the Victorians. Sir Nigel Loring is a heroic character in *The White Company* (1891), a historical romance by Sir Arthur Conan Doyle.

NIKOLAUS
German for Nicholas, q.v.

NILS
Scandinavian for Neil, q.v.

NOACH
Dutch for Noah, q.v.

NOAH
From the Hebrew, meaning 'long-lived'. The name of the Biblical

hero who built the ark, at the behest of the Almighty, to ensure the survival of the patriarch, his family and two of each kind of animal at the time of the Great Flood. It was used by Puritans in the seventeenth century and taken to America by them.

Noah Claypole brings about the murder of Nancy by Bill Sikes in Charles Dickens' novel, *Oliver Twist*.

NOAK
Swedish for Noah, q.v.

NOÉ
Spanish and French for Noah, q.v.

NOEL
From the French, meaning 'Christmas'. Used as a baptismal name for both boys and girls born on Christmas Day during the Middle Ages, it has been a male name from the seventeenth century.

Noel Coward (1899–1973), writer, actor and playwright of such plays as *Blithe Spirit* and *Private Lives* is a well-known bearer of the name.

NOLAN
An Irish surname, meaning 'descendant of a noble', now used as a first name.

NOLL
An old variant of Oliver, q.v.

NORBERT
From the Old German, meaning 'famous in the north'. St. Norbert (1080–1134) was a German courtier who became a bishop and founder of the Premonstratensian Canons. The name has been used in Britain since the late nineteenth century, when there was great enthusiasm for medieval names.

NORMAN
From the Old English, meaning 'Northman'. The name was popular in England before the Norman Conquest and continued so until the 1300s. It was revived by the Victorians.

The British actor Norman Wisdom (b.1915) and the fashion designer Norman Hartnell (1901–1979) are well-known bearers of the name.

NORRIS
From the Old French meaning 'northerner'. A surname, now used as a first name.

NYE
A variant of Aneurin, q.v.

OCTAVIUS
From the Latin, meaning 'eighth child'.

OLAF
From the Norse Olafr, meaning 'old relic'. This name is mentioned in the Domesday Book and has been the name of some of the kings of Norway.

OLAV
A variant of Olaf, q.v.

OLIVER
From the Old Norse, meaning 'ancestor'. Oliver is a close friend to the eponymous hero of the popular medieval romance *Song of Roland,* in which both are knights of Charlemagne.

Oliver Cromwell (1599–1658), Puritan leader and Lord Protector of the Realm after the execution of Charles I, caused the name to fall into disfavour until the nineteenth century.

Oliver Twist, or The Parish Boy's Progress (1837), which tells of a boy who emerges unscathed from the criminal underworld to be happy ever after, remains one of the most popular of the novels of Charles Dickens.

OLIVERIO
Spanish for Oliver, q.v.

OLIVIER
French for Oliver, q.v.

OLIVIERO
Italian for Oliver, q.v.

OMAR
From the Persian, meaning 'first born'.

ONEFRE
Spanish for Humphrey, q.v.

ONEFREDO
Italian for Humphrey, q.v.

ONFROI
French for Humphrey, q.v.

ORAZIO
Italian for Horace, q.v.

ORLANDO
The Italian form of Roland, q.v. The English composer Orlando Gibbons (1583–1625) was organist at Westminster Abbey. His church anthems, keyboard works and madrigals are still performed today.

ORVILLE
From the French, meaning 'of the golden place'.

OSBERT
From the Anglo-Saxon, meaning 'God's brightness'.

OSBORN
From the German, meaning 'divine spear'.

OSCAR
From the Old English, meaning 'god-spear'. James Macpherson (1736–1796) published poems purporting to have been composed by the mythical Gaelic bard Ossian, who had a son named Oscar. The

popularity of this work revived the name.

Napoleon bestowed it on his godson, who went on to become Oscar I, king of Sweden and Norway.

Oscar Fingal O'Flahertie Wills Wilde (1854–1900), writer and playwright, penned the delightful *The Importance of Being Earnest,* now considered his masterpiece.

OSMOND

From the Old English, meaning 'God's protection'. This is the Norman version of a name used in England before the Norman Conquest.

St. Osmond (d. 1099) came to England as Chancellor to William the Conqueror, later becoming a bishop. The name was revived in the late nineteenth century.

OSMUND

A variant of Osmond, q.v.

OSWALD

From the Old English, meaning 'divine power'. St. Oswald I of Northumbria (605–641) who was the first Anglo-Saxon king to be canonised and St. Oswald (d.992), Archbishop of York, ensured the popularity of the name. It was revived by the Victorians.

Oswald Bastable is the hero of several classic books by the children's writer, Edith Nesbit (1858–1924). If you have not already read these, you have a treat in store.

OTIS

From the Old German, meaning 'riches'. A surname derived from Otto, now used as a first name.

OTTO

From the Old German, meaning 'riches'. The nomadic tribe of Magyars was defeated by King Otto the Great of Germany in 955 and settled down to farm the land which we call Hungary. The name was introduced to Britain by the Normans and is mentioned in the Domesday Book. The name was revived in the mid-nineteenth century.

OWEN

A Welsh name, derived from Eugene, now in general use. Owen Glendower (1359–1416) was a Welsh chieftain who fought for Welsh independence from the English. He was defeated by the future Henry V in 1405.

PABLO
Spanish for Paul, q.v.

PADDY
A variant of Patrick, q.v.

PAOLO
Italian for Paul, q.v.

PASCAL
From the Old English, meaning 'Easter'. Given to boys born in the Easter season, this has been used as a baptismal name since the Middle Ages, particularly in Cornwall.

PAT
A diminutive of Patrick, q.v.

PATRICE
French for Patrick, q.v.

PATRICIO
Spanish for Patrick, q.v.

PATRICK
From the Latin, meaning 'nobleman'. The patron saint of Ireland, St. Patrick (c.385–461), whose original name was Sucat, was taken as a slave to Ireland at the age of sixteen from his home on the Severn Estuary. After six years he managed to escape, but was called in a dream to go back to Ireland as an evangelist. Thought of as an Irish name, it has been used in the North of England since the twelfth cen-

123

tury and is now generally popular.

Patrick Macnee is well known as John Steed, the male hero of the cult television series, *The Avengers,* first shown in the 1960s.

PATRIZIO
Italian for Patrick, q.v.

PATRIZIUS
German for Patrick, q.v.

PAUL
From the Latin, meaning 'small'. St. Paul, Apostle to the Gentiles, converted to Christianity by a vision while on the road to Damascus and writer of fourteen Epistles included in the New Testament, made the name very popular among the early Christians. The name occurred in England before the Norman Conquest and has been used steadily since then.

PAYNE
From this surname, meaning 'pagan or countryman'.

PEDRO
Spanish for Peter, q.v.

PEPIN
From the Teutonic, meaning 'to endure'. Pepin was the father of Charlemagne.

PERCIVAL
This seems to have been invented by Chretien de Troyes, a French poet of the twelfth century, for the hero of his epic poem *Percevale, a knight of King Arthur,* written c.1175. Alfred, Lord Tennyson (1809–1892) included Sir Percival in his immensely popular poem *Idylls of the King,* which led to a great resurgence in the name.

PERCY
A place name and aristocratic surname, now used as a first name. The Percy family are descended from William de Perci who accompanied William the Conqueror to England.

The great Romantic poet Percy Bysshe Shelley (1792–1822) was born near Horsham and went to Eton. He was the friend of Lord Byron and John Keats; his second wife, Mary, wrote *Frankenstein.* Shelley drowned off Viareggio in Italy at the age of twenty-nine, leaving behind a large amount of poetry to give him immortality.

PEREGRINE
From the Latin, meaning 'stranger'. A name common among the Early Christians, it has been the name of three saints and used in England since the Middle Ages.

Peregrine Pickle, written by Tobias Smollett in 1751, made the name well known.

PERRY
A surname, meaning 'a man who lives by a pear tree', now used as a first name.

PETE
A diminutive of Peter, q.v.

PETER
From the Greek, meaning 'rock'. An apostle of Christ and the first pope, St. Peter wrote two Epistles included in the New Testament. Tradition states that he was martyred in Rome, in A.D. 67, by being crucified upside down. There are over one thousand British churches dedicated to St. Peter and it was the commonest name to be given to boys in the Middle Ages.

The play *Peter Pan: or the Boy Who Would Not Grow Up* (1904), written by James Matthew Barrie, made the name immensely popular and this has continued.

PETRUS
German for Peter, q.v.

PHIL
A diminutive of Philip, q.v.

PHILEMON
From the Greek, meaning 'friendly'.

PHILIP
From the Greek, meaning 'fond of horses'. It was the name of an apostle and several saints and is a regal name, especially in France and Spain. Philip II, King of Macedonia (382–336 B.C.), was father to Alexander the Great.

The poet, scholar and soldier Sir Philip Sidney, who died so nobly at Zutphen in 1586, was considered the perfect Renaissance gentle-

125

man. His poem *Astrophel and Stella* made the sonnet very fashionable.

PHILIPPE
French for Philip, q.v.

PHINEAS
From the Greek, meaning 'mouth of the serpent'.

PIERCE
From the French Piers, q.v.

PIERRE
French for Peter, q.v.

PIERS
This is the French version of Peter, brought to England by the Normans. William Langland wrote the long and rambling poem *The Vision of Piers Plowman* c.1362 which begins when the poet falls asleep in the Malvern Hills.

PIETER
Dutch for Peter, q.v.

PIETRO
Italian for Peter, q.v.

PIP
An old variant of Philip, q.v.

PRESLEY
From the Anglo-Saxon, meaning 'one who dwells at the priest's meadow'.

PRESTER
Meaning 'one who is a priest'.

PRESTON
An Old English place name, meaning 'priest's farm', and surname, used as a first name since the nineteenth century. It is the surname of the viscounts Gormanston.

Oliver Cromwell defeated the Royalists at Preston in 1648, and the Old Pretender was proclaimed king in its town square.

PRICE
A surname meaning 'son of Rhys', now used generally as a first name.

PUGH
From the Welsh, meaning 'son of Hugh'.

QUENTIN
From the Latin, meaning 'fifth'. St. Quentin was martyred in the third century and gave his name to the town of St. Quentin in northern France. The Normans introduced the name to England at the Norman Conquest.

Quentin Durward, the romantic novel set in fifteenth century France, written by Sir Walter Scott (1771–1832), revitalised the name.

QUILLER
From the Gaelic, meaning 'cub'.

QUINCY
From the French, meaning 'connected to the fifth son'.

QUINN
From the Irish, meaning 'wise'.

QUINTON
A variant of Quentin, q.v.

RAB
A Scottish form of Robert, q.v.

RABAN
From the Old German, meaning 'raven'.

RADLEY
From this surname, meaning 'one who lives by the red meadow'.

RAFAEL
Spanish for Raphael, q.v.

RAFAELLE
Italian for Raphael, q.v.

RAFE
A popular medieval variant of Ralph (q.v.), now enjoying a resurgence.

RAIMONDO
Italian for Raymond, q.v.

RAIMUND
German for Raymond, q.v.

RALEIGH
From the Old English, meaning 'clearing with roe deer'. A place name and surname, now used as a first name.

The flamboyant Sir Walter Raleigh (c.1552–1618), favourite of Elizabeth I, poet and pirate, writer and explorer, ended a tumultuous life in Old Palace Yard, Westminster, where he was beheaded.

RALPH

From the Old English, meaning 'wolf counsel'. This has been used in Britain since before the Norman Conquest. The Eton headmaster Nicholas Udall (1505–1566) wrote the first English comedy, entitled *Ralph Roister-Doister,* for his pupils. The swaggering hero attempts to make a wealthy marriage.

RALSTON

A place name and surname, used as a first name since the nineteenth century.

RAMON

Spanish for Raymond, q.v.

RAMSAY

A place name and aristocratic surname, now used as a first name. Allan Ramsay (1713–1784) was a Scottish painter much favoured by George III. He is most famous for his portraits of women: the National Gallery of Scotland has the fine *Margaret Lindsay, the Painter's Wife* in its collection.

James Ramsay MacDonald (1866–1937) became the first Labour Prime Minister in 1924.

RANALD

A Scottish form of Ronald, q.v.

RANDAL

From the Old English, meaning 'wolf shield'. Both Randal and Ranulph were the popular medieval forms of Randolph, now used in their own right.

RANDALL

A variant of Randal, q.v.

RANDOLPH

From the Old English, meaning 'wolf shield'.

RANULF

A variant of Randolph, q.v.

RANULPH

A popular medieval variant of Randolph (q.v.), now used in its own right.

RAOUL

The French version of Ralph (q.v.), used regularly in Britain. Raoul Island is one of a group of uninhabited volcanic islands off the coast of the North Island of New Zealand.

RAPHAEL

From the Hebrew, meaning 'healing of God'.

RASTUS

A variant of Erastus, q.v.

RAWNSLEY

This name means 'one who lives by the raven's meadow'.

RAY

A diminutive of Raymond, q.v.

RAYMOND

From the Old French, meaning 'wise protection'. Another of the names brought to England at the Norman Conquest, two saints have borne this name. St. Raymond Nonnatus (d.1240) voluntarily sold himself into slavery to save others and was later made a cardinal in Rome. He is the patron saint of midwives.

The American writer Raymond Chandler (1888–1959) created the private detective Philip Marlowe. *The Big Sleep* and *Farewell, My Lovely* are two of his best-known novels.

RAYNE

A variant of Rayner, q.v.

RAYNER

From the Scandinavian, meaning 'mighty army'.

REDMOND

From the Anglo-Saxon, meaning 'protecting counsel'.

REECE

A variant of Rhys, q.v.

REEVE

From this surname, meaning 'bailiff'.

REG
A diminutive of Reginald, q.v.

REGGIE
A diminutive of Reginald, q.v.

REGINALD
From the Old English, meaning 'power force'. This is a medieval name revived in the nineteenth century. Reggie is a character in the once-popular Victorian novel, *Love Me Little, Love Me Long* (1859), written by Charles Reade.

REID
A surname meaning 'red haired', now used as a first name. The British novelist Thomas Mayne Reid (1818–1883) was a popular writer of 'rattling good yarns' for boys, such as *The Scalp Hunters* and *The Headless Horseman*.

REINHOLD
Danish and Swedish for Reginald, q.v.

REINOLD
Dutch for Reginald, q.v.

REINWALD
German for Reginald, q.v.

REMUS
From the Latin, meaning a 'power'. Romulus and Remus are said to have founded Rome.

RENALDO
Spanish for Ronald, q.v.

RENATO
Spanish for Reginald, q.v.

RENAULT
French for Reginald, q.v.

RENDLE
A variant of Randal, q.v.

RENÉ
French for Reginald, q.v.

REUBEN
From the Hebrew, meaning 'behold a son'. In the Bible, the name given to the eldest son of Jacob and one of the twelve tribes of Israel. Always popular in the Jewish community, the Puritans brought it into general use in the seventeenth century.

The drunkard Reuben Smith came to a bad end in the classic children's story *Black Beauty,* written by Anna Sewell (1820–1878).

REX
From the Latin, meaning 'king' or 'ruler'. Its use as a first name seems to have begun in the twentieth century.

Rex Carey Harrison (1908–1990), the British actor who starred in the classic films *Blithe Spirit* and *My Fair Lady,* made the name known worldwide.

REY
Spanish for Rex, q.v.

RHYS
From the Welsh, meaning 'ardour'. A name famous in Welsh history: King Rhys ap Tewdwr ('son of Tewdwr') paid William the Conqueror £40 per annum to ensure his position as ruler was acknowledged.

RICARDO
Spanish for Richard, q.v.

RICCARDO
Italian for Richard, q.v.

RICHARD
From the Old German, meaning 'powerful ruler'. Brought to England at the time of the Norman Conquest, it has remained popular since then. St. Richard of Chichester (1197–1253) was a reforming bishop, merciless towards nepotism and very generous to the poor.

Richard I (1157–1199), Coeur de Lion, led the Third Crusade and is the complete antithesis of Richard III (1452–1485), who has become the archetypal royal villain, thanks to the play by William Shakespeare.

Richard Steele (1672–1729) founded the periodicals *The Tatler* and *The Spectator* and wrote plays and essays. Sir Richard Arkwright (1732–1792) invented the spinning frame for cotton mills.

Richard A. Butler (1902–1982), Education Minister in 1944, instigated free education for all.

RICHIE
A Scottish variant of Richard, q.v.

RICK
A diminutive of Richard, q.v.

RICKY
A diminutive of Richard, q.v.

RIDER
From the Anglo-Saxon, meaning 'horseman'.

RIGG
From this surname, meaning 'one who lived by the ridge'.

RIK
A variant of Rick, diminutive of Richard, q.v.

RINALDO
Italian for Reginald, q.v.

RIORDAN
From the Irish, meaning 'bard'.

RITCHIE
A variant of Richard, q.v.

ROB
A diminutive of Robert, q.v.

ROBBIE
A diminutive of Robert, q.v.

ROBBY
A diminutive of Robert, q.v.

ROBERT
From the Old German, meaning 'fame bright'. The French form of an

Anglo-Saxon name, it has remained popular since the Middle Ages. Robert, nicknamed 'the Devil', was the father of William the Conqueror, and brother-in-law to King Canute.

Sir Robert Peel (1788–1850) was twice Prime Minister, but is famous for forming the Metropolitan police, nicknamed 'Bobbies'.

Rob Roy was the title of a novel by Sir Walter Scott, based on a true character, Robert MacGregor (1671–1734), a legendary Scottish outlaw.

Robert Bridges (1844–1930) was appointed Poet Laureate in 1913. His most famous work is a long poem entitled *The Testament of Beauty.*

ROBERTO
Spanish and Italian for Robert, q.v.

ROBIN
A popular pet-form of Robert (q.v.) in the Middle Ages, this name is now seen as independent.

English literature, from the stories of the famous outlaw Robin Hood down to Christopher Robin Milne, owner of Winnie the Pooh, shows its popularity. Robin Goodfellow is a mischievous sprite in Shakespeare's play, *A Midsummer Night's Dream.*

ROBINSON
From this surname, meaning 'son of Robin'.

ROD
A diminutive of Roderick, q.v.

RODDY
A diminutive of Roderick, q.v.

RODERICH
German for Roderick, q.v.

RODERICK
From the Old German, meaning 'famous rule'. Roderick was the last Visigoth King of Spain, dying in battle against the Saracens in A.D. 711. He is the hero of a novel by Sir Walter Scott and a poem by Robert Southey (1774–1843), entitled *Roderick, the Last of the Goths.* (On a lighter note, Sir Roderick Glossop is a perpetual enemy to Bertie Wooster, hero of the stories by P.G. Wodehouse.)

RODGER

A variant of Roger, q.v.

RODNEY

A place name and surname, now used as a first name. It was made popular by Admiral Lord Rodney (1719–1792), who defeated the French at Le Havre and beat the Spanish fleet off Cape St. Vincent. Sir Arthur Conan Doyle wrote the novel *Rodney Stone* (1896).

RODOLFO

Spanish and Italian for Rudolph, q.v.

RODOLPHE

French for Rudolph, q.v.

RODRIGO

Italian for Roderick, q.v.

RODRIGUE

French for Roderick, q.v.

ROELAND

Dutch for Roland, q.v.

ROGER

From the Old German, meaning 'illustrious warrior'. The name was brought to England at the Norman Conquest and remained a favourite throughout the Middle Ages. It was revived in the nineteenth century.

Roger of Salerno, an Italian surgeon, wrote the first textbook of surgery in 1170. Sir Roger de Coverley is the name of an English country dance and a character who typified an eighteenth century gentleman in the writings of Steele.

ROGERIO

Spanish for Roger, q.v.

ROHAN

A French place name and aristocratic surname, now used as a first name.

ROLAND

From the Old German, meaning 'famous throughout the land'. The nephew of Charlemagne, Roland was a chivalrous knight about whom many stories were told. The twelfth century *Song of Roland* made the name very popular.

ROLANDO
Spanish for Roland, q.v.

ROLF
The Scandinavian version of Rudolph, now generally used. Rolf, son of Rognvald of Norway, sailed to France and besieged Paris. He was given the land now known as Normandy and ruled it well. He died in 932. William the Conqueror is descended from him.

ROLLO
A diminutive of Roland, q.v.

ROLPH
A variant of Rolf, q.v.

ROLY
A diminutive of Roland, q.v.

RON
A diminutive of Ronald, q.v.

RONALD
The Scottish version of the medieval name Reynold, used generally since the nineteenth century.

Two film stars, Ronald Colman (1891–1958), and Ronald Reagan, the latter better known as a former President of the U.S.A., kept the name before the public.

RONAN
From the Irish, meaning 'little seal'. The Irish St. Ronan worked as a missionary in Cornwall in the fifth century. He was later consecrated Bishop by St. Patrick.

RORY
From the Gaelic, meaning 'red'. Originally a Scottish name, it is now generally used.

ROSCOE
From the Norse, meaning 'one from the forest of deer'.

ROSS

A Scottish place name, meaning 'promontory', and a surname, now used as a first name. The British physician Sir Ronald Ross (1857–1932) received the Nobel Prize for Medicine in 1902 for his work on discovering the cause of malaria.

Sir John Ross, and his nephew Sir James Ross, discovered the north magnetic pole in 1831.

ROWAN

Either derived from the Gaelic, meaning 'red', or from the rowan tree (mountain ash), notable for its small scarlet berries.

ROWE

A variant of Roland (q.v.) and of Rowley (q.v.).

ROWLAND

A variant of Roland, q.v. Sir Rowland Hill (1795–1879) was the originator of the penny post in 1840.

ROWLEY

From the Anglo-Saxon, meaning 'one who dwells by the old meadow'.

ROY

Experts disagree over this name, so you may choose to believe (a) it is the anglicised version of Rory *or* (b) it is taken from the French word for 'king' *(roi).*

RUBÉN

Spanish for Reuben, q.v.

RUDI

A variant of Rudolph, q.v.

RÜDIGER

German for Roger, q.v.

RUDOLF

German for Rudolph, q.v.

RUDOLPH

From the Teutonic, meaning 'famous wolf'.

RUDY

A variant of Rudolph, q.v.

RUDYARD

From the Anglo-Saxon, meaning 'from the area of the reeds'.

RUFUS

From the Latin, meaning 'red-haired'. William Rufus (1056–1100), third son of William the Conqueror and Matilda of Flanders, became king of England on his father's death. A warlike man, he was murdered while out hunting in the New Forest, shot in the back by an arrow. He is buried in Winchester Cathedral. The name was revived in the nineteenth century.

RUGGIERO

Italian for Roger, q.v.

RUPERT

The anglicised version of Rupprecht, introduced to England by Prince Rupprecht of the Rhine (1619–1682), who came to help his uncle, the unfortunate Charles I, in the English Civil War. He was decisively beaten at Marston Moor in 1644 and Naseby in 1645, but, more happily, was a founder member of the Royal Society.

Rupert Brooke (1887-1915) was the most famous poet of the First World War, remembered for *The Great Lover* and *Grantchester.* (And children are very fond of Rupert the Bear, who lives in Nutwood.)

RUSS

A variant of Russell, q.v.

RUSSELL

From a French nickname, meaning 'a little man with red hair', which became an aristocratic surname and is now used as a first name. It is the surname of the dukes of Bedford and four other peers.

RUTGER

Dutch for Roger, q.v.

RUY

Spanish for Roderick, q.v.

RYAN

An Irish surname, now used as a first name. The port of Stranraer is situated on Loch Ryan in Dumfries.

SALOMO
Dutch and German for Solomon, q.v.

SALOMON
French for Solomon, q.v.

SALOMONE
Italian for Solomon, q.v.

SALVADOR
From the Spanish, meaning 'the Saviour'.

SALVATORE
Italian for Salvador, q.v.

SAM
A diminutive of Samuel, q.v.

SAMPSON
A variant of Samson, q.v.

SAMSON
From the Hebrew, meaning 'as the sun'.

SAMUEL
From the Hebrew, meaning 'name of God'. The prophet Samuel lived in the eleventh century B.C. He anointed the shepherd boy David to be successor to Saul as the King of Israel. The name became popular at the Reformation and has been given to many famous men. Samuel

Johnson (1709–1784), the English lexicographer, essayist and poet (and prodigious tea drinker) was the most famous literary character in the eighteenth century.

Samuel Pepys (1633–1703), politician and diarist; Samuel Richardson (1689–1761), writer of *Clarissa Harlowe,* the longest novel in the English language; Samuel Palmer (1805–1851), landscape painter and Samuel Morse (1791–1872), American inventor of Morse code are just a few of many who added lustre to the name.

SAMUELE
Italian for Samuel, q.v.

SANCHO
From the Spanish, meaning 'sanctified'.

SANDERS
This name means 'son of Alexander-defender'.

SANDY
The medieval pet-form of Alexander (q.v.), now considered an independent name. It was particularly popular in Scotland.

SANSÓN
Spanish for Samson, q.v.

SANSONE
Italian for Samson, q.v.

SAUL
From the Hebrew, meaning 'who is asked for'.

SAVEUR
French for Salvador, q.v.

SCOTT
A surname describing nationality – 'a Scot' – now used as a first name. The English explorer Robert Falcon Scott (1868–1912) died with his companions after failing to be the first to reach the South Pole. His son, Sir Peter Scott, was an artist, writer and founder of the Wildfowl Trust. The American (Francis) Scott Fitzgerald (1896–1940) wrote novels and short stories of the 'Jazz Age' or 1920s, notably *The Great Gatsby.*

SEAN
The Irish version of John, q.v. The Irish writer Sean O'Casey (1880–1964) is best remembered for the play *Juno and the Paycock.*

SEATON
From this surname, meaning 'one who lives at a sea town'.

SEBASTIAN
St. Sebastian was a Roman army officer, martyred in 288 for declaring himself to be a Christian. He was sentenced to death, by being shot with arrows; and the scene was a popular subject with medieval artists.

Sebastian is the name given to two characters in Shakespeare's *Twelfth Night* and *The Tempest.*

SEBASTIANO
Italian for Sebastian, q.v.

SÉBASTIEN
French for Sebastian, q.v.

SELBY
From the Anglo-Saxon, meaning 'one who lives by the willows'.

SELWYN
From the Old French, meaning 'savage'. A surname, used as a first name since the nineteenth century.

Selwyn College, Cambridge was named after the Englishman George Augustus Selwyn (1809–1878), who went to be the first bishop of New Zealand.

SEPTIMUS
This name means 'seventh son'.

SETH
From the Hebrew, meaning 'founder'. Seth was the third son of Adam and Eve, born after his eldest brother Cain had killed Abel.

The Bible states that he was born when Adam was one hundred and thirty years old. It was used as a first name after the Reformation.

SETON
A variant of Seaton, q.v.

SEWALD
A variant of Sewell, q.v.

SEWELL
From the Anglo-Saxon, meaning 'powerful sea man'.

SEYMOUR
A French place name and aristocratic surname, now used as a first name. It is the surname of the dukes of Somerset.

Sir Seymour Hicks (1871–1949), actor-manager and playwright, is best remembered as son-in-law to the actor William Terriss, who was assassinated by a madman in 1897 and reputedly haunts Covent Garden tube station!

SHAMUS
The Irish for James, q.v.

SHANE
An anglicised version of Sean, q.v. This was made popular by the classic Western film *Shane* (1953), starring Alan Ladd.

SHAUN
A variant of Sean, q.v.

SHAW
From the Anglo-Saxon, meaning 'of the wood'.

SHERIDAN
An Irish surname, used as a first name since the mid-nineteenth century. The playwright Richard Brinsley Sheridan (1751–1816) is best-known for his brilliant comedies of manners *The School For Scandal* and *The Rivals*. Arrested for debt in 1813, seriously ill for several years before his death, he found a last resting place in Westminster Abbey.

SHERLOCK
This name means 'of the white or shorn locks'.

SHERMAN
From the Anglo-Saxon, meaning 'wool man'.

SHOLTO
From the Gaelic, meaning 'sower'.

SID
A diminutive of Sidney, q.v.

SIDNEY
A French place name and aristocratic surname, now used as a first name. The family came to England in 1154 with the French-born King Henry II – William Sidney was his Chancellor. 'Quo fata vocant', translated as 'Wherever fate may summon me', is the appropriate family motto.
   Sir Philip Sidney (1554–1586), the poet and soldier fatally wounded at Zutphen, gave his own water bottle to a dying foot soldier, saying 'Thy necessity is greater than mine'.

SIEGFRIED
From the Teutonic, meaning 'victorious'. Siegfried was a hero in some of the German legends.

SIFFRE
French for Siegfried, q.v.

SIGISMOND
French for Sigmund, q.v.

SIGISMONDO
Italian for Sigmund, q.v.

SIGISMUND
From the Teutonic, meaning 'protector of victory'.

SIGISMUNDO
Spanish for Sigmund, q.v.

SIGISMUNDUS
Dutch for Sigmund, q.v.

SIGMUND
From the Teutonic, meaning 'protector of victory'.

SIGVARD
Norwegian for Siegfried, q.v.

SILAS
From the Aramaic, meaning 'asked of God'. In the New Testament,

Silas, a Roman citizen, accompanied Paul on his second journey to Corinth. Later he became secretary to St. Peter. The name came into use after the Reformation.

SILVESTER
From the Latin, meaning 'of the forests'.

SILVESTRE
Spanish and French for Silvester, q.v.

SILVESTRO
Italian for Silvester, q.v.

SILVIO
Spanish and Italian for Silvanus, q.v.

SIM
A diminutive of Simeon, q.v.

SIMEON
From the Hebrew, meaning 'one who hearkens'.

SIMON
From the Greek, meaning 'snub-nosed'. The New Testament mentions nine men with this name, the most famous being Simon Peter, the chief Apostle. The Syrian St. Simon Stylites (c.390—459) spent thirty-six years on top of a pillar in prayer and fasting.

The dashing Simon Templar is the hero of 'the Saint' novels by Leslie Charteris, the first of which, *Enter the Saint*, appeared in 1930.

SIMONE
Italian for Simon, q.v.

SINCLAIR
A French place name and aristocratic surname, used as a first name since the nineteenth century.

Sinclair Lewis (1885–1951), the first American writer to be awarded the Nobel Prize for Literature in 1930, is best known for his novel *Elmer Gantry,* later filmed.

SOL
A diminutive of Solomon, q.v.

SOLLY
A diminutive of Solomon, q.v.

SOLOMON
From the Hebrew, meaning 'peaceful'.

SOMERSET
From this surname, and from the county.

SPENCER
From the Old English, meaning 'steward' or 'butler'. An aristocratic surname, now used as a first name. The British politician Spencer Perceval (1762–1812) became Prime Minister in 1809 and was assassinated in the lobby of the House of Commons on 11th May 1812 by a bankrupt merchant named John Bellingham.

ST. JOHN
From Saint John, usually pronounced 'Sinjon'.

STAFFORD
From the Anglo-Saxon, meaning 'from the landing place'.

STAMFORD
A variant of Stanford, q.v.

STAN
A diminutive of Stanley, q.v.

STANFORD
An English place name, meaning 'stony ford', and surname, now regularly used as a first name. The extremely prolific British composer Sir Charles Stanford (1852–1924) is the best known bearer of the name.

STANISLAUS
From the Polish, meaning 'glorious'.

STANLEY
A place name, meaning 'stony meadow', and aristocratic surname, now used as a first name. Its popularity began in the 1870s when Henry Morton Stanley (*real* name John Rowlands) greeted the long-lost African explorer David Livingstone with the famous words, 'Doctor Livingstone, I presume!'

Sir Stanley Matthews (b.1915) was the first footballer to receive a knighthood.

STEFAN
German and Swedish for Stephen, q.v.

STEFANO
Italian for Stephen, q.v.

STEPHEN
From the Greek, meaning 'crown'. The name of the first Christian martyr and several other saints, it was made popular by the Normans. William the Conqueror dedicated the Abbey built at Caen to St. Stephen.

Stephen I (c.977–1038) was the first Christian ruler of Hungary and later canonised. Stephen Bathory was elected king of Poland in 1575 and ruled for eleven years.

STEVE
A diminutive of Stephen, q.v.

STEVEN
A variant of Stephen, q.v.

STEVIE
A diminutive of Stephen, q.v.

STEWART
A variant of Stuart, q.v.

STRATFORD
From the Anglo-Saxon, meaning 'one who lives by the ford – near the street'.

STUART
From the Old English, meaning 'steward'. The Stuart family were rulers of Scotland from 1371 until 1603 and of both England *and* Scotland from 1603–1714. It became popular as a first name in the nineteenth century.

SUTTON
This name means 'one who comes from a southern town'.

SYD
A diminutive of Sydney, a variant of Sidney, q.v.

SYDNEY
A variant of Sidney, q.v. Sydney Carton, the dissipated hero of Dickens' novel, *A Tale of Two Cities* (1859), dies on the guillotine with the lines, 'It is a far, far better thing that I do, than I have ever done; it is a far, far better rest that I go to, than I have ever known', ensuring floods of tears from the reader.

SYLVANUS
From the Latin, meaning 'of the forests'.

SYLVESTER
From the Latin, meaning 'of the forests'.

TADDEO
Italian for Thaddeus, q.v.

TADEO
Spanish for Thaddeus, q.v.

TAFFY
From the Welsh, meaning 'one who is loved'. A form of David, q.v.

TALBOT
An aristocratic surname, now used as a first name. Richard Talbot came to England with William the Conqueror. It is the surname of the earls of Shrewsbury.

TARQUIN

The family name of a legendary line of early Roman kings, seven in number. Lucius Tarquinius Superbus, the seventh and last king of Rome, was sent, with his family, into exile in 510 B.C. and a republic established.

TAYLOR

An occupational surname, now a first name bestowed on both boys and girls. John Taylor (1580–1653) was a poet who achieved fame by sailing from London to Queensborough in Kent in a paper boat. (He also walked from London to Edinburgh.)

TED

A diminutive of Edward, q.v.

TEDDIE

A diminutive of Edward, q.v.

TEDDY

A diminutive of Edward, q.v.

TEOBALDO

Italian and Spanish for Theobald, q.v.

TEODORO

Italian and Spanish for Theodore, q.v.

TERENCE

The anglicised version of the Irish Turlough. Terence (185–159 B.C.), the comic playwright of Ancient Rome, was taken to Rome from Carthage as a slave to the senator Terentius Lucanus. The senator helped him to study and freed him: the former slave then took the owner's name as a mark of gratitude.

TERENCIO

Spanish for Terence, q.v.

TERRY

A diminutive of Terence, q.v.

THADDAUS

German for Thaddeus, q.v.

THADDEUS
From the Greek, meaning 'praiseworthy'.

THANE
From the Old English, meaning 'servant'. A thane held land given by the king and ranked with an earl's son. It was the title of a clan chief in Scotland. Used as a first name since the nineteenth century.

THEO
A diminutive of Theodore (q.v.) and of Theobald (q.v.).

THEOBALD
From the Teutonic, meaning 'of the bold people'.

THEODOR
Swedish, Danish and German for Theodore, q.v.

THEODORE
From the Greek, meaning 'God's gift'. It was a popular name with the early Christians and borne by several saints. St. Theodore of Canterbury (602–690) was a Greek monk sent by Pope St. Vitalian to be Archbishop of Canterbury in 667. The name was revived by the Tractarians in the mid-nineteenth century and now seems to be gaining in popularity.

THEODORUS
Dutch for Theodore, q.v.

THIBAUT
French for Theobald, q.v.

THOMAS
From the Aramaic, meaning 'twin'. The name of one of the Twelve Apostles and many saints, it was made popular by St. Thomas à Becket (1118–1170), murdered in Canterbury Cathedral as a result of some harsh words by Henry II. Thomas has been one of the commonest names for boys, as is shown in the expression 'every Tom, Dick and Harry'.

The poet Thomas Gray (1716–1771), who wrote *Elegy written in a Country Churchyard*; Thomas Hardy (1840–1928), poet and author of *Tess of the D'Urbervilles* and *Far from the Madding Crowd*; and Thomas Gainsborough (1727–1788), portrait and landscape painter, are just three of those who have borne the name with distinction.

TIBOLD
German for Theobald, q.v.

TIEBOUT
Dutch for Theobald, q.v.

TIM
A diminutive of Timothy, q.v.

TIMMY
A diminutive of Timothy, q.v.

TIMOTEO
Italian for Timothy, q.v.

TIMOTHÉE
French for Timothy, q.v.

TIMOTHEUS
German for Timothy, q.v.

TIMOTHY
From the Greek, meaning 'honouring God'. The New Testament St. Timothy was converted by St. Paul, whose helper and companion he became.

Tradition states that he was beaten to death by a mob in A.D. 97 for opposing the worship of the goddess Diana. The name came into use in Britain after the Reformation. *The Tale of Timmy Tiptoes* (1911) by Beatrix Potter is the story of a fat grey squirrel.

TITE
French for Titus, q.v.

TITUS
The Biblical St. Titus was a gentile disciple of St. Paul. The Roman Emperor Titus (40–81), who served as a military tribune in Britain, captured and destroyed Jerusalem in A.D.70. He was responsible for the building of the Colosseum in Rome. The name was used in Britain after the Reformation.

TOBIA
Italian for Tobias, q.v.

TOBIAS
From the Hebrew, meaning 'the Lord is good'. The apocryphal story of 'Tobias and the Angel' was a favourite with renaissance artists.

The surgeon and novelist Tobias Smollet (1721–1771), notorious for becoming involved in controversy and being outrageously malicious, is remembered for the novels *Roderick Random, Peregrine Pickle* and *Humphrey Clinker*.

TOBIE
French for Tobias, q.v.

TOBIN
A variant of Tobias, q.v.

TOBY
Toby is the anglicised version of Tobias, q.v.

TODD
A surname, meaning 'fox', now used as a first name.

TOM
A diminutive of Thomas, q.v.

TOMAS
Spanish for Thomas, q.v.

TOMASO
Italian for Thomas, q.v.

TOMMY
A diminutive of Thomas, q.v.

TONY
A diminutive of Anthony, q.v.

TORQUIL
From the Old Norse, meaning 'Thor's cauldron'. It was brought to England by the Danes before the Norman Conquest.

TRAVERS
A variant of Travis, q.v.

TRAVIS

An occupational surname for a toll-keeper, now used as a first name.

TRENT

From the Celtic, meaning 'one who lives by a stream'.

TREVOR

A place name, meaning 'large settlement', and surname, now used as a first name. The actor Trevor Howard, best remembered for his part in the film *Brief Encounter* (1945), helped to make the name known.

TRISTRAM

An anglicised version of the Celtic Tristan, used in English since the twelfth century.

Sir Tristram of Lyoness was one of the bravest knights of the Round Table, second only to Sir Lancelot. Sent by his uncle, King Mark of Cornwall, to collect his intended bride the beautiful princess Isolt from Ireland, Tristram and Isolt drank a potion that caused them to fall eternally in love with each other. Alfred, Lord Tennyson, included the story in his immensely popular poem, *The Idylls of the King*.

The English novelist and clergyman Laurence Sterne (1713–1768) wrote the chaotic classic novel *Tristram Shandy*.

TROY

A surname meaning, 'descendant of a foot soldier', now used as a first name. (Should you love the classics, you will ignore the mundane and think only of the ancient city in Asia Minor, besieged by the Greeks for ten years and immortalised by Homer.)

TUDOR

The Welsh version of Theodore. Edmund Tudor, 1st Earl of Richmond, was the father of Henry VII (1457–1509), the first Tudor king.

TYRONE

The name of a county in Northern Ireland, 'Owen's land'. The name was popularised by the American film star Tyrone Power (1913–1958), swashbuckling star of *The Mark of Zorro* and many others.

UBERTO
Italian for Hubert, q.v.

UGO
Italian for Hugh, q.v.

ULISES
Spanish for Ulysses, q.v.

ULRIC
From the Old English, meaning 'wolf power'. Mentioned in the Domesday Book, it has been the name of three saints.

The English St. Ulric (d. 1154) was a priest in Wiltshire who ended his life as a recluse at Haselbury.

ULYSSES
From the Greek, meaning 'one who hates'.

URBAINE
French for Urban, q.v.

URBAN
From the Latin, meaning 'of the town'. The Urban of the New Testament was greeted by St. Paul in his letter to the Romans. Several early saints and eight popes have borne the name.

URBANO
Italian and Spanish for Urban, q.v.

URIAH
From the Hebrew, meaning 'light of God'

VAL
A diminutive of Valentine, q.v.

VALENTIJN
Dutch for Valentine, q.v.

VALENTIN
French, Spanish, German, Danish and Swedish for Valentine, q.v.

VALENTINE
From the Latin, meaning 'strong'. A third century martyr, about whom little is known, inextricably linked to Valentine cards and treacly endearments in the 'Personal' columns of newspapers on his feastday, 14th February.

Valentine and Orson was a French romance about twin brothers published in England in 1550 and much imitated. Abandoned in a forest, Orson was carried off and raised by a bear while the rescued Valentine grew up at the court of King Pepin, later marrying the sister of a giant.

VALENTINO
Italian for Valentine, q.v.

VAN
A Dutch forename, meaning 'from . . .'.

VANCE
From the Anglo-Saxon, meaning 'young'.

VASSILY
Russian for Basil, q.v.

VAUGHAN
A Welsh surname, meaning 'little', now used as a first name. The English composer Ralph Vaughan Williams (1872–1958), noted especially for *Fantasia on a Theme by Thomas Tallis* and *The Lark Ascending*, is a well-known bearer of the name. (He also wrote the music for the 1948 film *Scott of the Antarctic!*)

VERE
A French place name and aristocratic surname, used as a first name since the seventeenth century.

VERNON
A French place name, meaning 'place of alders', and aristocratic surname, now used as a first name. It is the surname of the barons Lyveden.

Richard de Vernon was yet another companion to William the Conqueror at the Norman Conquest (1066).

VIC
A diminutive of Victor, q.v.

VICENTE
Spanish for Vincent, q.v.

VICTOR
From the Latin, meaning 'conqueror'. Popular with the early Christians, it has been the name of several early martyrs and a pope. Rare in the Middle Ages, it became most popular in the nineteenth century, presumably in honour of Queen Victoria.

The pianist and comedian Victor Borge is a well-known bearer of the name.

VILHELM
Swedish for William, q.v.

VINCE
A diminutive of Vincent, q.v.

VINCENT
From the Latin, meaning 'to conquer'. There are several saints with this name, the most revered being the Frenchman St. Vincent de Paul (c.1580–1660). He devoted his life to the service of the poor, especially abandoned children and galley-slaves, and founded the

Daughters of Charity.

The world-famous Dutch painter Vincent Van Gogh (1853–1890), who sold only one painting in his lifetime, is remembered for *Sunflowers, The Yellow Chair* and *Starry Night.*

VINCENTE
Italian for Vincent, q.v.

VINCENTIUS
Dutch for Vincent, q.v.

VINCENZ
German for Vincent, q.v.

VINNY
A variant of Vincent, q.v.

VIRGIL
From the Latin, meaning 'staff bearer'.

VIRGILIO
Italian and Spanish for Virgil, q.v.

VITORIO
Spanish for Victor, q.v.

VIVIAN
From the Latin, meaning 'alive'. The name of an obscure Christian martyr of the fifth century, it has been used in Britain since the Middle Ages. Originally the masculine form, it is now bestowed on both boys and girls.

Vivian Grey (1826) was the first novel of the future Tory Prime Minister, Benjamin Disraeli.

WADE
An Old English place name, meaning 'ford', and surname, used as a first name since the nineteenth century.

WALDO
From the Teutonic, meaning 'ruler'. One notable bearer of this name was the American poet Ralph Waldo Emerson.

WALLACE
A Scottish surname, meaning 'stranger', used generally since the nineteenth century.
   The Scottish patriot William Wallace (c. 1270–1305), known as 'the Scourge of England', fought for Scottish independence but was betrayed to the English and hanged, drawn and quartered in Westminster Hall.

WALLACHE
German for Wallace, q.v.

WALLIS
A variant of Wallace, q.v.

WALLY
A diminutive of Walter, q.v.

WALT
A variant of Walter, q.v.

WALTER
From the Old German, meaning 'folk-ruler'. This was a popular name with the Normans and brought by them to England.

The British Impressionist painter Walter Sickert (1860–1942) is well-known for his portraits and pictures of the London streets.

WALTHER
German for Walter, q.v.

WARD
An occupational surname, meaning 'watchman', and aristocratic surname, used as a first name since the nineteenth century. It is the surname of the earls of Dudley.

WARNE
A variant of Warner, q.v.

WARNER
From the Teutonic, meaning 'warrior'.

WARREN
The name of a noble French family, brought to England at the Norman Conquest. The English statesman Warren Hastings (1732–1818) made the name popular in England. Governor General of India, he was impeached at the bar of the House of Lords for corruption and cruelty. After a trial lasting seven years, he was found innocent.

The actor Warren Beatty (b.1937), star of *Bonnie and Clyde*, *Shampoo* and *Dick Tracy* among others, has kept the name a favourite.

WARWICK
A place name, meaning 'farm beside a weir', and aristocratic surname, used as a first name since the nineteenth century.

WASHINGTON
From this Anglo-Saxon place name.

WAT
A variant of Walter, q.v.

WAYNE
An occupational surname, meaning 'carter'. Its use as a first name in the twentieth century appears to rest on the great popularity of the American actor Marion Michael Morrison, far better known as John Wayne, the star of so many Westerns and war films. His stage name

was derived from a general of the American Revolution, Anthony Wayne (1745–1796).

WEBSTER
From the Anglo-Saxon, meaning 'weaver'.

WENCESLAUS
From the Slav, meaning 'crowned with glory'.

WENDELL
From the Teutonic, meaning 'wanderer'.

WERNER
German for Warner, q.v.

WESLEY
An English place name, meaning 'western wood', and surname, now used as a first name. This was made popular by John Wesley (1703–1791), the founder of Methodism. His nephews Charles and Samuel Wesley were well-known organists and prolific composers who did much to spread a knowledge of Bach in England.

WHITNEY
From the Anglo-Saxon, meaning 'one who lives at the west meadow'.

WHITTAKER
From the Anglo-Saxon, meaning 'one who lives at the white acre'.

WILBUR
From the Teutonic, meaning 'one who is brilliant'.

WILFRED
From the Old English, meaning 'desiring peace'. St. Wilfred of York (634–709), about whom it was said 'a quick walker, expert in all good works, with never a sour face', was made Bishop of York in 669 and was the first Englishman to carry a lawsuit to the Roman courts. A delightful legend states that he taught the men of Sussex to fish. There are fifty churches dedicated to him in Britain. The name was revived by the Tractarians of the nineteenth century.

WILFRID
A variant of Wilfred, q.v.

WILHELM
German for William, q.v.

WILL
A diminutive of William, q.v.

WILLEM
Dutch for William, q.v.

WILLIAM
From the Old German, meaning 'helmet of resolution'. William Duke of Normandy, later William I, known as the Conqueror (1027–1087), first cousin once removed to Edward the Confessor, fought the only battle known to everybody ('Battle of Hastings 1066' all in one breath) on 14th October and killed Harold II.

He was crowned King of England on Christmas Day of the same year at Westminster Abbey. (Unfortunately, William IV lingers in the memory for being nicknamed 'Silly Billy' and having a head shaped like a pineapple.)

A royal name past and present, it has been borne by many famous men. William Shakespeare (1564–1616), William Wordsworth (1770–1850), the visionary poet and painter William Blake (1757–1827), William Makepeace Thackeray (1811–1863), William Camden the historian (1551–1623), the politician William Gladstone – who was notorious for addressing Queen Victoria, 'as if I were a public meeting!' – William Wilkie Collins (1824–1889), writer of *The Woman in White* and the first English detective story, *The Moonstone,* . . . the list of luminaries seems endless.

WILLOUGHBY
A place name, meaning 'farm beside the willow trees', and aristo-cratic surname, now used as a first name.

The fickle Willoughby is the most interesting character in *Sense and Sensibility* (1811) by Jane Austen.

WILLY
A diminutive of William, q.v.

WILMER
From the Teutonic, meaning 'famous'.

WILSON
From this surname, meaning 'Will's son'.

WINSTON

An Old English place name, meaning 'friend's farm', and surname, now used as a first name.

The first Winston Churchill was born in 1620, his mother's maiden name being bestowed upon him at baptism: he became the father of the great Duke of Marlborough, victor at the Battle of Blenheim.

WOLF

From the Anglo-Saxon, meaning 'wolf'.

WOLFE

A variant of Wolf, q.v.

WOLFGANG

From the Anglo-Saxon, meaning. 'bold wolf'.

WOODROW

From the Anglo-Saxon, meaning 'one who lives by the hedge row'.

WYNDHAM

A Norfolk place name, meaning 'Wyman's homestead', and surname, used as a first name since the nineteenth century.

(Percy) Wyndham Lewis (1882–1957), novelist and painter, is a well-known bearer of the name. 'John Wyndham' was the pen name of John Beynon Harris, the writer of the science fiction novel *The Day of the Triffids* (1951).

WYNN

From the Celtic, meaning 'white'.

WYNNE

A variant of Wynn, q.v.

WYSTAN

From the Old English, meaning 'battle-stone'. The name of a ninth century boy saint, King of Mercia. The best-known bearer of the name in modern times was Wystan Hugh Auden (1907–1973), the English poet and dramatist.

XAVIER
From the Arabic, meaning 'bright'. St. Francis Xavier (1506–1552), the great Basque missionary to India, Sri Lanka and Japan, popularised the name. His feast day is 3rd December.

YALE
A Welsh place name, meaning 'fertile upland', and surname. Now used as a first name.

Yale University, the third oldest in America and founded in 1701, was named after Elihu Yale whose family came from Denbighshire.

YEHUDI
From the Hebrew, meaning 'the Lord praises'.

YVES
From the Old Breton, meaning 'well born'.

ZACARIAS
Spanish for Zachary, q.v.

ZACCARIA
Italian for Zachary, q.v.

ZACHARIAH
A variant of Zachary, q.v.

ZACHARIAS
German for Zachary, q.v.

ZACHARIE
French for Zachary, q.v.

ZACHARY
From the Hebrew, meaning 'Jehovah has remembered'. The elderly Zachary was the father of John the Baptist.
   St. Zachary (d.752) was elected Pope in 741. He was an implacable enemy to the trade in Christian slaves.

ZAK
A diminutive of Zachary, q.v.

ZAKARIAS
Swedish for Zachary, q.v.

ZANE
A variant of John, q.v.

ZEBEDEE
From the Greek, meaning 'my gift'.

Girls' Names

ABBIE
A diminutive of Abigail, q.v.

ABBY
A diminutive of Abigail, q.v.

ABIGAIL
From the Hebrew, meaning 'father rejoices'. The Old Testament contains two Abigails: one the sister and the other the second wife of King David.

Popular in England since the Reformation, it fell from favour when the name was given to a servant in a play by Beaumont and Fletcher, *The Scornful Lady* (1616), and became the slang term for a lady's maid.

Mrs. Abigail Masham was the influential confidante of Queen Anne in the eighteenth century.

ADA
From the Early English Acada, meaning 'happy one'.

ADDIE
A diminutive of Adelaide, q.v.

ADDY
A diminutive of Adelaide, q.v.

ADEL
A variant of Adelaide, q.v.

ADELA

From the Old German, meaning 'noble'. This was brought to England by the Normans, the name of the fourth daughter of William the Conqueror. It was revived by the Victorians.

ADELAIDE

From the Old German, meaning 'noble one'. St. Adelaide (931–999) was married to Otto the Great and became Empress of the Holy Roman Empire. St. Odilo described her as 'a marvel of beauty and goodness'. The name became popular in England when Princess Adelaide of Saxe-Meiningen married the future William IV in 1818. The city of Adelaide, capital of South Australia, was named in her honour.

ADÈLE

The French diminutive of Adelaide, now generally used. Adèle is the name of the ward of Edward Rochester, hero of *Jane Eyre* (1847), written by Charlotte Brontë.

ADELHEID

German for Adelaide, q.v.

ADELICIA

A variant of Adelaide, q.v.

ADELINA

French, Spanish and Italian for Adela, q.v.

ADELINE

A variant of Adela, q.v.

ADELLE

A variant of Adelaide, q.v.

ADRIANA

The feminine form of Adrian, q.v. Adriana is the wife of Antipholus of Ephesus in *The Comedy of Errors* by William Shakespeare.

ADRIANE

A German feminine form of Adrian, q.v.

ADRIENNE

A feminine form of Adrian, q.v.

AGATA
Italian for Agatha, q.v.

AGATHA
From the Greek, meaning 'good'. A Sicilian martyr of the third century, St. Agatha is the patron saint of bell-founders. Although greatly venerated, little is known of her life. Her feast day is 5th February.

The name was brought to England at the Norman Conquest by a daughter of William the Conqueror.

Agatha Christie (1891–1975) is famous for her many detective novels, including *The Murder of Roger Ackroyd* and *Murder on the Orient Express.*

(And P.G. Wodehouse created an unforgettable literary character in the terrifying Aunt Agatha, scourge of Bertie Wooster.)

AGATHE
French for Agatha, q.v.

AGGIE
A diminutive of Agatha, q.v.

AGNES
From the Greek, meaning 'pure'. St. Agnes was the most famous of all Roman Christian martyrs, executed by being stabbed in the throat in 304, aged thirteen. Her emblem in art is a lamb. There are five churches dedicated to her in Britain. Agnes was one of the commonest English names in the Middle Ages.

Agnes Grey (1847), the story of an ill-treated governess, was one of two novels written by Anne Brontë.

AGNETA
Danish and Swedish for Agnes, q.v.

AGUEDA
Spanish for Agatha, q.v.

AIDA
A variant of Ada, q.v.

AILEEN
The anglicised form of the Irish name Aibhlin, used generally since the beginning of the twentieth century.

AILSA

The Ailsa Crag is an island rock in the Firth of Clyde on the west coast of Scotland. Originally bestowed by Scottish parents on their daughters, the name is now generally used.

AIMÉE

French for Amy, q.v.

ALAINE

A variant of Alana, q.v.

ALANA

A twentieth century feminine version of Alan, q.v.

ALARICE

From the Old German, meaning 'ruler'.

ALBERTA

The feminine form of Albert, q.v.

ALBERTINA

A variant of Alberta, the feminine form of Albert, q.v.

ALEJANDRA

Spanish for Alexandra, q.v.

ALENA

A variant of Adela, q.v.

ALENE

A variant of Aileen, q.v.

ALESSANDRA

Italian for Alexandra, q.v.

ALEX

A diminutive of Alexandra, q.v.

ALEXANDRA

The feminine form of Alexander, used in Britain since the thirteenth century. The beautiful Princess Alexandra of Denmark (1844–1925), daughter of King Christian IX, made the name very popular when she came to England to marry the future Edward VII in 1863. She founded the Queen Alexandra's Royal Army Nursing Corps and the charitable Alexandra Rose Day.

The Princess Alexandra, Mrs Angus Ogilvie (b. 1936), cousin to Elizabeth II, continues the royal connection.

ALEXANDRINA
A variant of Alexandra, q.v.

ALEXANDRINE
French for Alexandra, q.v.

ALEXIS
The Russian version of Alexander. This name is given to both boys and girls, but is usually considered feminine in this country.

St. Alexis (d.430) lived by begging, sharing all he received with other poor people. On his death it was discovered that he was a Roman nobleman, who left his bride on his wedding day to live in poverty in Syria. St. Alexis was a favourite saint in the Middle Ages.

ALFONSINE
From the Old German Adalfuns, meaning 'noble and ready'.

ALFREDA
A feminine form of Alfred, q.v.

ALICE
From the Old German, meaning 'nobility'. The name was brought to England by the Normans, remaining popular throughout the Middle Ages in the form of Alys.

It was revived in the nineteenth century. Queen Victoria gave the name to her third child in 1843. Lewis Carroll (Charles Lutwidge Dodgson) wrote *Alice's Adventures in Wonderland* (1865) and *Through the Looking Glass* (1872) to please Alice Liddell, the daughter of Henry Liddell, Dean of Christ Church, Oxford.

ALICIA
A variant of Alice, q.v.

ALIE
A diminutive of Alison, q.v.

ALIMA
From the Arabic, meaning 'lover of music and dancing'.

ALINA
A variant of Alana, q.v.

ALINE
Used originally in the Middle Ages as a pet-form of Adeline, it now stands as an independent name.

ALISON
A pet-form of Alice, used as an independent name since the thirteenth century. Alison is a character in the *Miller's Tale*, a part of *The Canterbury Tales* by Geoffrey Chaucer (1343–1400).

ALIX
A variant of Alexandra, q.v.

ALLANNAH
A variant of Alana, q.v.

ALLEGRA
From the Italian, meaning 'cheerful, sprightly'. The best-known bearer of the name was Lord Byron's illegitimate daughter by Claire Clairmont, Shelley's sister-in-law. Born in Bath in 1817, her short and turbulent life ended in Italy in 1822, where she succumbed to typhus.

ALLIE
A diminutive of Alison, q.v.

ALLY
A diminutive of Alison, q.v.

ALLYS
A variant of Alice, q.v.

ALMA
From the Latin, meaning 'kindly'. The name became fashionable in Britain after the Battle of Alma (1854), so called from the Russian river, during the Crimean War.

(It is also the Spanish word for 'soul' or 'ghost'.)

ALMIRA
A name which comes from the Middle East, meaning 'truthful'.

ALOISE
The female version of Aloysius, used in England since the seventeenth century.

The Italian St. Aloysius (1568–1591), son of the Marquis of Castiglione, was intended for a military career. He chose instead to become a Jesuit priest, dying of plague while working to assist those stricken with the disease in a Roman hospital.

ALTHEA
From the Greek, meaning 'a flower'.

ALYS
A variant of Alice, q.v.

AMABEL
From the Latin, meaning 'lovable'. A very common name in the twelfth and thirteen centuries, it was revived in the nineteenth century when the passion for medieval names was at its height.

AMALIA
Dutch, German and Spanish for Amelia, q.v.

AMANDA
This seems to have been invented by the architect and playwright Sir John Vanbrugh (1664–1726) for the heroine of his play, *The Relapse*. Another literary Amanda married the eponymous hero of *Peregrine Pickle* (1751) by Tobias Smollett.

AMARYLLIS
From the Greek, meaning 'rippling stream'.

AMATA
Spanish, Swedish and Italian for Amy, q.v.

AMBER
From the gemstone, one of the jewel names which became popular in the late nineteenth century. Amber beads have been prized in Britain since the thirteenth century - for their sweet smell as well as their beauty!

AMELIA
From the Old German, meaning 'work'. Shakespeare includes a character named Aemilia in *A Comedy of Errors,* but the name

171

became popular in the eighteenth century with the birth of Princess Amelia (1783–1810), the youngest daughter of George III.

Amelia Edwards (1831–1892) was forty-three when she visited Egypt for the first time: from this adventure came a book, the founding (with Sir Erasmus Wilson) of the Egypt Exploration Society and funding for the first Chair of Egyptology in Britain.

AMELIE
French for Amelia, q.v.

AMETHYST
From the Greek, meaning 'of wine colour'.

AMY
From the Old French, meaning 'loved'. Used in Britain since the Middle Ages, the name became popular in the nineteenth century on the publication of *Little Dorrit* (1855) by Charles Dickens. Amy Dorrit was the saintly little seamstress of the Marshalsea Prison.

Amy Johnson (1903–1941) was the first woman to fly solo from England to Australia in 1930.

ANASTASIA
From the Greek, meaning 'resurrection'. A fourth century martyr, the name was popular in the Middle Ages when legend attributed the name to the midwife of the Blessed Virgin Mary.

More recently, the ill-fated Russian Grand Duchess Anastasia (1901–1918) was executed with her family in the cellar at Ekaterinburg by the Bolsheviks.

ANASTASIE
French for Anastasia, q.v.

ANDREA
The female form of Andrew (q.v.), used since the seventeenth century.

ANGELA
From the Greek, meaning 'messenger'. St. Angela of Brescia (1474–1540) founded the Ursuline nuns, the first teaching order of women. The name Angel or Angela was sometimes given to children born on the feast of St. Michael and All Angels, 29th September. It was revived by the Tractarians in the nineteenth century.

172

ANGELE
French for Angela, q.v.

ANGELICA
From the Latin, meaning 'angelic'. Princess Angelica is the object of desire in the epic *Orlando Furioso*, by the Italian poet Lodovico Ariosto (1474–1533).

ANGELIKA
Greek for Angelica, q.v.

ANGELINA
A variant of Angela, q.v.

ANGELINE
A variant of Angela, q.v.

ANGELIQUE
French for Angelica, q.v.

ANGHARAD
From the Welsh, meaning 'much loved'. Angharad is the lady of *Peredur, son of Efrawg*, a medieval Welsh tale included in the *Mabinogion*.

ANGIE
A diminutive of Angela, q.v.

ANITA
The popular Spanish version of Anne, used all over Britain.

ANN
A variant of Anne, q.v.

ANNA
The Greek version of Hannah (q.v.). Anna is the sister of Dido, Queen of Carthage in the *Aeneid* of Virgil, and the unwitting cause of the queen's death. Henri I of France (1031–1060) married the Russian princess Anna, which made the name popular in Europe.

Anna Sewell (1820–1878) wrote the classic children's novel *Black Beauty*, which did so much to improve the treatment of horses.

ANNABEL
A medieval variant of Amabel (q.v.), now considered an independent name.

Edgar Allan Poe (1809–1849) wrote the haunting poem *Annabel Lee* on the death of his young wife, Virginia.

ANNABELLA
A variant of Annabel, q.v. Anabella Drummond (d.1401) was married to the crippled Scottish king, Robert III.

ANNE
The French form of Hannah (q.v.), used since the Middle Ages and interchangeable with Ann. Fourteenth century devotion to St. Ann, traditionally the mother of the Blessed Virgin Mary, made the name very popular indeed from then on.

Queen Anne (1665–1714), sadly remembered for bearing seventeen children, of whom only one survived to the age of eleven, was the last Stuart monarch.

A Canadian novelist, Lucy Maud Montgomery (1874–1942) wrote *Anne of Green Gables,* and a string of sequels, which became a success worldwide.

The Princess Royal, christened Anne Elizabeth Alice Louise (b. 1950), is the most eminent modern bearer of the name.

ANNELIES
The German version of Anne, now generally popular. Annelies Marie Frank (1929–1944) is the full name of the girl who wrote *The Diary of Anne Frank* which has sold eighteen million copies worldwide since being published in 1947.

ANNETTE
A variant of Anne, q.v.

ANNIE
A variant of Anne, q.v.

ANNIS
The medieval version of Agnes (q.v.), now used independently.

ANTHEA
From the Greek, meaning 'flowery'. Used in Classical Greece as a name applied to the goddess Hera, wife of Zeus, it was used by English poets of the seventeenth century. *To Anthea Who May*

Command Him Anything by Robert Herrick (1591–1674) is a typical example.

ANTOINETTE
French for Antonia, q.v.

ANTONETTA
Italian for Antonia, q.v.

ANTONIA
The feminine form of Anthony, q.v. The daughter of Mark Antony and great-grandmother of Nero, Antonia Augusta was the most influential Roman matron of her time.

Antonia Fraser, writer of historical biographies such as *Cromwell, Our Chief of Men*, is the best-known modern bearer of the name.

ANTONIE
German for Antonia, q.v.

ANUSHKA
The Russian pet-form of Ann (q.v.) now used in Britain.

APRIL
A name which became popular in the early twentieth century, mostly for girls born in that spring month. Avril, the French word for April, is equally favoured.

ARABELA
Spanish for Arabella, q.v.

ARABELLA
Originally a medieval Scottish name, meaning 'moved by prayer', now generally used. It was at its most popular in the eighteenth century, when Lord Petre cut off a lock of hair belonging to Arabella Fermor. This prompted Alexander Pope (1688–1744) to write his well-known poem, *The Rape of the Lock*.

ARABELLE
German for Arabella, q.v.

ARAMINTA
The name was invented by Sir John Vanbrugh (1664–1726), architect of Blenheim Palace and playwright, for his comedy *The Confederacy*.

ARIADNE
From the Greek, meaning 'very holy one'. In Greek mythology, Ariadne fell in love with Theseus, who came to Crete to kill the Minotaur. She gave him a sword, and a ball of thread with which to trace his path through the labyrinth. Ariadne later married the god Dionysus. There is an obscure early Christian martyr with the name.

ARLEEN
From the Gaelic, meaning 'a promise'.

ARLENE
A variant of Arleen, q.v.

ARLETTE
A variant of Arleen, q.v.

ARLINE
A modern name which seems to have come from America, possibly derived from Marlene or Charlene.

ARTEMIS
One of the twelve deities who lived on Mount Olympus, twin sister to Apollo, Artemis was the goddess of hunting and defender of children and all weak things. She is a main character in three plays by Euripides. The name has been used in England since the eighteenth century, when the love for the classical was at its height.

ASHLEIGH
From the Old English, meaning 'ash wood'. A place name and a surname, now used as a first name for both girls and boys, although the spelling Ashley is preferred for boys.

ASTRA
From the Greek, meaning 'star'.

ASTRID
From the Old Norse, meaning 'divinely beautiful'. Astrid was the wife of St. Olaf (995–1030), King of Norway, and it has remained a popular royal name in that country. It has been used in Britain since the beginning of the twentieth century.

ATALANTA
In Greek mythology, Atalanta was a beautiful huntress who said that

176

she would marry any suitor who could out-run her, but anyone who could not do so must die. She was finally beaten by Melanion, who dropped three golden apples given to him by Venus. Atalanta stopped to pick them up and so lost the race and married the winner. Algernon Charles Swinburne wrote a famous poem, *Atalanta in Calydon* (1865), about her.

AUDREY

From the Old English name, Etheldreda, used as an independent name since the sixteenth century. St. Etheldreda (630–679) founded a monastery for both monks and nuns at Ely: the present Ely Cathedral stands on its site. She was the most revered of all Anglo-Saxon women saints. Audrey is a country lass in *As You Like It* by Shakespeare.

AUGUSTA

The female form of Augustus, q.v. Popular as an aristocratic name in Germany, it was brought to England by the Hanoverians.

George III named two daughters, Charlotte Augusta Matilda, Princess Royal (b.1766), and Augusta Sophia (b.1768), after his mother, Augusta of Saxe-Gotha-Altenburg. The name became very popular in the nineteenth century and has been used steadily since then.

AURIAL

A variant of Auriel, q.v.

AURIEL

From the Latin, meaning 'golden'. A name used in Ancient Rome, it was revived in the nineteenth century.

AURORA

The Roman goddess of the Dawn, sister to the Sun and the Moon. This has been used in Europe since the Renaissance.

Lady Aurora Sydney was travelling in a carriage stopped by the highwayman, Claude Duval. Part of his plunder was restored to her on condition that she danced a coranto with him on the heath. (He was hanged at Tyburn in 1670.)

AVA

From the Latin, meaning 'birdlike'.

AVELINE
French for Hazel, q.v.

AVRIL
The French word for the month of April, used as a first name since the early twentieth century.

BABE
A variant of Babette or Barbara, q.v.

BABETTE
A variant of Barbara, q.v.

BABS
A variant of Barbara, q.v.

BARBARA
From the Greek, meaning 'strange' or 'foreign'. (The ancient Greeks believed that the language of foreigners was unintelligible, sounding like nothing but 'bar-bar-bar'.) St. Barbara, probably martyred in the third century, became very popular in the Middle Ages. The patron saint of architects and miners, she was invoked for protection against lightning. The name was revived in the late nineteenth century.

BARBE
French for Barbara. q.v.

BARBRA
A variant of Barbara, q.v.

BEA

A diminutive of Beatrice, q.v.

BEATRICE

From the Latin, meaning 'bringer of joy'. The name of a Christian martyr in the fourth century, it was common in Britain during the Middle Ages and is mentioned in the Domesday Book. Princess Beatrice (1857–1944) was the youngest daughter of Queen Victoria, and the name has been bestowed on the elder daughter of Prince Andrew, Duke of York.

Beatrice Portinari was the guide through Paradise to God for the Italian poet Alighieri Dante (1265–1321), in his epic poem, *The Divine Comedy*. A painting in the Tate Gallery in London, entitled *Beata Beatrix*, by Dante Gabriel Rossetti, depicts her death. And the writer and illustrator Beatrix Potter (1866–1943), of 'Peter Rabbit' fame, should not be forgotten.

BEATRIX

A variant of Beatrice, q.v.

BEATTIE

A variant of Beatrice, q.v.

BECKY

A diminutive of Rebecca, q.v. Becky Sharp is the interesting but far from pleasant main character in *Vanity Fair* (1848) by William Makepeace Thackeray.

BELINDA

It was used by Alexander Pope as the name of the beautiful heroine of his epic poem, *The Rape of the Lock* (1712), which made it fashionable.

'If to her share some female errors fall,
   Look on her face and you'll forget 'em all'.
The name has been used regularly since then.

BELITA

Spanish for Elizabeth, q.v.

BELLA

Diminutive of the following (q.v.): Isabel, Isabella, Arabella and Annabella.

179

BELLE
Diminutive of: Isabel, Isabella, Arabella and Annabella (q.v.).

BELLITA
A variant of Belle, q.v.

BENEDETTA
Italian for Benedicta, q.v.

BENEDICTA
A feminine form of Benedict, q.v.

BENEDIKTA
German for Benedicta, q.v.

BENITA
A variant of Benedicta, q.v.

BENOITE
French for Benedicta, q.v.

BERENICE
From the Greek, meaning 'bringer of Victory'. Popular in Ancient Greece and Rome, the New Testament Berenice was the daughter of Herod Agrippa. It has been used in Britain since the Reformation. *Berenice* was the title of a tragedy by the French playwright Jean Racine (1639–1699).

BERNADETTE
The French female version of Bernard. This became well-known when the very poor and sickly Bernadette Soubirous (1844–1879) had several visions of the Blessed Virgin in 1858 at the grotto in Lourdes, now celebrated as a place of pilgrimage for the sick. St. Bernadette was canonised in 1933.

BERNADINE
A variant of Bernadette, q.v.

BERNARDINA
Spanish and Italian for Bernadette, q.v.

BERNICE
From the Greek, meaning 'one who brings victory'.

BERNIE
A variant of Bernice, q.v.

BERTHA
From the German, meaning 'bright'.

BERTHE
French and German for Bertha, q.v.

BERYL
A green gemstone, first used as a name for girls by the Victorians. (Medieval Parisian jewellers sometimes pretended these stones were diamonds, which did not please the buyers at all!)

BESS
A variant of Elizabeth. q.v.

BESSIE
A variant of Elizabeth. q.v.

BETH
A variant of Elizabeth. q.v.

BETHAN
A variant of Bethany, q.v.

BETHANY
A traditional Welsh girls' name. Also a modern name taken from a town situated on the Mount of Olives. It was the Biblical home of Lazarus, whom Christ raised from the dead.

BETSY
A variant of Elizabeth, q.v.

BETTE
A variant of Elizabeth, q.v.

BETTINA
A variant of Elizabeth, q.v.

BETTY
A variant of Elizabeth, q.v.

BEULAH
From the Hebrew, meaning 'married'.

BEVERLEY
A Yorkshire place name, meaning 'beaver stream', and surname, used as a first name since the eighteenth century. It is given to both boys and girls.

BIANCA
The Italian version of Blanche, meaning 'white'. In Shakespeare's play *The Taming of the Shrew*, Bianca is the younger sister of Katharina, as gentle and meek as her sister is irascible: while in Shakespeare's *Othello,* Bianca is a courtesan.

BIDDY
A variant of Bridget, q.v.

BILLIE
A variant of Wilhelmina, q.v.

BINNIE
A variant of Benedicta, q.v.

BLAISE
From the Latin, meaning 'stammerer'.

BLANCA
Spanish for Blanche. q.v.

BLANCHE
From the French, meaning 'white'. The name was brought to England by Blanche of Artois on her marriage to Prince Edmund (d.1296), a son of Henry III. It was revived in the nineteenth century.

BLANKA
German for Blanche, q.v.

BLOSSOM
This name means 'like a blossom'.

BOBBIE
A variant of Roberta, q.v.

BOBETTE
A variant of Roberta, q.v.

BONNIE
An affectionate Scottish term, meaning 'pretty', now used as a first name. Two films may have helped to popularise the name. Scarlett O'Hara's daughter was given the nickname Bonnie in *Gone With The Wind;* while Bonnie Parker was the murderous accomplice to Clyde Barrow in *Bonnie and Clyde* (1967).

BRENDA
From the Norse, meaning 'sword'. Popular in Scotland, it became generally used in the nineteenth century. Sir Walter Scott gave the name to a character in his novel *The Pirate* (1822).

BRIDGET
The anglicised version of the Irish Brighid, meaning 'the high one'. St. Bridget (450–523), patroness of Ireland, founded the first religious community for women in that country. Her cult spread to England and Scotland, where churches were dedicated in her honour in the medieval form of St. Bride. (A well-known example, 'the printers' church', stands in Fleet Street in London.)

BRIDIE
A variant of Bridget, q.v.

BRIGITTE
The French version of Bridget, q.v. The best-known bearer of the name is Brigitte Bardot (b.1934), the former film star who now devotes her life to animals.

BRIONY
A variant of Bryony, q.v.

BRITTANY
A French province of north-west France, an independent duchy until 1532, now used as a first name.

BRONWEN
From the Welsh, meaning 'white-breast'. Bronwen is the daughter of the sea god in ancient legend.

BROOKE
A place name, meaning 'dweller by a stream', and surname, now used as a first name by both girls and boys.

BRYONY
A botanical name, used as a first name since the beginning of the twentieth century. A climbing plant, the white bryony has large yellow flowers and poisonous red berries.

BUNNY
A variant of Bernice, q.v.

CADENCE
From the Latin, meaning 'one who is rhythmic'.

CADENZA
Italian for Cadence, q.v.

CALANDRA
From the Greek, meaning 'a lark'.

CALANDRE
French for Calandra, q.v.

CALANDRIA
Spanish for Calandra, q.v.

CALANTHA
From the Greek, meaning 'fair blossom'.

CALANTHE
French for Calantha, q.v.

CALLIOPE
From the Greek, meaning 'one with a lovely voice'.

CAMILA
Spanish for Camilla, q.v.

CAMILLA
The feminine form of Camillus, a family name of Ancient Rome. In Virgil's *Aeneid*, Camilla was a warrior maiden so fleet of foot that she could run across a field of corn without bending a single blade. She was killed in battle with the Trojans. The name was first used in England in the thirteenth century. Fanny Burney (1752–1840) wrote the novel *Camilla* (1814) which helped to revive the name.

CAMILLE
The French version of Camilla (q.v.), now generally used.

CANDACE
A title given to the Queens of Ethiopia, also mentioned in the New Testament. The name has been used in Britain since the seventeenth century.

CANDICE
A variant of Candace, q.v.

CANDIDA
From the Latin, meaning 'white'. The name of an early Christian martyr, not used in Britain until the twentieth century. Candida Morell is the heroine of the play *Candida* (1903), written by George Bernard Shaw, which brought the name into favour.

CANDIDE
French for Candida, q.v.

CANDY
A variant of Candace, q.v.

CARA
From the Italian, meaning 'dear'. A popular modern name.

CARINA
A variant of Cara, q.v.

CARISSA
From the Latin, meaning 'dear one'.

CARLA
The feminine version of Carl, the German for Charles, q.v.

CARLOTA
Spanish for Charlotte, q.v.

CARLOTTA
Italian for Charlotte, q.v.

CARLY
A variant of Carla, q.v.

CARMEL
From the Hebrew, meaning 'garden'.

CARMELA
Italian for Carmel, q.v.

CARMELITA
Spanish for Carmel, q.v.

CARMEN
From the Latin, meaning 'song' and from the Spanish, meaning 'crimson'.

CARMENCITA
Spanish for Carmen, q.v.

CAROL
Originally a pet-form of Caroline, used independently since the late nineteenth century. This is sometimes given to girls born in the Christmas season, in association with the carol, a song for the festivity.

CAROLE
A variant of Carol, q.v.

CAROLINA
Spanish and Italian for Caroline, q.v.

CAROLINE
The feminine Italian form of Charles. Caroline Wilhelmina of Brandenburg-Anspach (1683–1737), wife of George II, made the name a great favourite in the eighteenth century and this popularity has continued. Another royal Caroline was married to George IV; her turbulent life included an abortive attempt at divorce and being forcibly excluded from her husband's coronation in Westminster Abbey.

CAROLYN
A variant of Caroline, q.v.

CARRIE
A variant of Caroline, q.v.

CASEY
An Irish surname, now used as a first name by both girls and boys. See the entry in the boys' section.

CASSANDRA
In Greek legend, she was the beautiful daughter of King Priam. When she rejected the god Apollo, he cursed her so that her prophecies would never be believed. She died in the fall of Troy. The story was popular in the Middle Ages and has been used regularly since then.

Cassandra was the beloved elder sister of the novelist Jane Austen (1775–1817), the recipient of many of her surviving letters.

CASSIE
A diminutive of Cassandra, q.v.

CATALINA
Spanish for Catherine, q.v.

CATARINA
Italian for Catherine, q.v.

CATH
A diminutive of Catherine, q.v.

CATHARINE
A variant of Catherine, q.v.

CATHERINE
From the Greek, meaning 'pure'. The name of many saints, the most famous of whom is St. Catherine of Alexandria (d.307). Refusing to deny her faith, a vain attempt was made to break her on a wheel (thus giving us the firework 'catherine wheel') and she was beheaded. The angels carried her body to Mount Sinai, where the monks of the orthodox monastery there still guard her shrine. Her cult was brought to Britain by returning Crusaders and many churches were dedicated to her.

Henry VIII (1491–1547) was particularly partial to the name. Catherine of Aragon, Katherine Howard and Katherine Parr were unfortunate enough to be married to him.

The name has been, and remains, a great favourite.

CATHIE
A variant of Catherine, q.v.

CATHLENE
A variant of Catherine, q.v.

CATHY
A variant of Catherine, q.v.

CATRINA
A variant of Catriona, q.v.

CATRIONA
The Gaelic diminutive of Catherine, now used all over Britain. *Catriona* (1893) is the name of a novel written by Robert Louis Stevenson, sequel to the more famous *Kidnapped*.

CECILE
French for Cecilia, q.v.

CECILIA
From the Latin, meaning 'blind', the feminine form of Cecil. An early Christian martyr in Rome, St. Cecilia has been revered in Europe since the sixth century. She is the patron saint of musicians. The name was brought to England at the Norman Conquest by a daughter of William I.

Cecily Cardew is the ward of Jack Worthing in the classic play, *The Importance of Being Earnest* (1895), by Oscar Wilde.

CECILY
A variant of Cecilia, q.v.

CELESTE
From the Latin, meaning 'heavenly'. The name of two (male) saints, but considered exclusively feminine in Britain.

CELIA
The feminine form of an ancient Roman family, the name became popular when Shakespeare included it in *As You Like It*. Celia is the daughter of Duke Frederick.

The poet Ben Jonson (1572–1637) wrote the well-known poem *To Celia*, which includes the lines:
'Drink to me only with thine eyes,
And I will pledge with mine;'

CERYS
From the Welsh, meaning 'to love'.

CHANEL
The world-famous French perfume, now used as a first name. The French dress designer Gabrielle ('Coco') Chanel (1883–1971) opened her first fashion house in 1914. Her life was portrayed in a musical comedy entitled *Coco* in 1969.

CHANTAL
This name was originally used in honour of St. Jeanne de Chantal (1572–1641), the charming co-founder of the Order of the Visitation. She was described by another saint as 'one of the holiest people I have ever met on this earth'. It has been used in Britain since the beginning of the twentieth century.

CHANTELLE
A variant of Chantel, q.v.

CHARIS
From the Greek, meaning 'grace'. Charis was one of the three Graces, attendants to Aphrodite, mentioned in Homer's *Iliad*. She was married to Hephaestus, the lame god of fire and metal-working. The name was used after the Reformation.

CHARISSA
A variant of Charis, q.v.

CHARITY
From the Latin Charitas, meaning 'charitable'.

CHARLENE
A feminine version of Charles, in use since the 1950s.

CHARLIE
A diminutive of Charlotte, q.v.

CHARLOTTA
Swedish for Charlotte, q.v.

CHARLOTTE
The French feminine form of Charles. The name was unusual in Britain until the marriage of Charlotte Sophia of Mecklenburg-Strelitz (1744–1818) to George III in 1761 made it fashionable. Her grand-daughter, Princess Charlotte (1796–1817), daughter of the Prince Regent, died in childbirth, generating a great wave of public grief. There is a beautiful monument to her in St. George's Chapel, Windsor.

The writer Charlotte Brontë (1816–1855), author of *Jane Eyre*, *The Professor*, *Shirley* and *Villette* is a famous bearer of the name, as is the poet Charlotte Mew (1869–1928).

CHARMAIN
A variant of Charmaine, q.v.

CHARMAINE
From the Latin, meaning 'singer'.

CHELSEA
A place name in west London, meaning 'a landing place for limestone', now used as a first name. The singer Joni Mitchell had a success with her song *Chelsea Morning*, which may have helped.

CHELSIE
A variant of Chelsea, q.v.

CHERRIE
A variant of Cherry, q.v.

190

CHERRY
Sometimes considered the anglicised form of the French word for 'darling' (cherie), it was originally a pet-form of Charity. Charity and Mercy, daughters of Mr. Pecksniff in *Martin Chuzzlewit* (1844), are called Cherry and Merry.

CHERYL
A variant of Cherry, q.v.

CHIARA
Italian for Clara, q.v.

CHIQUITA
From the Spanish, meaning 'little one'.

CHLÖE
From the Greek, meaning 'green shoot'. The New Testament Chlöe lived in Corinth and was mentioned by St. Paul. It was popular with the Puritans of the seventeenth century as they searched the Bible for names for their children.

Daphnis and Chlöe, a Greek pastoral poem of the fourth century by Longus, has inspired many imitations. Maurice Ravel wrote the music for a ballet of the same name.

CHRIS
A diminutive of Christina, q.v., or Christine.

CHRISSIE
A diminutive of Christina, q.v., or Christine.

CHRISTABEL
This name means 'beautiful Christian'.

CHRISTEN
A variant of Christina, q.v.

CHRISTIANA
A variant of Christina, q.v.

CHRISTINA
The feminine abbreviation of Christian (q.v.), used regularly since the eighteenth century. The enigmatic poet Christina Rossetti (1830–1894) must be the most famous bearer of the name. *In the*

Bleak Midwinter, now used as a carol, was written by her.

CHRISTINE
The French version of Christina (q.v.), favoured in Britain since the end of the nineteenth century.

CHRISTY
A variant of Christina, q.v.

CHRYSTAL
A variant of Crystal, q.v.

CICELY
A variant of Cecilia, q.v.

CILLA
A variant of Priscilla, q.v.

CINDY
The pet-form of Cynthia or Lucinda, now used as an independent name.

CIS
A variant of Cecilia, q.v.

CISSIE
A variant of Cecilia, q.v.

CLAIRE
A variant of Clare, q.v.

CLARA
This name means 'renowned'.

CLARABEL
A variant of Clare, q.v.

CLARE
From the Latin, meaning 'bright'. St. Clare of Assisi (1194–1253), the friend of St. Francis and founder of the Poor Clare contemplative nuns, made the name well-known. She is the patron saint of television; owing to her having seen and heard a mass being celebrated far away, which illness had prevented her from attending.

CLARIBEL
A variant of Clare, q.v.

CLARICE
A variant of Clarissa, q.v.

CLARINDA
A variant of Clara, q.v.

CLARISSA
From the Latin, meaning 'renowned'. A form of Clarice, made famous by the book *Clarissa Harlowe* by Samuel Richardson (1689–1761), the longest novel in the English language. Clarissa rejects the man her tyrannical family wish her to marry, elopes with the unsuitable Robert Lovelace and it all ends in tears.

CLARITA
Spanish for Clara, q.v.

CLARRIE
A variant of Clara, q.v.

CLARY
A variant of Clara, q.v.

CLAUDETTE
A variant of Claudia, q.v.

CLAUDIA
The feminine form of Claudius, the name of an ancient Roman family. The name is mentioned in the New Testament as that of a Roman convert. It has been used in Britain since the seventeenth century.

CLAUDINE
French for Claudia, q.v. Claudine is the heroine of four semi-autobiographical novels written by 'Colette' (Sidonie Gabrielle Colette) between 1900–1903.

CLEMENCE
French for Clemency, q.v.

CLEMENCY
From the Latin, meaning 'merciful', the feminine form of Clement. The name has been used in England since the thirteenth century: seventeenth century Puritans liked the abstract nouns of Clemency, Prudence and Patience.

CLEMENTIA
A variant of Clemency, q.v.

CLEMENTINA
A variant of Clemency, q.v.

CLEMENTINE
A variant of Clemency, q.v.

CLEMMIE
A diminutive of Clemency, q.v.

CLEO
A diminutive of Cleopatra, q.v.

CLEOPATRA
From the Greek, meaning 'fame and glory'. Cleopatra was Queen of Egypt from 69–30 B.C.

CLIO
From the Greek, meaning 'praise'. In Greek mythology, the inventor of heroic and historical poetry, one of the nine Muses, daughters of Zeus and Mnemosyne.

CLODAGH
From the river in County Tipperary. A modern first name.

CLORINDA
From the Latin, meaning 'renowned'.

CLOVER
A botanical name, used as a first name since the nineteenth century. Clover Carr is the sister of the eponymous heroine of the classic children's books, *What Katy Did* and *What Katy Did Next* by Susan Coolidge (1835–1905; real name Sarah Chauncey Woolsey).

COLETTE
The feminine French diminutive of Nicholas, q.v. St. Colette (1381–1447) was born when her mother was sixty years of age. She became a hermit and, later, a reformer of the Poor Clares. The name has been used in England since the thirteenth century.

COLLEEN
From the Irish, meaning 'maiden'.

CONCHITA
A Spanish name, meaning 'the beginning'.

CONNIE
A variant of Constance, q.v.

CONSTANCE
From the Latin, meaning 'firmness'. A saint's name, it was brought to England by the Normans, the name of a daughter of William the Conqueror.
    Lady Constance Lytton (1869–1923) was a militant suffragette whose health was permanently impaired by forcible feeding: she wrote a book about her experiences.

CONSTANTA
A variant of Constance, q.v.

CONSTANTIA
A variant of Constance, q.v.

CONSTANZA
Spanish and Italian for Constance, q.v.

CONSUELA
A Spanish name, meaning 'consolation'.

CONSUELO
Italian for Consuela, q.v.

CORA
From the Greek, meaning 'maiden'. The name was not used until the nineteenth century, apparently brought to public attention by a character in the novel *The Last of the Mohicans* (1826), by James Fenimore Cooper. Cora Munro is in love with Uncas, the last of the

Mohicans, and it ends in suicide.

CORAH
A variant of Cora, q.v.

CORAL
Used as a girl's name since the late nineteenth century, when there was a passion for jewel names. Italian babies of the fourteenth century wore pieces of coral mounted with silver around their necks: this can be seen in several medieval paintings of the Virgin and Child.

CORALIE
French for Coral, q.v.

CORDELIA
From the Latin, meaning 'heart'. Cordelia is the only faithful daughter of Shakespeare's *King Lear,* and marries the King of France.
   To her are applied the lines:
      'Her voice was ever soft, gentle and low,
      an excellent thing in a woman'. (!!!)

CORDELIE
A variant of Cordelia, q.v.

CORINA
Spanish for Cora, q.v.

CORINNA
From the Greek, meaning 'maiden'. Corinna was a Greek poet of the fourth century B.C. Robert Herrick used the name in his well-known poem, *Corinna's Going A-Maying* (1648).

CORINNE
A variant of Corinna, q.v. The French writer Madame de Stael (1766–1817) wrote the romantic novel, *Corinne.*

CORRIE
A variant of Cora, q.v.

COSIMA
From the Greek, meaning 'harmony'. Cosima Wagner (1837–1930), the daughter of Franz Liszt and wife of Richard Wagner, is the best-known bearer of the name.

COURTNEY
An aristocratic surname, originating from Courtenay in France, now bestowed as a first name on both girls and boys.

CRESSIDA
Both Chaucer and Shakespeare wrote about the legend of 'Troilus and Cressida'. Cressida, the daughter of a Trojan priest, vowed eternal fidelity to Troilus but threw him aside for Diomedes, thus making herself a byword for infidelity. A favourite name in the twentieth century.

CRISTINA
Spanish and Italian for Christina, q.v.

CRYSTAL
Another of the gem names, popular since the late nineteenth century. The word is derived from the Greek 'krystallos', meaning 'ice'.

CYNTHIA
A title of the goddess Diana, meaning 'of Cynthus', the mountain on which she was born. It has been used in England since the sixteenth century.

DAISY
From the flower, which in Old English means 'the eye of day'. The Victorians began the vogue for flower names in the latter part of the nineteenth century.

   Daisy Miller is the eponymous unsophisticated American heroine of a novelette by Henry James (1843–1916).

And 'top of the pops' c. 1902 was:
'Daisy, Daisy, give me your answer do,
I'm half crazy, all for the love of you'.

DAMARIS

From the Greek, meaning 'heifer', implying gentleness. In the New Testament Damaris was an Athenian woman converted by St. Paul. Along with Priscilla and Dorcas, it was one of the most popular of all Puritan names in the seventeenth century.

DANA

This name means 'one who came from Denmark'.

DANIELA

A variant of Danielle, q.v.

DANIELLE

The French feminine form of Daniel (q.v.), very popular indeed since the 1960s.

DANNIE

A diminutive of Danielle, q.v.

DAPHNE

From the Greek, meaning 'laurel'. In Greek mythology, Daphne, the daughter of a river-god, was loved by Apollo. Pursued by him, she appealed to her father to save her and was transformed into a laurel tree. This was believed to be so holy as to protect all beneath its shade from lightning. The name came into fashion in Britain in the late nineteenth century and is now enjoying a revival.

Daphne du Maurier (1907–1989), author of such popular novels as *Rebecca* and *Jamaica Inn,* is the best-known bearer of the name.

DARA

From the Hebrew, meaning 'pearl of wisdom'. A male name in the Old Testament, shown in a genealogical list as 'one of the five sons of Zerah, grandson of Judah' (I Chronicles, ch. 2 v.6), it is used as a girl's name in modern times.

DARCEY/DARCY

A French place name and surname, brought to England by Norman D'Arcy, a companion of William the Conqueror.

It is now bestowed on both girls and boys; a compliment to the fine ballerina Darcey Bussell, perhaps.

DARIA
The feminine form of Darius. Darius I (558–486 B.C.) was one of seven Persian chiefs who overthrew the usurper, Smerdis, and won the throne by a trick. He invaded Greece and was defeated at the battle of Marathon in 490 B.C.

DARRYL
Generally considered a male name, but occasionally bestowed on girls.

DAVIDA
The feminine form of David, q.v.

DAVINA
The Scottish feminine version of David (q.v.), now generally used.

DAWN
This name has been used since the early twentieth century; the English version of the goddess Aurora, who was married to the Titan Astraeus and gave birth to the stars, the winds and Eosphorus, the Morning Star.

DEANE
A variant of Dena, q.v.

DEANNA
A variant of Diana, q.v.

DEB
A diminutive of Deborah, q.v.

DEBBIE
A diminutive of Deborah, q.v.

DEBORAH
From the Hebrew, meaning 'bee'. In the Old Testament there are two women with this name. The first was nurse to Rebecca and accompanied her when she married Isaac. The second Deborah was the prophetess, whose wisdom made her leader of the Israelites as they fought successfully against the Canaanites.

The Puritans of the seventeenth century favoured the name and it has been used since then. The blind poet John Milton (1608–1674) bestowed it on his youngest daughter.

DEBRA
A variant of Deborah, q.v.

DEE
This name is used as a variant of Deborah, q.v.

DEIRDRE
The heroine of Irish legend, Deirdre, the most beautiful woman in the land, fled to Scotland with the man she loved and his two brothers. Persuaded to return and betrayed, the three men were murdered and *Deirdre,* by the poet W.B. Yeats (1865–1939), and *Deirdre of the Sorrows* by J.M. Synge (1871–1909), have made the name popular since the early years of the twentieth century.

DELIA
From the Greek island of Delos, birthplace of the goddess Diana. Delia was the shepherdess in the *Eclogues* of Virgil (70–19 B.C.) and the name was used in many poems of the seventeenth and eighteenth centuries, including *Sonnets to Delia* by Samuel Daniel (1562–1619).

DELILAH
This name means 'delicate'. In the Bible Delilah was the betrayer of Samson.

DELLA
A variant of Adelaide, q.v.

DENA
From the Old English, meaning 'valley'. This is considered to be the feminine version of Dean and has been used since the 1950s.

DENISE
The French feminine form of Dennis, q.v. The name was brought to England at the Norman Conquest and in use until the eighteenth century, when it disappeared to be revived in the early twentieth century.

DESIRÉE
From the French, meaning 'desired'. The Puritans of the seventeenth century gave the name Desire to their daughters, but it was never

popular. The French version appears to have been used in Britain since the beginning of the twentieth century. (It is also the name of the rather delicious potato!)

DIANA

The Latin name for the goddess of the moon, it became fashionable in Britain in the sixteenth century when there was much interest in classical literature.

Diana of the Crossways (1885) was a novel by George Meredith; the heroine of which disliked her 'pagan' name!

Diana, Princess of Wales (1961–1997) greatly increased the name's popularity.

DIANE

A variant of Diana, q.v. Diane de Poitiers (1499–1566) was the mistress of the French king, Henry II, and allowed unlimited power when he ascended the throne. She was created the Duchesse de Valentinois, but expelled from court on his death.

DIANNA

A variant of Diana, q.v.

DIDO

The legendary founder and Queen of Carthage, whose husband was murdered by her brother, Pygmalion.

In Virgil's *Aeneid*, she falls in love with Aeneas when he and other Trojans are shipwrecked on her shores. Finally abandoned by him, she commits suicide.

Christopher Marlowe and Thomas Nashe collaborated on the play *Dido, Queen of Carthage* (1593), and the English Baroque composer Henry Purcell (1659–1695) wrote one opera, *Dido and Aeneas.*

DILYS

From the Welsh, meaning 'genuine'. It has been used as a name since the latter part of the nineteenth century.

DINAH

From the Hebrew, meaning 'judged'. In the Old Testament, the unhappy daughter of Jacob and Leah. Another of the names adopted by the Puritans of the seventeenth century and used regularly since then. (An unusual literary Dinah was the cat of Alice of Wonderland fame!)

DIONE
A variant of Dionne, q.v.

DIONNE
In Greek mythology, Dione was a consort of the god Zeus and the mother of Aphrodite. Another of the same name was a daughter of Atlas who married the unfortunate Tantalus. The American singer Dionne Warwick brought the name back into the limelight.

DIXIE
A variant of Benedicta, q.v.

DODO
A pet-form of Dorothy, q.v.

DOLL
A pet-form of Dorothy, q.v.

DOLLY
A pet-form of Dorothy, q.v.

DOLORES
From the Spanish, meaning 'sorrows'. A title of the Blessed Virgin, 'Maria de los Dolores', which commemorated seven sad episodes in her life.

DOMINGA
Spanish for Dominica, q.v.

DOMINICA
This name means 'of the Lord'.

DOMINIQUE
French for Dominica, q.v.

DOÑA
Spanish for Donna, q.v.

DONNA
From the Italian, meaning 'lady', literally mistress of the household. An Italian title, it has been used as a first name in Britain since the 1930s.

DORA

A shortened form of Theodora and Dorothy, used as an independent name since the beginning of the nineteenth century.

David Copperfield, the eponymous hero of the novel by Charles Dickens (1812–1870) is hopelessly in love with Dora Spenlow who appears to be besotted only with her dog, Jip. He later marries his 'child-wife', who fortunately does not long survive. This rather idiotic character made the name very popular.

DORCAS

From the Greek, meaning 'gazelle'. In the New Testament, Dorcas is the Greek translation of the Aramaic name, Tabitha, a woman who was 'full of good works and almsdeeds', and raised from the dead by St. Peter (Acts IX v.36–41). This was first used by the Puritans of the seventeenth century.

DOREEN

An Irish version of Dora. It has been used in Britain since the beginning of the twentieth century; possibly prompted by the novel *Doreen* (1894) written by Edna Lyall.

DORETTA

A variant of Dora, q.v.

DORINDA

A name invented in the eighteenth century, used by both poets and playwrights. Dorinda, the daughter of Lady Bountiful, marries Thomas Aimwell, one of the two beaux in the play *The Beaux' Stratagem* by the comic dramatist George Farquhar (1678–1707).

DORIS

From the Greek, meaning 'of the sea'. In Greek mythology, Doris was married to the sea-god Nereus, and mother to fifty daughters known as Nereids or sea-nymphs.

For reasons unfathomable the name became very popular in Britain in the late nineteenth century.

The American film star Doris Day (b.1924) is well known.

DOROTEA

Spanish and Italian for Dorothy, q.v.

DOROTHEA

German for Dorothy and a variant for Dorothy in Britain, q.v.

DOROTHY

From the Greek, meaning 'gift of God'. St. Dorothy (d.303) was martyred during Diocletian's persecution of the Christians. On her way to execution a lawyer mocked her, asking her to send him fruit and flowers from Paradise: a child promptly appeared and gave him a basket of apples and roses. The lawyer became a Christian and a martyr himself.

The name has been used in Britain since the fifteenth century. It was so common in the sixteenth century that the diminutive Doll was given to the child's toy.

The English detective-story writer Dorothy L. Sayers (1893–1957) created Lord Peter Wimsey and wrote the religious play, *The Man Born To Be King* (1942).

DORRIE

A variant of Dora (q.v.) and of Dorothy (q.v.).

DOT

A variant for Dorothy, q.v.

DRUSILLA

From the Latin, meaning 'of the family of Drusus'.

DUANA

From the Irish Gaelic, meaning 'little dark girl'.

DULCIE

From the Latin, meaning 'sweet'. This was a name coined in the late nineteenth century, perhaps based on the medieval Dowsabel, now obsolete.

EARTHA
From the Old English, meaning 'of the earth'.

ECHO
In Greek mythology, the goddess Hera was infuriated by the incessant chatter of a nymph named Echo. As a punishment the goddess deprived her of speech, allowing her only the ability to repeat the last words spoken by someone else. Echo fell in love with the beautiful youth Narcissus, but her love was unrequited. She pined away, leaving nothing behind but her voice.

EDIE
A variant of Edith, q.v.

EDITA
Italian for Edith, q.v.

EDITH
From the Old English, the two syllables meaning 'wealthy' and 'war'. The name of three Anglo-Saxon saints, it survived the Norman Conquest and has been used regularly since then.

Queen Edith (d.1075), daughter of the Earl of Wessex, was married to St. Edward the Confessor.

The actress Dame Edith Evans (1888–1975), famous for her Lady Bracknell in Oscar Wilde's *The Importance of Being Earnest,* and the writer and poet Dame Edith Sitwell (1887–1964), are the best-known modern bearers of the name.

EDMUNDA
A feminine form of Edmund, q.v.

EDNA

From the Hebrew, meaning 'delight'. Edna was married to Raguel, a relative of Tobit, in the Apocryphal *Book of Tobit*. It came into use in Britain in the mid-nineteenth century.

Two best-selling literary ladies have borne the name: the Victorian novelist Edna Lyall and Edna Ferber, the American writer remembered for *Show Boat* and *Giant*.

EDWINA

The feminine form of Edwin q.v., first used in the nineteenth century.

EILEEN

The Irish form of Helen (q.v.), used in England since the late nineteenth century. Ruth McKenney wrote the amusing *My Sister Eileen* (1938), later filmed, which helped to popularise the name.

EIRWEN

From the Welsh, meaning 'golden-fair', used since the early years of the twentieth century.

ELAINE

The Old French form of Helen (q.v.), now used independently. Arthurian romance mentions two ladies named Elaine. The first, daughter of King Pelles, fell in love with Sir Lancelot and assumed the likeness of Queen Guinevere for one night in order to deceive him. Sir Galahad was the result of their union.

The second died of unrequited love for Sir Lancelot and her story is included in the poems, *Idylls of the King* by Alfred, Lord Tennyson (1809–1892), and *The Lady of Shalott*. These poems made the name a favourite with parents.

ELEANOR

A variant of Helen (q.v.), brought to England by the ebullient Eleanor of Aquitaine (1122–1204), who married Henry II at Bordeaux Cathedral. She was mother to Richard the Lionheart and the 'baddie', King John.

Queen Eleanor of Castile (1244–1290), wife of Edward I, accompanied her husband on the Crusades and saved his life by sucking poison from a wound. Twelve memorial crosses (of which four remain), were erected by him to mark her body's resting place at each halt on her last journey from Harby, in Nottinghamshire, to burial in Westminster Abbey.

ELEANORA
Italian for Eleanor, q.v.

ELEANORE
Danish and German for Eleanor, q.v.

ELENA
Italian for Helen, q.v.

ELGA
From the Norse, meaning 'holy'.

ELINOR
A variant of Eleanor, q.v. Elinor Dashwood is the heroine of *Sense and Sensibility* (1811) by Jane Austen.

ELISA
Italian for Elizabeth, q.v.

ELISABET
Swedish for Elizabeth, q.v.

ELISE
A variant of Elizabeth, q.v.

ELIZA
A variant of Elizabeth, q.v.

ELIZABETH
From the Hebrew, meaning 'God's promise'. The Biblical Elizabeth was cousin to the Blessed Virgin Mary and mother to John the Baptist.

Queen Elizabeth I (1533–1603) made the name immensely popular, which is indicated by the very many variants used. In the twentieth century, the name continued firmly regal when borne by Elizabeth Bowes Lyon (b.1900), wife of George VI, and bestowed upon Queen Elizabeth II (b.1926). The poet Elizabeth Barrett Browning (1806–1861), whose tyrannical father prompted the most famous elopement in literary history, is just one of the many famous bearers of this favourite name.

ELLA
From the Old German, meaning 'all'. This was brought to England at

the Norman Conquest and was popular during the Middle Ages. It was revived in the nineteenth century, chiefly by the Pre-Raphaelites in their enthusiasm for the medieval.

The jazz singer Ella Fitzgerald is a well-known modern bearer of the name.

ELLEN

An English form of Helen (q.v.), used as an independent name since the thirteenth century. Ellen Montgomery was the heroine of the Victorian tearjerker, *The Wide, Wide World* by Elizabeth Wetherell.

ELLERIE

A variant of Ellery, q.v.

ELLERY

A surname, now used as a first name by both girls and boys.

ELLICE

The feminine form of Ellis, q.v.

ELLIE

A pet-form of Eleanor (q.v.), now used independently.

ELMA

From the Greek, meaning 'pleasant'.

ELOISE

A variant of Louise, q.v.

ELSA

From the Old German, meaning 'noble maiden'. Elsa, princess of Brabant, is a heroine of German romances. Lohengrin, the Knight of the Swan, marries her on the understanding that she should know neither his name nor his lineage. Of course, on her wedding night she *does* ask, is told, and Lohengrin leaves, accompanied by a swan.

Richard Wagner wrote an opera, *Lohengrin* (1850), on the subject.

ELSIE

A Scottish diminutive of Elizabeth (q.v.), used as an independent name since the eighteenth century.

Oliver Wendell Holmes wrote *Elsie Venner: A Romance of Destiny* (1861), whose heroine has the qualities of a snake and a repellent nature!

And Elsie Marley is the girl of nursery rhyme who refuses to feed the pigs and

'lies in bed till eight or nine.

Lazy Elsie Marley'.

Who can find it in their heart to blame her?

ELSPETH
Another Scottish diminutive of Elizabeth (q.v.), in use since the nineteenth century.

ELVINA
From the Anglo-Saxon, meaning 'friend of the elf'.

ELVIRA
A Spanish name, brought to public attention as the wife of Don Juan in the opera *Don Giovanni* (1787) by Mozart.

Elvira is the deceased first wife of the novelist Charles Condomine in the Noël Coward play *Blithe Spirit* (1941), later a highly successful film.

ELVIRE
French for Elvira, q.v.

ELYSIA
From the Greek, meaning 'blissful'. In Greek mythology, Elysium was the abode of the blessed dead.

EMA
Spanish for Emma, q.v.

EMELIA
A variant of Amelia, q.v.

EMELINE
A variant of Amelia, q.v.

EMERALD
From the gem stone, another of the jewel names so liked by the Victorians. Dr. William Drennan (1754–1820) was the first to describe Ireland as the 'Emerald Isle' in his poem *Erin*. The Emperor Nero (A.D. 37–68) wore emerald spectacles to aid his sight.

EMILIA
Spanish, Dutch and Italian for Emily, q.v.

EMILIE
French for Emily, q.v.

EMILY
From the Latin, meaning 'eager'. It is derived from Aemilius, the name of an ancient Roman family and was a popular name with the early Christians.

Geoffrey Chaucer (1343–1400) included a character named Emelye in *The Knight's Tale,* part of *The Canterbury Tales.*

St. Emily De Rodat (1787–1852) was the French foundress of the Congregation of the Holy Family, who now run schools all over the world, including Great Britain.

Two writers, Emily Brontë (1818–1848), author of *Wuthering Heights,* and the reclusive American poet, Emily Dickinson (1830–1886), who had only seven poems published in her lifetime, add lustre to the name. And Emily Davies (1830–1921), founder of Girton College, Cambridge, should not be forgotten.

EMMA
From the Old German, meaning 'universal'. The name was brought to England by Emma of Normandy (d.1052) who married King Ethelred II ('the Unready'), in 1002. A widow, she married King Canute in 1017. She was the mother of St. Edward the Confessor.

Emma by Jane Austen (1775–1817) has the delightful and infuriating Emma Woodhouse as heroine. Gustave Flaubert's *Madame Bovary* (1857) is a very different character. Emma Bovary is an adulteress, overwhelmed by debt, who finally commits suicide. A classic novel, naturally.

ENA
From the Gaelic, meaning 'fiery'.

ENGELBERTA
A feminine form of Engelbert, q.v.

ENGRACIA
Spanish for Grace, q.v.

ENID
From the Welsh, meaning 'life'. Alfred, Lord Tennyson included Enid and her husband Geraint in his verse epic, *Idylls of the King* (1859), thus popularising the name.

The phenomenal children's writer Enid Blyton (1897–1968), created 'Noddy' and 'The Famous Five' and published over seven hundred books!

ERICA
The feminine version of Eric, q.v. Erica is the Latin botanical name for heather.

ERIKA
This, the Swedish form of Erica (q.v.), has been used in Britain since the nineteenth century.

ERIN
From the Gaelic, meaning 'isle of the west', a poetic term for Ireland. The name became popular during the Celtic revival of the nineteenth century. *Erin* was the title of a poem written by Dr. William Drennan (1754–1820).

ERMA
From the Teutonic, meaning 'noble maid'.

ERMINTRUDE
From the Teutonic, meaning 'mighty and beloved'.

ERNESTINE
A feminine form of Ernest, q.v.

ESME
From the French, meaning 'esteemed'. Introduced to Britain in the sixteenth century by the Duke of Lennox, Esme Stuart (1542–1583), it is now considered a purely feminine name.

ESMERALDA
Spanish for 'this gem'.

ESTELLA
A variant of Estelle, q.v. Estella is the haughty ward of Miss Havisham in Dickens' novel *Great Expectations* (1860). The hero, Pip, remains hopelessly in love with her, even when he discovers that

she is the illegitimate daughter of the convict, Magwitch, and Jagger's housekeeper, Molly the murderess.

ESTELLE
From the French, meaning 'star'.

ESTER
Spanish and Italian for Esther, q.v.

ESTHER
From the Persian, meaning 'star'. The Biblical Esther became the favourite of the Persian King Ahasuerus and managed to save her fellow Jews from death, thwarting the plans of the evil Haman, who was hanged. Orthodox Jews celebrate this deliverance at the feast of Purim.

Esther Summerson is the kindly narrator of Dickens' *Bleak House* (1852), the illegitimate daughter of Lady Dedlock.

ESTRELLA
Spanish for Estelle, q.v.

ETHEL
From the Anglo-Saxon Aethel, meaning 'noble'.

ETTA
A variant of Henrietta, q.v.

ETTIE
A variant of Henrietta, q.v.

ETTY
A variant of Henrietta, q.v.

EUGENIA
A variant of Eugenie, q.v.

EUGENIE
The French feminine form of Eugene (q.v.), revived by Princess Eugenie (b. 1990), the daughter of the Duke of York.

Empress Eugenie (1826–1920) was the wife of Napoleon III of France. After he surrendered to the Prussians at Sedan, she fled to England, living first at Chislehurst, then Farnborough.

EUNICE
From the Greek, meaning 'good victory'. The New Testament Eunice was the mother of St. Timothy, first bishop of Ephesus. It came into use in England in the seventeenth century, a favourite of the Puritans.

EVA
A variant of Eve, q.v.

EVADNE
From the Greek, meaning 'high born'.

EVANGELINE
This name appears to have been invented by Henry Wadsworth Longfellow (1807–1882) for his long narrative poem *Evangeline, a Tale of Acadie* (1847). This tells the story of Evangeline Bellefontaine and Gabriel Lajeunesse, starcrossed lovers separated by the British.

Evangeline St. Claire (better known as 'little Eva') was cared for by the noble Uncle Tom in *Uncle Tom's Cabin* (1852) by Harriet Beecher Stowe.

EVE
From the Hebrew, meaning 'life'. The Biblical first woman, helpmate to Adam, the first man. It has been used in England since the twelfth century. Eva is a character in *Die Meistersinger,* an opera by Richard Wagner (1813–1883).

EVELINA
A variant of Evelyn, q.v. *Evelina* (1778) is the name of the best-selling novel by Fanny Burney (1752–1840), in which the heroine, Evelina Anville, is introduced into high society and marries Lord Orville after many trials.

EVELINE
A variant of Evelyn, q.v.

EVELYN
From the Old German, meaning 'hazel nut'. The name was brought to Britain by the Normans. It is bestowed upon both girls and boys.

EVIE
A variant of Eve, q.v.

EVONNE
An alternative spelling for Yvonne.

FAITH
First used after the Reformation, when the abstract virtues of Faith, Hope and Charity became favourite names.

FANNY
A variant of Frances, q.v.

FAY
A shortened version of Faith, first used in the late nineteenth century. The wicked sorceress Morgan le Fay disclosed the liaison between Queen Guinevere and Sir Lancelot to her brother, King Arthur.

Fay Wray, the American film star, is best remembered for screaming so piercingly at the sight of the great ape who loved her in the original *King Kong* (1933).

FAYE
A variant of Fay, q.v.

FEDERICA
Italian for Frederica, q.v.

FEDORA
Russian for Theodora, q.v.

FELICE
A variant of Felicity, q.v.

FELICIA
A variant of Felicity, q.v.

FELICITY
From the Latin, meaning 'happy'. St. Felicity (d.203), a slave girl, was a Christian martyr who died in the arena at Carthage with her friend, St. Perpetua. *The Passion of Saints Perpetua and Felicity* is the most moving of all the authentic narratives of early martyrs.

It came into use in Britain in the seventeenth century, the Puritans taking it to their hearts in its Latin meaning.

FELIPA
Spanish for Philippa, q.v.

FENELLA
The anglicised version of an Irish name, meaning 'white shoulder', used since the nineteenth century.

Fenella Fielding, the actress with a truly memorable voice, is a well-known bearer of the name.

FERN
This has been used as a first name since the late nineteenth century, when the passion for botanical names was at its height. There are over ten thousand species of the beautiful non-flowering plant.

Shakespeare, in *Henry IV, Part I,* mentions the old belief that fern seed bestowed invisibility on whoever carried it.

FIFI
French for Josephine, q.v.

FILIDE
Italian for Phyllis, q.v.

FILIPPA
Italian for Philippa, q.v.

FIONA
From the Gaelic, meaning 'fair'. The Scottish writer William Sharp (1855–1905) wrote under the pen-name 'Fiona Macleod', a name he invented as a feminine version of Finn.

FLAVIA
From the Latin, meaning 'yellow', the feminine form of the name of

an ancient Roman family.

St. Flavia Domitilla was a Christian of the first century A.D., exiled and put to death for her faith during the persecution of the Roman Emperor Domitian, of whose family she was a member.

FLEUR
From the French, meaning 'flower'. This was made popular by Fleur Forsyte, a main character in a series of novels called *The Forsyte Saga* by John Galsworthy (1867–1933).

FLO
A diminutive of Florence, q.v.

FLORA
The ancient Roman goddess of flowers, whose festival was celebrated from 28th April until 3rd May. The name has been used in Britain since the Renaissance.

Flora MacDonald (1722–1790) helped Prince Charles Edward Stuart to escape after his defeat at the battle of Culloden, disguised as her maid. She went to live in America, where her husband fought on the English side during the American Revolution of 1776.

FLORENCE
From the Latin, meaning 'flourishing'. The capital of Tuscany, an old Roman colony rebuilt by Julius Caesar in 59 B.C. to guard the river crossing. (During the Middle Ages, the name was used for both girls and boys.)

'The Lady With the Lamp', Florence Nightingale (1820–1910), received the name because she was born in the city. After her pioneering work for the sick and injured of the Crimean War, she founded the school of nursing at St. Thomas's Hospital, London. Her statue can be seen on the Crimean War Memorial off Pall Mall.

FLORRIE
A variant of Florence, q.v.

FLOSS
A variant of Florence, q.v.

FLOSSIE
A variant of Florence, q.v.

FRAN
A diminutive of Frances, q.v.

FRANCES
The feminine version of Francis, q.v. St. Frances Cabrini (1850–1917), foundress of the Missionary Sisters of the Sacred Heart, was the first citizen of the United States of America to be canonised.

FRANCESCA
Italian for Frances, q.v.
   Francesca da Rimini fell in love with her husband's brother, Paola, and both were put to death: their history is included in Dante's *Inferno*. The name has been used in Britain since Tudor times.

FRANCISCA
Spanish for Frances, q.v.

FRANZISKA
German for Frances, q.v.

FREDA
A pet-form of Winifred (q.v.) or Frederica (q.v.), used as an independent name since the late nineteenth century.

FREDERICA
From the Teutonic, meaning 'peaceful ruler'.

FRÉDÉRIQUE
French for Frederica, q.v.

FREYA
The anglicised version of the Swedish name Freja, used in Britain in the twentieth century and now very popular.
   Freya was the Nordic goddess of love, wife of Odin. She travelled in a chariot drawn by cats and wept tears of gold when her husband was absent.

FRIEDERIKE
German for Frederica, q.v.

FULVIA
From the Latin, meaning 'of the yellow hair'.

GABBY
A diminutive of Gabriella (q.v.) and of Gabrielle (q.v.).

GABRIELLA
The Italian feminine version of Gabriel (q.v.), popular in the U.K.

GABRIELLE
The French feminine version of Gabriel (q.v.), generally popular.
   Gabrielle Adorno is a character in the Verdi opera, *Simon Boccanegra* (1881).

GABY
A diminutive of Gabriella (q.v.) and of Gabrielle (q.v.).

GAIL
A shortened form of Abigail (q.v.) used as an independent name since the mid-twentieth century.

GAY
This name means 'gay or light-hearted one'.

GAYNA
A variant of Gaynor, q.v.

GAYNOR
A medieval form of Guinevere, the name of the wife of King Arthur, now enjoying a revival.

GEMMA
From the Italian, meaning 'precious stone'. St. Gemma Galgani

(1875–1903), an Italian stigmatic and visionary, brought the name to public attention. It was first used in Britain in the thirteenth century. Gemma Craven (b. 1950) is a well-known actress.

GENE
A variant of Eugenia, q.v.

GENEVIEVE
Popular in France as the name of the saintly patroness of Paris, it has been used in Britain since the nineteenth century.

Genevieve is a character in the opera *Pelléas and Mélisande* by Achille Claude Debussy (1862–1918).

GEORGE
A diminutive of Georgina, q.v.

GEORGETTE
French for Georgia, q.v.

GEORGIA
A variant of Georgina, q.v.

GEORGIANA
A variant of Georgina, q.v.

GEORGINA
The feminine version of George, q.v. This has been popular in Britain since the eighteenth century, when the very first of the six British King Georges arrived reluctantly from Hanover, speaking only French and German, to be crowned at Westminster Abbey on 20th October 1714.

GERALDINE
The feminine form of Gerald; supposedly invented by Henry Howard, Earl of Surrey (1517–1547), in his poems to the 'fair Geraldine' (really Lady Elizabeth Fitzgerald, grand-daughter of the ninth Earl of Kildare). The name came into general use at the beginning of the nineteenth century.

GERDA
From the Norse, meaning 'shielded'.

GERHARDINE
German for Geraldine, q.v.

GERMAINE
From the German, meaning 'of Germany'.

GERTRUD
German for Gertrude, q.v.

GERTRUDA
Italian for Gertrude, q.v.

GERTRUDE
From the Old German, meaning 'ruler of the spear'. The German mystic St. Gertrude the Great (1256–1302) made the name popular in the Middle Ages. It was revived in the nineteenth century.

The writer and artist Gertrude Jekyll (1843–1932) is best known for her garden design, collaborating with the architect Edwin Lutyens for a 'Lutyens house' with a 'Jekyll garden'. Her portrait hangs in the National Portrait Gallery in London.

GERTRUDIS
Spanish for Gertrude, q.v.

GILL
A diminutive of Gillian, q.v.

GILLIAN
The English form of Juliana, common in the Middle Ages. It came back into favour in the twentieth century.

Gillian Avery is a well-known modern writer for children; *The Warden's Niece* (1957) and *The Elephant War* (1960) have become classics.

GILLY
A diminutive of Gillian, q.v.

GINA
A pet-form of Georgina, used independently since the early twentieth century. Gina Lollobrigida (b.1927), the Italian actress, is a well-known bearer of the name.

GINGER
This name means 'one who is auburn haired'.

GIORGIA
Italian for Georgia, q.v.

GIOVANNA
Italian for Jane, q.v.

GIRALDA
Italian for Geraldine, q.v.

GISELA
Spanish and Italian for Giselle, q.v.

GISELE
French for Giselle, q.v.

GISELLE
From the Old German, meaning 'pledge'. The Adam ballet *Giselle* (1841) made the common French name widely known.

GIUDITTA
Italian for Judith, q.v.

GIULETTA
Italian for Julia, q.v.

GIUSTINA
Italian for Justine, q.v.

GLADYS
The anglicised version of a Welsh name, meaning 'princess'. It came into general use in the second half of the nineteenth century, helped by being bestowed on the heroines of several popular novels of the time.

GLENDA
From the Welsh, meaning 'holy and good'. Glenda Jackson (b. 1937) is a fine actress who turned to politics and became a Labour M.P.

GLORIA
From the Latin, meaning 'glory'. Gloria was a character in the play

You Never Can Tell (1898) by George Bernard Shaw, and the name appears to have been coined by him.

GLORIANA
A variant of Gloria, q.v.

GLYNIS
From the Gaelic, meaning 'narrow valley'. The actress Glynis Johns is best remembered for her portrayal of the mermaid heroine in the film *Miranda* (1947).

GOLDIE
From the Anglo-Saxon, meaning 'golden-haired'.

GRACE
The name came into use after the Reformation and was favoured by the Puritans. In Roman mythology, the Three Graces embodied charm and beauty and have been a favourite subject for painters.

Grace Darling (1815–1842) was the daughter of the lighthouse keeper on Longstone, one of the Farne Islands. At great risk to themselves, she and her father rescued nine people from the *Forfarshire*, sailing from Hull to Dundee when wrecked off the Longstone lighthouse in 1838. Her heroism engendered an immense fame which popularised the name.

GRANIA
The anglicised version of the Irish name Grainne, used since the 1970s. In Irish legend, Grainne was the second wife of Finn MacCool and eloped with his nephew.

GRAZIA
Italian for Grace, q.v.

GREER
A variant of Gregoria, q.v.

GREGORIA
A feminine form of Gregory, q.v.

GRETA
A variant of Margaret, q.v.

GRETAL
German for Margaret, q.v.

GRETCHEN
German for Margaret, q.v.

GRISELDA
From the German, meaning 'battle maid'.

GRISHILDE
Dutch and German for Griselda, q.v.

GUGLIELMA
Italian for Wilhelmina, q.v.

GUIDA
From the Italian, meaning 'teacher'.

GUILLELMINA
Spanish for Wilhelmina, q.v.

GUILLELMINE
French for Wilhelmina, q.v.

GUNHILDA
From the German, meaning 'war maid'.

GWEN
From the Welsh, meaning 'white'. A shortened form of Gwendolen, now generally used.

The artist Gwen John (1876–1939), born in Wales and a graduate of the Slade School of Art who spent most of her working life in France, was described as 'the greatest woman artist of her age'.

GWENDA
A variant of Gwendolen, q.v.

GWENDOLEN
An ancient Welsh name, used in Britain since the mid-nineteenth century. George Eliot's last novel, *Daniel Deronda* (1876), has a heroine Gwendolyn Harleth who is hopelessly in love with the eponymous hero, to no avail.

And Gwendolen Fairfax, daughter of Lady Bracknell in Oscar

Wilde's play, *The Importance of Being Earnest* (1895), carries her diary with her at all times in order to have something sensational to read!

GWENDOLYN
A variant of Gwendolen, q.v.

GWYNNETH
From the Welsh, meaning 'happiness'.

HANNAH
From the Hebrew, meaning 'grace'. In the Old Testament, Hannah was the mother of the prophet Samuel. It has been used in Britain since the seventeenth century.

Hannah More (1745–1833), writer, dramatist and philanthropist, was a friend of Dr. Johnson, Horace Walpole and Joshua Reynolds. Her play *Percy* was performed at Drury Lane for fourteen nights – a long run in those days. Her later years were spent in attempts to improve conditions for the poor of Somerset.

HARRIET
The feminine version of Harry, used regularly since the eighteenth century. The writer Harriet Martineau (1802–1876) worked very hard, producing nearly fifty books on subjects as diverse as education, hypnotism and the abolition of slavery. She is renowned as a political economist and feminist.

Harriet Smith is an ingenuous young girl who suffers from the attempts of Emma Woodhouse to improve her and to find her a husband in Jane Austen's *Emma* (1816).

224

HATTIE
A variant of Harriet (q.v.) and of Henrietta (q.v.).

HAYLEY
A place name, meaning 'hay field', and surname, popularised as a first name by the actress Hayley Mills, daughter of Sir John Mills, who made her debut in *Tiger Bay* (1959).

HAZEL
Another of the botanical names first bestowed upon girls in the late nineteenth century. The hazel-wand represented both protection and wisdom in ancient times.

HEATHER
From the plant name, first used in the late nineteenth century and now very popular.

HEBE
The Greek goddess of youth, daughter of Zeus and Hera. Cupbearer to the gods, she married the deified Heracles and both were worshipped in Athens. (Her Latin name was Juventas, now more familiar as a football team!) It has been used in Britain since the nineteenth century and is now enjoying a revival.

HEIDI
The pet-form of the German name Adalheid, more familiar in Britain as Adelaide, q.v. The children's classic *Heidi*, written by the Swiss author Johanna Spyri (1829–1901), inspired its use.

HELEN
From the Greek, meaning 'light'. In Greek mythology, the beautiful Helen was wife of King Menelaus of Sparta. Her elopement with Paris precipitated the Trojan War. St. Helena (c. 255–330), mother of Constantine the Great, is best remembered for her reputed discovery of the True Cross and was much revered in the Middle Ages.

Helen Adams Keller (1880–1968), deaf and blind since the age of nineteen months, learned to speak, wrote several books and lectured all over the world on behalf of the blind.

HELENA
A variant of Helen, q.v.

HELENE
A variant of Helen, and German and French for Helen, q.v.

HELGA
From the Norse, meaning 'holy'.

HÉLOISE
Héloise (1101–1164) is remembered as the beloved of Pierre Abelard, a French philosopher and theologian. Their tragic lives and famous love letters made their history a popular romantic subject in literature.

Jean Jacques Rousseau's best-selling novel, *La Nouvelle Héloise* (1761), revived the name and it has been used steadily since then.

HENDRIKA
Dutch for Henrietta, q.v.

HENRIETTA
The name was brought to Britain by the daughter of Henry IV of France, Henrietta Maria (1609–1669), who married the unfortunate Charles I in 1625.

HERMIONE
In Greek mythology, the daughter of the beautiful Helen and King Menelaus, abandoned by her mother at the age of nine when Helen eloped to Troy with Paris. Hermione later married her cousin, Orestes. She is the rival to Andromache in a tragedy of that name by the Greek playwright Euripides (480–405 B.C.).

Shakespeare's Hermione was Queen of Sicily in *The Winter's Tale*.

HESTER
A medieval variation of Esther q.v., once interchangeable but now quite independent. Hester Thrale (1741–1821) is remembered for her friendship with Dr. Johnson and his break with her when she married the musician Gabriel Piozzi (a foreigner!!). Her diaries are an invaluable source of biographical information.

Hester Prynne is the heroine of Nathaniel Hawthorne's masterpiece, *The Scarlet Letter* (1850).

HETTIE
A variant of Henrietta, q.v.

HETTY
A variant of Henrietta, q.v.

HILARY
From the Latin, meaning 'cheerful'. Once bestowed on both boys and girls, it is now considered purely feminine.

St. Hilary of Poitiers (315–367) was a French bishop who devoted his life to the fight against Arian heresy. His feast day (on January 13th in the Anglican Church) gives the name to Hilary Term, one of the four portions of the year in which the High Court sits. (The other terms are Michaelmas, Easter and Trinity.)

HILDA
From the Old German, meaning 'battle'. The greatly revered St. Hilda (614–680), grand-niece of King Edwin of Northumbria, founded an Abbey at Whitby. She ruled over both men and women religious, one of whom was the poet Caedmon.

The name was revived by the Tractarians of the nineteenth century, although it had never completely dropped from favour in the north of England.

HILDEGARD
From the Teutonic, meaning 'strong in battle'.

HOLLY
From the plant, used as a first name since the late nineteenth century. Pagans believed that holly prickles would repel witches and evil spirits; being an evergreen, it also symbolised immortality and good fortune.

HONEY
From the Anglo-Saxon, meaning 'sweet'.

HONOR
The shortened form of Honoria (q.v.), brought to England at the Norman Conquest. Puritans of the seventeenth century bestowed it on both males and females, but it is now used only for girls.

The actress Honor Blackman is a well-known bearer of the name.

HONORIA
From the Latin, meaning 'one of honour'.

HOPE

One of the three main Christian virtues (together with Faith and Charity), used as a first name by the Puritans and still popular today.

The English metaphysical poet Richard Crashaw (1612–1649) wrote *On Hope*, from which came the following lines:

'Dear Hope! Earth's dowry and Heaven's debt,

The entity of things that are not yet.

Subtlest but surest being!'

HORATIA

The feminine form of Horace, q.v.

HORTENSE

From the Latin, meaning 'of the garden'.

HORTENSIA

Dutch, German and Danish for Hortense, q.v.

HUBERTA

The feminine form of Hubert, q.v.

HYACINTH

In Greek mythology, the young boy Hyacinth was beloved by Apollo, who accidentally killed him while throwing the discus. The distraught god caused a flower to grow from Hyacinth's blood. Several early Christian martyrs have borne this name.

Considered exclusively female in Britain, it came into use in the late nineteenth century when flower names for girls were all the rage.

HYACINTHE

French for Hyacinth, q.v.

HYACINTHIE

German for Hyacinth, q.v.

HYPATIA

From the Greek, meaning 'highest'.

IANTHE

From the Greek, meaning 'violet flower'. The name of a sea nymph, daughter of the sea god Oceanus, it was the name given to the daughter of the poet Shelley and his wife, Harriet Westbrook.

Walter Savage Landor (1775–1864) wrote the poem *Ianthe* for his early love, Sophia Jane Swift.

IDA

From the Teutonic, meaning 'prosperous'.

IMELDA

The Italian form of Irmhilde, meaning 'universal battle', now generally used. A well-known modern bearer of the name is the actress Imelda Staunton.

IMOGEN

From the Latin, meaning 'image'. Imogen is the daughter of Cymbeline, King of Britain, in Shakespeare's play *Cymbeline,* the faithful wife of Posthumus Leonatus. (And, if you are an opera fan, you will know that Imogen is a character in Vincenzo Bellini's *Il Pirata,* first produced at La Scala in 1827.)

The name became popular in Britain in the twentieth century.

INA

A variant of a number of names ending in 'ina', particularly used in Scotland, such as Georgina and Wilhelmina.

INDIA

The country; from the Greek 'indos', meaning the river Indus. A name increasing in favour in modern times.

INEZ
Spanish for Agnes, q.v.

INGA
A Scandinavian variant of Ingrid, q.v.

INGE
A Scandinavian variant of Ingrid, q.v.

INGRID
From the Old Norse, meaning 'Ing's ride'. The name was mentioned in the Domesday Book but soon vanished, to be revived in the twentieth century.

Ingrid Bergman (1915–1982), the beautiful Swedish film star best remembered for her part in the classic *Casablanca,* popularised the name.

IOLANTHE
From the Greek, meaning 'violet'. Iolanthe is the chief character in one of Gilbert and Sullivan's light operas.

IOLE
In Greek mythology, Iole was the daughter of King Eurytus. Heracles won her as a prize in an archery contest, but her father refused to give her up. She later married Hyllus, Heracles' son. The Victorians revived this name in the late nineteenth century.

IONA
From the small Hebridean island. St. Columba founded a monastery on Iona and sent missionaries from there throughout Scotland in the sixth century. Considered a holy place, it became the burial ground for Scots, Irish and Norse kings.

A modern name and very popular.

IRENA
A variant of Irene, q.v.

IRENE
From the Greek, meaning 'peace'. St. Irene (d.304) was martyred at Salonika with her two sisters for refusing to eat food offered to the gods and for reading Christian books. It appears to have been used in Britain since the late nineteenth century.

IRIS
From the Greek, meaning 'the rainbow'. In Greek mythology she was the messenger of the gods, who used the rainbow as a bridge between the heavens and earth. She was married to Zephyrus, the West Wind, and mother of Eros.

It came into vogue at the end of the nineteenth century, when plant names were very fashionable.

IRMA
From the German, meaning 'noble one'.

ISA
A diminutive of Isabel (variant of Isabella, q.v.).

ISABEAU
French for Isabel, q.v.

ISABEL
A variant of Isabella, q.v.

ISABELLA
A variant of Elizabeth (q.v.), used regularly in Britain since the twelfth century. There have been three queens of England with this name: Isabella of Angouleme (d.1246), second wife of King John; Isabella (1292–1358), daughter of King Philip III of France, wife of Edward II; and Isabella (1389–1409), daughter of Charles VI of France, second wife of Richard II.

The beautiful and virtuous Isabella is the heroine of Shakespeare's play, *Measure for Measure*.

ISABELLE
German for Isabel (variant of Isabella, q.v.).

ISADORA
From the Greek, meaning 'gift of Isis'. One well-known bearer of the name was the dancer Isadora Duncan.

ISEULT
From the Welsh, meaning 'one who is fair'.

ISIS
From the Egyptian, meaning 'goddess supreme'.

231

ISLA
Taken from the Scottish river, a modern name.

ISOBEL
The Scottish form of Isabel (variant of Isabella, q.v.).

ISOLDE
From the Welsh, meaning 'one who is fair'.

IVY
From the Anglo-Saxon, and from the plant of this name.

JACALYN
A variant of Jacqueline, q.v.

JACINTA
Spanish for Hyacinth, q.v.

JACINTHA
From the Greek, meaning 'like a hyacinth'.

JACINTHE
A variant of Jacintha, q.v.

JACKIE
A variant of Jacqueline, q.v.

JACOBA
The Jacobites of the eighteenth century had no time for the upstart
Hanoverians, clinging to the Stuarts as the true kings of Great Britain.

Jacoba and Jacobina were the names given to their infant daughters to demonstrate their feelings. These are now enjoying a revival.

JACOBINA
A variant of Jacoba, q.v.

JACQUELINE
The French feminine form of Jacques (James), used in Britain since the thirteenth century.

Samuel Rogers (1763–1855), poet and patron of men of letters, wrote the poem *Jacqueline*.

The cellist Jacqueline du Pre is best remembered for her filmed rendition of Elgar's *Cello Concerto in E Minor*.

JACQUETTA
A variant of Jacqueline, q.v.

JACQUI
A variant of Jacqueline, q.v.

JADE
From the precious stone, used as a first name since the 1970s. In Chinese Taoism, the Jade Emperor is Father of Heaven, usually depicted seated on a throne wearing green robes decorated with dragons. Chinese emperors made yearly offerings of silk and jade to him in the Temple of Heaven in Beijing.

JAIMIE
An extremely popular modern feminine form of James, q.v.

JAN
A variant of Janet, q.v.

JANE
A form of Johanna (see Joan), used regularly in Britain since the sixteenth century. Jane Seymour (1509–1537), Queen of England, the third wife of Henry VIII, was the mother of the frail Edward VI and died a few days after his birth. She is buried with her husband in St. George's Chapel, Windsor Castle.

Jane Austen (1775–1817), who left only six completed novels, was one of our greatest writers. Her home in Chawton, Hampshire, is now a museum. And Jane Welsh Carlyle (1801–1866), long-suffering wife of the dyspeptic Thomas Carlyle, is vividly alive in her many fascinating and acerbic letters. Leigh Hunt wrote the poem *Jenny Kissed Me* in her honour.

JANET
A diminutive of Jane, once exclusively Scottish but now generally used.

JANETTE
A variant of Janet (and thereby of Jane, q.v.).

JANEY
A variant of Jane, q.v.

JANICE
A variant of Jane, q.v.

JANIE
A variant of Jane, q.v.

JANINE
A variant of Jane, q.v.

JANIS
A variant of Jane, q.v.

JASMIN
A variant of Jasmine, q.v.

JASMINE
From the sweet scented flower, first used at the end of the nineteenth century.

JAYNE
A variant of Jane, q.v.

JEAN
A medieval variation of the French name Jehanne. The prolific 'Jean Plaidy' (1910–1993), writer of some two hundred books, mostly fictionalised history, is well-known. (Her *real* name was Mrs Eleanor Hibbert.)

JEANETTE
An old Scottish diminutive of Jane, now generally used.

Jeanette MacDonald (d. 1965) trilled her way happily through such musical films as *Rose Marie* (1936) and *Sweethearts* (1938), aided and abetted by Nelson Eddy.

JEM
A diminutive of Jemima, q.v.

JEMIMA
From the Hebrew, meaning 'dove'. The Old Testament Jemima was one of the three beautiful daughters of the later, prosperous Job.

The eponymous hero of *The Tale of Jemima Puddleduck* (1910) by Beatrix Potter is nearly killed by the fox in her attempt to find somewhere to lay her eggs.

JENNA
A variant of Jennifer, q.v.

JENNIE
A variant of Jennifer, q.v.

JENNIFER
This was originally an exclusively Cornish form of Guinevere, wife of King Arthur, but has been used generally since the beginning of the twentieth century.

JENNY
A variant of Jennifer, q.v.

'The Swedish Nightingale', the soprano Jenny Lind (1820–1887), later a British subject, sang worldwide for over forty years.

At the other end of the spectrum, Jenny Diver (1705–1740), the most noted pickpocket of her time, was twice transported before being executed at Tyburn. She is mentioned by Macheath in *The Beggar's Opera*.

JESS
A variant of Jessica, q.v.

JESSAMY
A variation of Jasmine, used since the 1920s.

JESSICA
From the Hebrew, meaning 'he beholds'. The name given to

Shylock's rebellious daughter who eloped with Lorenzo in *The Merchant of Venice* by Shakespeare; this seems to have begun the use of the name.

Jessica Landseer (1807–1880), devoted companion to her famous brother Edwin, painted miniatures and landscapes and had ten pictures hung at the Royal Academy.

Hesba Stretton (really Sarah Smith) was responsible for the phenomenally successful children's story of slum life, *Jessica's First Prayer* (1867), which was translated into every European language and many Asiatic and African ones as well.

JESSIE
Either a Scottish pet-name for Janet or a shortened form of Jessica, but sturdily independent.

JESSYE
A variant of Jessie, q.v.

JILL
A pet-form of Gillian, used since the Middle Ages. Its age is shown by the nursery rhyme *Jack and Jill*, who were both so unfortunate in their excursion to fetch water.

And Puck, as he squeezes juice on the eyes of Lysander in Shakespeare's *A Midsummer Night's Dream*, includes
'Jack shall have Jill;
Nought shall go ill'
in his spell.

JINNIE
A variant of Jane, q.v.

JO
A diminutive of Josephine, q.v.

JOAN
The medieval feminine form of John, q.v. It was revived at the end of the nineteenth century. The 'bad' King John appears to have liked the name. He had two daughters on which this was bestowed: the first (d. 1237) married the Welsh ruler Llywelyn the Great; the second (d. 1238) married the Scottish King Edward II.

And the 'Fair Maid of Kent', so called on account of her great beauty, was Joan, daughter of Edmund, Earl of Kent, who married the Black Prince and became the mother of Richard II.

JOANNA
A variant of Joan, q.v.

JOANNE
A variant of Joan, q.v.

JOCASTA
In Greek legend, the mother and unwitting wife of Oedipus. She is the tragic heroine of many dramas, from Sophocles' *Oedipus Rex* to Stravinsky's opera of the same name (1927). It seems to have been used first by the late Victorians.

JOCELYN
Brought to England at the Norman Conquest and originally a masculine name, it is now bestowed on both girls and boys.

The French writer Alphonse Lamartine (1790–1869) wrote a long narrative poem entitled *Jocelyn*.

JODIE
A modern name derived from Judy; made popular by the actress Jodie Foster, who made her debut in the exuberant children's musical *Bugsy Malone*.

JOHANNA
A variant of Joan, q.v.

JORDAN
Crusaders of the twelfth century brought back bottles of water from the River Jordan to be used in the baptism of their children. (The royal family continue the tradition today.) It has always been a name given to both girls and boys.

JORDYN
A variant of Jordan, q.v.

JOSE
A variant of Josephine, q.v.

JOSEFA
Spanish for Josephine, q.v.

JOSELINE
A variant of Jocelyn, q.v.

JOSEPHA
German for Josephine, q.v.

JOSEPHINE
The French female form of Joseph, q.v. The lady responsible for its popularity, the Empress Josephine (1763–1814), first wife of Napoleon, was actually named Marie Josèphe Rose Tascher de la Pagerie. (She preferred her pet-name.)

Josephine Butler (1828–1906), the fierce campaigner against the exploitation and degradation of women, is a well-known bearer of the name. And Jo is the best-loved of the four March sisters, heroine of Louisa May Alcott's classic novel *Litile Women* (1868) and its three sequels.

JOSETTE
A variant of Josephine, q.v.

JOSIE
A variant of Josephine, q.v.

JOSLYN
A variant of Jocelyn, q.v.

JOY
From the Latin, meaning 'merry'. Used in the Middle Ages, it was revived by the Victorians. Two lines by the mystic poet, William Blake (1757–1827), are appropriate.
'I happy am,
Joy is my name'.

JOYCE
From the Latin, meaning 'merry'. A French hermit saint of the seventh century made the name a favourite for both men and women until the Middle Ages. It was revived in the late nineteenth century.

Joyce Grenfell, the actress and writer, is best remembered for her nursery school monologues.

JUANITA
Spanish for Jane, q.v.

JUDIE
A diminutive of Judith, q.v.

JUDITH

From the Hebrew, meaning 'praise'. In the Old Testament, Judith was a Hittite woman who married Esau, to the dismay of his parents. The heroine of the apocryphal *Book of Judith* saved her people by beheading the Assyrian leader, Holofernes.

The name was introduced early into England when Judith, daughter of King Charles the Bald of the Franks, married King Ethelwulf (d.858).

William Shakespeare gave the name to his second daughter (d.1662), twin sister to Hamnet.

JUDY

A diminutive of Judith, q.v.

Judy Garland (1922-1967), whose real name was Frances Gumm, is best remembered as Dorothy in *The Wizard of Oz* (1939).

JULIA

The feminine form of Julius, which became very popular in Britain in the eighteenth century. Robert Herrick (1591–1674), clergyman and poet, addressed many of his poems to Julia, notably *Upon Julia's Voice* and *Upon Julia's Clothes*.

Julia Cameron (1815–1879) was a brilliant and dedicated amateur photographer whose work now commands high prices. (And she did not begin until nearly fifty years of age!)

JULIANA

A variant of Julia, q.v.

JULIANNE

A variant of Julia, q.v.

JULIE

A variant of Julia, q.v. Julie d'Etanges is the heroine of Rousseau's very successful novel *Julie ou La Nouvelle Héloise* (1761).

JULIET

The English version of the Italian Giulietta, whose popularity began with Juliet Capulet, starcrossed lover of Romeo in the Shakespeare play.

JULIETA

Spanish for Julia, q.v.

JULIETTE
French for Julia, q.v.

JUNE
From the sixth month, used as a first name since the early twentieth century. It was named after the Roman goddess Juno, wife of Jupiter, and was supposedly an auspicious month for marriages.

JUSTINA
Spanish for Justine, q.v.

JUSTINE
The French feminine form of Justin (q.v.). *Justine* (1957) is the first of the four novels which make up the *Alexandria Quartet* by Lawrence Durrell.

KARA
A popular version of Cara, from the Italian, meaning 'dear'. (The Kara Sea is one of the coldest seas in Russia, notorious for its dense fogs and frequent storms!)

KAREN
The Danish form of Catherine, now generally used. Baroness Karen Blixen (1883–1962), the Danish writer of *Out of Africa* and other books, used the pen-name Isak Dinesen.

KARLI
A variant of Carla, q.v.

KARLOTTE
German for Charlotte, q.v.

KAROLINE
German for Caroline, q.v.

KATE
This diminutive of Catherine/Katherine has been used since the sixteenth century, as have its variants Katie and Katy.

The illustrator Kate Greenaway (1846–1901), friend of John Ruskin, drew perfect children wearing immaculate frills, pinafores, bonnets and sashes in an arcadian setting: no wonder she has remained a favourite!

KATERINA
A variant of Catherine, q.v.

KATEY
A variant of Kate, q.v.

KATH
A diminutive of Katharine, variant of Catherine, q.v.

KATHARINE
A variant of Catharine, q.v.

KATHERINE
A variant of Catherine, q.v.

KATHLEEN
The anglicised version of the Irish name Caitlin, used in Britain since the mid-nineteenth century

Kathleen Ferrier (1912–1953), the Lancashire-born contralto, is a famous bearer of the name.

KATHY
A variant of Katharine, variant of Catherine, q.v.

KATIE
A variant of Kate, q.v.

KATINKA
Russian for Catherine, q.v.

KATRINA
A variant of Catherine, q.v.

KATY
A variant of Kate, q.v. *What Katy Did* (1872) written by 'Susan Coolidge' – real name Sarah Chauncey Woolsey – is a classic of children's literature.

KAY
A pet-form of Katherine or Karen, now used independently. Kay Kendall (1927–1959), the actress and film star, is best remembered for her part in *Genevieve*.

KAYLEIGH/KYLIE
A modern conjunction of Kyle and Kelly, perhaps. (Or one can believe that Kylie is the Aborigine name for boomerang, as is often stated!)

KEELEY
A variant of Kelly, q.v.

KEIRA
From the Celtic, meaning 'black haired'.

KELLY
An Irish surname, meaning 'warlike one', now used as a first name for both boys and girls.

KERRY
From the county situated in the south-west of the Republic of Ireland. Originally bestowed upon boys when the name was first used in the mid-twentieth century, it is now considered exclusively feminine.

County Kerry possesses the highest range of mountains in Ireland, called MacGillycuddy's Reeks, to the west of Killarney.

KEZIAH
From the Hebrew, meaning 'cassia'. The Old Testament Keziah was the second of three daughters born to Job when he had been restored to health and prosperity. (Her two sisters were Jemima and Keren-Happuch.) The seventeenth century Puritans began the use of the name.

Keziah Wesley (d. 1741) was the youngest of the seven sisters of the founder of Methodism, whose short life was made unhappy by poverty and illness.

242

KIM
A diminutive of Kimberley, q.v., now used in its own right.

KIMBERLEY
A place name and a surname, used as a first name since the beginning of the twentieth century.

The South African diamond town of Kimberley was named after the English statesman, John Wodehouse, 1st Earl of Kimberley (1826–1902). During the Boer War it was besieged by the Boers from October 1899 until February 1900, when relieved by General Sir John French. It was this that began its use as a first name in Britain.

Rudyard Kipling wrote the novel *Kim* (1901), in which the hero, an Irish orphan named Kimball O'Hara, roams India with an old lama from Tibet and helps the English Secret Service!

KIRSTEEN
A variant of Kirsten, q.v. Margaret Oliphant wrote *Kirsteen* (1890), the eponymous heroine of which supports her large and snobbish family by working with her hands – which enables them to despise her.

KIRSTEN
The Danish form of Christine, popular in Scotland and now generally used.

KIRSTIE
A variant of Kirsty, q.v.

KIRSTIN
A variant of Kirsten, q.v.

KIRSTY
A Scottish pet-form of Christine, now generally popular.

KIT
A diminutive of Kitty, q.v.

KITTY
A medieval pet-form of Catherine (q.v.), regularly used since then. The Kitty of the nursery rhyme ('Lucy Locket lost her pocket, Kitty Fisher found it') was the mistress of several eminent men, an excellent horsewoman and a model for many artists. She died in 1767.

In Jane Austen's *Pride and Prejudice* (1813), Kitty Bennet is notable only for coughing!

KLARA
Germán for Clara, q.v.

KRISTEL
German for Christine, a variant of Christina, q.v.

KRISTIAN
The Danish form of Christian (q.v.), used in Britain for both girls and boys since the 1960s.

Oslo, the capital city of Norway, was named Kristiana until 1925. Destroyed by fire in 1625, the city was redesigned by the Danish King Kristian IV, hence the name.

KRYSTLE
A variant of Crystal, q.v.

KRYSTYNA
A variant of Christina, q.v.

KYLE
From the Gaelic, meaning 'channel between islands'. A place name and a surname, now used as a first name for both girls and boys.

(Should you be keen to travel 'over the sea to Skye', the Scottish village called Kyle of Lochalsh is your jumping-off point.)

KYLIE
A variant of Kayleigh, q.v.

KYRA
The Greek feminine version of Cyril, meaning 'lord'. St. Cyril (c.827–869), apostle to the Slavs, is the reputed inventor of the Cyrillic alphabet used by the Russians and Bulgarians.

LALAGE
From the Greek, meaning 'babble'. A literary favourite since the Roman poet Horace (65–8 B.C.) used the name in one of his famous Odes.

Lalage is a character in the *The French Lieutenant's Woman* by John Fowles.

LALITA
From the Sanscrit, meaning 'free of guile'.

LALLIE
A variant of Lalage, q.v.

LANA
A contracted form of Alana, brought to public attention by Lana Turner, the 1940's Hollywood film star.

LARA
The pet-form of the Russian name Larissa. Lara, a nymph whose father was the River Tiber, refused to help Jupiter in his amours. He retaliated by pulling out her tongue and sent her down to the Underworld. She was the mother of the Lares, the household gods of the Romans.

Lara was the heroine of Boris Pasternak's *Doctor Zhivago* (1957), later filmed, which made the name a favourite.

LARISSA
From the Greek, meaning 'cheerful'.

LAURA

From the Latin, meaning 'laurel'. The name has been used in Britain since the twelfth century.

Petrarch (1304–1374) wrote countless poems in honour of the beautiful and unattainable Laura, who died in the great plague of 1348. (And Thomas Campion (1567–1620) wrote of 'Rose-Cheeked Laura'.)

Dame Laura Knight (1877–1970), artist and Royal Academician, loved painting subjects connected with the circus, the theatre and the ballet.

LAUREL

From the trees and evergreen shrubs, used as a first name since the late nineteenth century, when the passion for plant names was at its height.

Universities had a custom of presenting a laurel wreath to graduates in rhetoric and poetry: Ben Jonson became the first Poet Laureate in Britain in 1619.

LAUREN

A modern feminine version of Laurence (q.v.), popularised by the actress Lauren Bacall (real name Betty Jean Perske). She first appeared in the film *To Have and Have Not* with her future husband Humphrey Bogart in 1944.

LAURIE

A variant of Laura, q.v.

LAVENDER

Named after this sweet smelling plant.

LAVINIA

In Roman mythology, the wife of Aeneas, from whom were descended Romulus and Remus, the founders of Rome. Lavinium, the ancient town to the south of Rome, was named after her.

The name became popular in England at the Renaissance. 'Gracious Lavinia, Rome's rich ornament', the daughter of Titus in Shakespeare's *Titus Andronicus* comes to a gruesome end.

LAYLA

A variant of Leila, q.v.

LEA
A variant of Leah, q.v.

LEAH
From the Hebrew, meaning 'gazelle'. The Old Testament Leah, whose eyes were weak, became the first wife of Jacob by a ruse. The Puritans of the seventeenth century began the use of the name in England.

LEANA
From the French, meaning 'one who clings'.

LEANNE
A modern name, perhaps taken from Julianne, first used in the 1960s.

LEANOR
Spanish for Eleanor, q.v.

LEANORE
A variant of Eleanor, q.v.

LEATRICE
A variant of Beatrice, q.v.

LEE
A variant of Leah, q.v.

LEETICE
French for Letitia, q.v.

LEIGH
From the Old English place name, meaning 'field' or 'pasture', the feminine version of Lee.

LEILA
From the Persian, meaning 'night'. Leila, beautiful concubine to the Caliph Hassan, is the heroine of Lord Byron's lengthy poem, *The Giaour* (1813), which brought the name to public attention. Leila is also the heroine of a book of the same name by Edward Bulwer-Lytton (1803–1873).

LELA
A variant of Leila, q.v.

LENA
A shortened form of Helena, used independently since the nineteenth century. The singer Lena Horne is a modern bearer of the name. (It is also the name of one of the largest rivers in Russia!)

LEONI
A variant of Leonie, q.v.

LEONIE
The French feminine form of Leon, used in Britain since the early years of the twentieth century.

LEONORA
This became popular in Britain in the nineteenth century, perhaps chosen by parents who were music lovers.

Three operas – *Leonora*, by Gaveaux, first produced in 1798; *Leonora or Wedded Love* by Ferdinando Paer; and the heroine of Beethoven's *Fidelio* (1814) – make the name unforgettable. (She is also a character in operas by Donizetti and Verdi!!)

LESLEY
A Scottish place name, meaning 'garden by a pool', and aristocratic surname, used as a first name since the nineteenth century.

LETICIA
Spanish for Letitia, q.v.

LETITIA
From the Latin, meaning 'gladness'. Lettice was the medieval version of the name, going out of favour in the eighteenth century to be replaced by Letitia. Both are now enjoying a revival.

Letitia Elizabeth Landon (1802–1838), English poet and novelist, is best remembered for her mysterious death in Africa. She accidentally overdosed on the prussic acid which she used to treat her spasms!

LETIZIA
Italian for Letitia, q.v.

LETTICE
A variant of Letitia, q.v.

LETTY
A variant of Letitia, q.v.

LEXIE
A variant of Alexandra, q.v.

LIANA
From the French, meaning 'one who clings'.

LIANNE
A variant of Leanne, q.v.

LIBBY
A pet-form of Elizabeth (q.v.), now used as an independent name.

LIDIA
Spanish and Italian for Lydia, q.v.

LILA
A variant of Lilian, q.v.

LILI
German for Lilian, q.v.

LILIAN
From the Latin name Liliana, meaning 'lily', used in Britain since the late nineteenth century.
   Lilian Baylis (1874–1934) was the manager of the Old Vic in London, turning it into the home of Shakespeare's plays. She was also responsible for reopening the Sadlers Wells Theatre in 1931.

LILIAS
Scottish for Lilian, q.v.

LILIBET
A variant of Elizabeth, q.v.

LILITH
From the Hebrew, meaning 'night-monster'. In Babylonian mythology, it is the name of a female demon who goes abroad on stormy

nights and is particularly dangerous to children. (Naughty ones, presumably!)

She is also mentioned as a night devil in Isaiah, Ch. 34 v.14, and included in Goethe's play, *Faust* (1808).

LILLI
A variant of Lily, q.v.

LILLIAN
A variant of Lilian, q.v.

LILY
From the name of the flower, used since the mid-nineteenth century. In tradition, the lily sprang from the tears of Eve as she was driven out of paradise. Christian art uses it as a symbol of purity.

Emilie Charlotte Langtry (1853–1929), British actress and society beauty, was always known as 'the Jersey Lily'.

LINA
A variant of Caroline, q.v., and of Adeline, q.v.

LINDA
From the Old German, meaning 'serpent'. This is no insult: serpents personified wisdom and were venerated by many ancient peoples, including the Pre-Hindu dwellers in India and the worshippers of a crowned snake goddess in Lower Egypt. (It is also the Spanish for 'pretty'.) The name has been used in Britain from the late nineteenth century.

LINDSAY
A variant of Lindsey, q.v.

LINDSEY
From the Old English, meaning 'Lelli's island'. A place name and aristocratic surname, now used as a first name for both girls and boys.

LINDY
A variant of Linda, q.v.

LINETTE
A variant of Lynette, q.v.

LINNET
A variant of Lynette, q.v.

LIS
French for Lilian (q.v.) and also short for Elizabeth (q.v.).

LISA
A variant of Liza, q.v.

LISABET
A variant of Elizabeth, q.v.

LISBETH
A variant of Elizabeth, q.v.

LISETTE
A variant of Elizabeth, q.v.

LISSA
A variant of Melissa, q.v.

LITA
From Carmelita, meaning 'of God's garden'.

LIVIA
A diminutive of Olivia, q.v.

LIZ
A variant of Liza, q.v.

LIZA
A shortened form of Elizabeth (q.v.), popular since the 1960s. *Liza of Lambeth* (1897) was the first novel of William Somerset Maugham, inspired by his experiences as a medical student in the London slums.

LOIS
From the Greek, meaning 'good'. The New Testament Lois was the Greek grandmother of St. Timothy, friend and helper of St. Paul. The Puritans of the seventeenth century began its use as they rejected all names not included in the Bible.

LOLA
A variant of Dolores, q.v.

LOLITA
A variant of Dolores, q.v.

LORA
A variant of Laura, q.v.

LOREN
A variant of Laura, q.v.

LORENZA
Italian for Laura, q.v.

LORETTA
A pet-form of Laura (q.v.), in use since the late nineteenth century. The beautiful film star Loretta Young, who won an Academy Award for her part in *The Farmer's Daughter* (1947), popularised the name.

LORI
A pet-form of Lorraine (q.v.), used independently. (A lory is also a brightly coloured Australian parrot which dines on the nectar and pollen of flowers!)

LORITA
A variant of Laura, q.v.

LORNA
A name invented by Richard Doddridge Blackmore (1825–1900), for the heroine of his best-known novel, *Lorna Doone*. The Doones are outlaws on Exmoor, but Lorna turns out to be the kidnapped daughter of the Earl of Dugal. (Yes reader, the hero then marries her. . .).

LORRAINE
From the region in north-east France and a surname, used as a first name since the late-nineteenth century.
    The Cross of Lorraine, a red cross with two horizontal crosspieces, was adopted by the French as an emblem of resistance to German occupation in the Second World War.

LORY
A variant of Lori, q.v.

LOTTIE

A pet-form of Charlotte, used independently since the nineteenth century.

Lottie Dod (1871–1960) won her first tennis singles title at Wimbledon in 1887 when she was not yet sixteen. (Her opponent was a Miss Bingley.) She also won the Women's Golf Championship in 1904.

LOU

A variant of Louise, q.v.

LOUELLA

A combination of Louise, q.v., and Ella, q.v.

LOUISA

A variant of Louise, q.v. Louisa May Alcott (1832–1888), the American novelist and poet, was a prolific writer but remains famous for the children's classic, *Little Women*. And Dame Louisa Aldrich Blake (1865–1925), who devoted her life to medicine, was the first woman to obtain the degree of Master of Surgery.

LOUISE

The feminine form of Louis (q.v.), fashionable in Britain since the eighteenth century.

St. Louise de Marillac (1591–1660) was the French co-founder of the Daughters of Charity, who care for the sick poor all over the world.

LUCE

A variant of Lucy, q.v.

LUCIA

Italian for Lucy, q.v.

LUCIE

A variant of Lucy, q.v.

LUCIENNE

French for Lucy, q.v.

LUCILLA

From the Latin, meaning 'light', the feminine version of Lucius. St. Lucius was an African Christian martyr, executed at Carthage in 259.

It has been used in Britain since the eighteenth century, when the passion for classical names was at its height.

LUCILLE
A variant of Lucilla, q.v.

LUCINDA
This was a literary variation of Lucia. The name was given to a character in *Don Quixote* (1605) by Miguel de Cervantes; it was later adopted by English poets of the eighteenth century.

James Thomson includes 'thy lov'd Lucinda, with soul to thine attuned' in his best-known work, *The Seasons* (1728). It has been used regularly since then.

LUCY
From the Latin, meaning 'light'. The virgin martyr St. Lucy (d.304), executed at Syracuse in Sicily, is the patron saint of those suffering with diseases of the eyes. She was greatly revered in the Middle Ages, which made the name a favourite. Lucie Manette was the heroine of Dickens' *A Tale of Two Cities* (1859). It was for her sake that the dissolute barrister Sydney Carton died on the guillotine.

LUISA
Italian and Spanish for Louise, q.v.

LUISE
German for Louise, q.v.

LULU
A variant of Louise, q.v.

LUZ
Spanish for Lucy, q.v.

LYDIA
From the Greek, meaning 'a woman of Lydia', a district of Asia Minor. The Biblical Lydia was a purple-dye seller, converted by St. Paul together with her household. The seventeenth century Puritans began the use of the name in Britain.

The feather-brained Lydia Languish is the heroine of Richard Brinsley Sheridan's comedy *The Rivals* (1775). Another Lydia in the same mould elopes with George Wickham in Jane Austen's *Pride and Prejudice* (1813).

LYDIE
French for Lydia, q.v.

LYN
A variant of Linda, q.v.

LYNDA
A variant of Linda, q.v.

LYNETTE
This was popularised by Alfred, Lord Tennyson's poem *Gareth and Lynette* (1872), part of his epic *Idylls of the King*. Linnet was the medieval version of the name, still in use today. (While the bird received its name from its passion for flax seeds, botanical name 'linum'.)

LYNN
A variant of Linda, q.v.

LYNNE
A variant of Linda, q.v.

LYNSEY
A variant of Lindsey, q.v.

LYSANDRA
From the Greek, meaning 'liberator'.

MAB
From the Gaelic, meaning 'joyful'. Mab was reputed to have been queen of the fairies.

MABEL
A shortened form of Amabel (q.v.), used as an independent name since the seventeenth century.

MABELLE
French for Mabel, q.v.

MADALENA
Spanish for Madeline, q.v.

MADDELENA
Italian for Madeline, q.v.

MADDISON
A variant of Madison, q.v.

MADELEINE
French for Madeline, q.v.

MADELINE
A medieval variation of Magdalen, used regularly since then. The beautiful Madeline is the beloved of Porphyro in John Keats' lengthy poem, *The Eve of St. Agnes*, a favourite subject for Pre-Raphaelite painters.

And the little girl who lived in an old house in Paris with eleven schoolmates and Miss Clavel is the heroine of the children's book *Madeline* (1952) and its sequels by Ludwig Bemelmans.

MADGE
A variant of Margaret, q.v.

MADISON
From the surname, meaning 'son of Maud', a modern first name for girls.

James Madison (1751–1836), fourth president of the United States of America, was in office when British troops captured Washington and burnt the White House in 1814. He is commemorated in Madison Avenue and Madison Square in New York.

MADY
German for Madeline, q.v.

MAE
A variant of May, q.v.

MAEVE
Irish for Mab, q.v.

MAGDA
German for Madeline, q.v.

MAGDALENA
From the Hebrew, meaning 'woman of Magdala', a town on the Sea of Galilee.

The Biblical St. Mary Magdalene was the first to whom the risen Christ appeared: there was a great devotion to her in the Middle Ages.

Magdalene College, Cambridge, possesses the manuscript of the diary of its most famous graduate, Samuel Pepys. Magdalene College, Oxford, has a beautiful tower from the top of which a Latin hymn is sung at sunrise on May Day.

MAGDALENE
A variant of Magdalena, q.v.

MAGGIE
A variant of Margaret, q.v.

MAIA
From the Greek, meaning 'nurse'. In Greek mythology, the daughter of Atlas and Pleione. She was the eldest and most beautiful of the Pleiades, mother of Hermes by Zeus.

The Romans also honoured an ancient divinity of Spring with this name. They offered sacrifices to her on the first day of May, naming the month after her.

MAIRI
Scottish for Mary, q.v.

MAISIE
The Scottish pet-form of Margaret (q.v.), now generally used and gaining in popularity.

What Maisie Knew (1897), a novel by Henry James, deals with the problems of the young Maisie Farange whose parents are divorced. (She finally decides to live with her governess.)

MAME
A variant of Mary, q.v.

MAMIE
A variant of Mary, q.v.

MANDY
A pet-form of Amanda (q.v.), used in Britain since the mid- twentieth century.

MANETTE
French for Mary, q.v.

MANON
A French diminutive of Mary (q.v.) best known as the eponymous heroine of the operas *Manon Lescaut* (1893) by Puccini and *Manon* (1884) by Massenet. The beautiful Manon Lescaut becomes a beautiful 'kept woman' and toast of the demi-monde; her life the usual wine, parties, rich men and, of course, a tragic death.

MARCIA
The feminine version of Marcus, ultimately derived from Mars, the god of war.

MARCIE
French for Marcia, q.v.

MARGARET
From the Greek, meaning 'pearl'. The name of at least five saints, one of whom, St. Margaret of Scotland (1045–1093), was married to Malcolm III and noted for her care of orphans and the poor. There have been several royal Margarets, both in Britain and in Europe, the latest being Princess Margaret Rose (b. 1930), the sister of Elizabeth II.

Dame Margaret Rutherford (1892–1972), actress and film star, is well remembered for her portrayal of the delightfully dotty Madame Arcati in *Blithe Spirit.*

Margaret Damer Dawson (1875–1920) was the founder of the Women's Police Service in 1914.

MARGARETE
Danish and German for Margaret, q.v.

MARGARETHA
Dutch for Margaret, q.v.

MARGARITA
Spanish for Margaret, q.v.

MARGERY
A variant of Marjorie, q.v.

MARGHERITA
Italian for Margaret, q.v.

MARGO
A variant of Margaret, q.v.

MARGOT
A variant of Margaret, q.v.

MARGUERITE
The French form of Margaret and a flower name, popular since the nineteenth century.

Marguerite of Navarre (1492–1549) was the sister of Francis I of France and the Queen of Navarre. A poet and a writer, she produced the first collection of French stories and the poetic *Les Marguerites de la Marguerite des Princesses* (1547).

Marguerite Gardiner (1789–1849) became the notorious Countess of Blessington, leading hostess of the day. Her *Conversations With Lord Byron* is still read.

MARI
An Irish form of Mary, q.v.

MARIA
Spanish and Italian for Mary (q.v.). It became fashionable in the eighteenth century in Britain. Maria Montessori (1870–1952), Italian educationalist, developed the theory of non-interference with the freedom and individuality of children so popular today.

MARIAN
A French variant of Marion, q.v.

MARIANA
Spanish for Marion, q.v.

MARIANNA
Italian for Marion, q.v.

MARIANNE
A French conjunction of Marie and Anne, used since the eighteenth century. The work of the painter and explorer Marianne North (1830–1890) can be seen in the Marianne North Gallery in Kew Gardens. Over eight hundred of her vivid botanical paintings cover the walls. Her interesting autobiography is called *Recollections of a Happy Life*.

MARIBELLA
A combination of Mary, q.v., and of Bella, q.v.

MARIE
French for Mary, q.v. It became fashionable in the nineteenth century in Britain.

MARIELLA
The Italian diminutive of Marie, now generally used.

MARIELLE
The French diminutive of Marie, now generally used.

MARIETTA
A French diminutive of Marie, used in Britain since the nineteenth century.
    Marietta is a character in Erich Korngold's opera *Die Tote Stadt* or *The Dead City* (1920).

MARIGOLD
From this flower name.

MARILDA
From the Germanic, meaning 'battle maid'.

MARILYN
A twentieth-century combination of Mary and the suffix 'lyn'.
    Norma Jean Mortenson (1926–1962), far better known as the film star Marilyn Monroe, starred in many films; notably *Gentlemen Prefer Blondes* (1953) and *Some Like It Hot* (1959).

MARINA
From the Latin, meaning 'of the sea'. In Shakespeare's *Pericles,* Marina is the daughter of Thaisa and Pericles, called so 'for I was born at sea'.

The Greek Princess Marina, Duchess of Kent (1906–1968), gave her name to a shade of blue and was the mother of Princess Alexandra and the present Duke of Kent.

MARION
A medieval diminutive of Mary, brought to England at the Norman Conquest. Marion was the famous legendary girlfriend of Robin Hood. In 1332 a puppet play *Robin et Marion* was performed by students at Angers: the origin of marionettes, puppets worked by strings.

MARJORIE
The medieval English version of Marguerite. Marjorie (d.1316) was the daughter of Scotland's national hero Robert the Bruce and his wife Isabella. (But the Marjorie Daw of children's nursery rhyme fame always springs to mind.)

MARJORY
A variant of Marjorie, q.v.

MARLENE
German for Madeline, q.v.

MARQUITA
A variant of Marcia, q.v.

MARSHA
A variant of Marcia, q.v.

MARTA
Spanish, Swedish and Italian for Martha, q.v.

MARTHA
From the Aramaic, meaning 'lady'. The New Testament Martha was the sister of Lazarus and Mary, all three the close friends of Christ. She is the patroness of housekeepers and all who care for the needy. It has been used in Britain since the Reformation. Martha is always associated in the U.S.A. with the name of the wife of the first President George Washington (1732–1799).

MARTINA

The feminine form of Martin, q.v. St. Martina was a Christian martyr of the third century; but nowadays the name is associated with the Czechoslovak-born tennis player Martina Navratilova (b.1956), winner of the Wimbledon tennis singles title an amazing nine times, and the Swiss player Martina Hingis who was named in her honour.

MARTINE

French for Martina, q.v.

MARTITA

A variant of Martha, q.v.

MARY

The English version of Miriam, from the Hebrew meaning 'bitterness'. There are seven women of this name in the New Testament; pre-eminent among them being the Blessed Virgin Mary, mother of Jesus. Considered too holy for common use, the name was not used in Britain until the thirteenth century.

The tragic Mary I of England (1516–1558), daughter of Henry VIII and Catherine of Aragon, was the second wife of King Philip II of Spain who was responsible for the Spanish Armada.

Mary Beale (b.1633), a protégée of Sir Peter Lely, was the first woman in Britain to earn her living as an artist.

(But the famous bearers of this ever-popular name are innumerable.)

MARYANN

A combination of Mary and Ann.

MARYLOU

A combination of Mary and Louise.

MATELDA

Italian for Matilda, q.v.

MATHILDE

French for Matilda, q.v.

MATILDA

From the Old German, meaning 'strength in battle'. The name was brought to England at the Norman Conquest by the wife of William the Conqueror. Matilda of Flanders was crowned Queen of England at Westminster Abbey in 1068.

The poet and painter Matilda Betham (1776–1852) was admired by Coleridge, who wrote a poem in her honour.

MATILDE
Spanish for Matilda, q.v.

MATTIE
A variant of Martha, q.v.

MAUD
The French medieval version of Matilda, revived in the nineteenth century. Tennyson's lengthy poem *Maud* (1855), with such lines as 'Maud with her exquisite face', was probably responsible. And Whittier's poem *Maud Muller* (1854) contains the memorable lines:
'For all sad words of tongue or pen,
The saddest are these: "It might have been".'

MAUDE
A variant of Maud, q.v.

MAURA
From the Irish for Mary, meaning 'bitter'.

MAUREEN
An anglicised version of the Irish name Mairin, meaning 'little Mary'. It became popular in Britain in the early twentieth century.

The Californian tennis player Maureen Connolly (1934–1969), better known as 'Little Mo', was the first woman to win the world's four major singles championships or 'Grand Slam' in 1953 – France, Australia, United States of America and Wimbledon.

MAURIZIA
Italian for Maureen, q.v.

MAVIS
From the Old French, meaning 'song thrush'.

Mavis Clare was the heroine of Marie Corelli's bestseller, *The Sorrows of Satan* (1894), reputedly an idealised portrait of the writer: this made the name a favourite with the Victorians.

MAXIE
A variant of Maxine, q.v.

MAXINE
A modern feminine version of Maximilian (q.v.).

MAY
A pet-form of Mary or Margaret used in the nineteenth century, but now associated with the fifth month. The Romans honoured an ancient divinity of the Spring named Maia. They offered sacrifices to her on the first day of May, having named the month after her.

MAYA
A variant of Maia, q.v.

MAYBELLE
This name means 'beautiful May'.

MEAVE
Irish for Mab, q.v.

MEG
A variant of Margaret, q.v.

MEGAN
The Welsh pet-form of Margaret, now generally used. Lady Megan Lloyd George (1902–1966), daughter of the Liberal Prime Minister, was also keen on politics. She became first a Liberal, and then a Labour, Member of Parliament.

MELANIE
From the Greek, meaning 'black'. There are two Roman saints of the fifth century bearing this name, grandmother and granddaughter, friends of St. Jerome. The name has been used in Britain since the seventeenth century.
    The gentle Melanie Wilkes is the only truly admirable character in Margaret Mitchell's bestselling novel, *Gone with the Wind* (1936).

MELINA
Italian for Carmel, q.v.

MELINDA
A name coined in the eighteenth century and used regularly since then.

MELISANDE
French for Millicent, q.v.

MELISENDA
Spanish for Millicent, q.v.

MELISSA
From the Greek, meaning 'a bee'; in Greek mythology, a nymph who introduced us to the pleasures of eating honey.

Melissa is a prophetess, living in Merlin's cave, in Ariosto's epic poem *Orlando Furioso*. The name came into favour in Britain in the nineteenth century.

MELODY
From the Greek, meaning 'singing of songs'. A modern name, although noted once or twice in the nineteenth century. (And if we have to deal with sleepless, shrieking babies, lines from John Keats' *Ode on a Grecian Urn* must spring to mind:
'Heard melodies are sweet, but those unheard
Are sweeter. . .'.)

MERCEDES
Spanish for Mercy, q.v.

MERCY
The virtue, used as a first name since the seventeenth century. Mercy, a neighbour, accompanies Christiana and her children to the Celestial City in the second part of *The Pilgrim's Progress* (1684) by John Bunyan.

MEREDITH
From the Welsh, meaning 'great lord'. A surname and male name, first used as a name for girls in the twentieth century.

MERIEL
From the Celtic, meaning 'sea bright'. This is a medieval version of Muriel, brought to England by the Normans. It was revived in the nineteenth century.

MERLE
From the French, meaning 'like a blackbird'.

MIA

The Danish pet-form of Mary, made popular by the American actress Mia Farrow, best remembered for her part in *Rosemary's Baby* (1968).

MICAELA

A variant of Michaela, q.v. Micaela is a character in Bizet's last opera, *Carmen* (1875).

MICHAELA

The feminine form of Michael, meaning 'Who is like God?', popular since the 1950s.

MICHAELLA

Italian for Michaela, q.v.

MICHELLE

The French feminine form of Michael (q.v.), now generally used. A ballad of the same name by the Beatles brought the name to public attention in the 1960s.

MICKIE

A variant of Michaela, q.v.

MIGNON

From the French, meaning a 'favourite'.

MIGNONETTE

A variant of Mignon, q.v.

MIGUELITA

Spanish for Michaela, q.v.

MILLICENT

From the German, meaning 'strong worker'. The name was brought to England by the Normans, being revived in the nineteenth century.

Dame Millicent Fawcett (1847–1929) was a leading figure in the women's suffrage movement for fifty years. At the age of eighty-one she attained success, when the House of Lords passed the Bill allowing women the same voting rights as men.

The singer Millicent Martin is a well-known modern bearer of the name. (And the ageless Milly-Molly-Mandy, heroine of so many children's stories by Joyce Lankester Brisley, is another.)

MILLIE
A variant of Millicent, q.v.

MILLY
A variant of Millicent, q.v.

MIMI
A French pet-form of Mary. The use of the name is generally linked to the heroine of Giacomo Puccini's opera, *La Bohème* (1896). The Parisian seamstress Mimi (whose tiny hand is frozen) loves the penniless poet of the Latin Quarter, Rodolfo, and expires beautifully.

(This is also the name given by the aborigines of Australia to an earlier culture, who appear to have died out. Their only legacy are numerous cave paintings of mysterious running figures.)

MINA
A variant of Minna, q.v.

MINETTE
French for Minerva, meaning 'one who thinks'.

MINNA
From the Old German, meaning 'small', or a pet-form of Wilhelmina. This may have been introduced to Britain by the eponymous heroine of *Minna von Barnhelm* (1767), a comic play by Gotthold Lessing or by Minna Troil, a character in *The Pirate* (1822) by Sir Walter Scott.

MINNIE
A Scottish form of Mary, q.v.

MIRA
A diminutive of Mirabel, q.v.

MIRABEL
From the Latin, meaning 'glorious'. A medieval name, revived in the early nineteenth century. Now a girl's name, it was given to the hero of William Congreve's masterpiece, *The Way of the World* (1700). Mirabell wishes to marry the beautiful Millamant, despite the opposition of Lady Wishfort, her aunt.

MIRABELLA
A variant of Mirabel, q.v.

MIRANDA

From the Latin, meaning 'worthy of admiration'. Shakespeare seems to have invented the name for Prospero's daughter in his last play, *The Tempest*. Raised without human companionship on an enchanted island, Miranda marries Ferdinand, the son of the King of Naples.

A popular name in the twentieth century.

MIRIAM

From the Hebrew, meaning 'bitterness'. The Old Testament Miriam watched over her infant brother Moses when he was hidden in the bulrushes. She led the music and dancing after the Israelites crossed the Red Sea in safety. The name came into use in Britain after the Reformation.

Miriam is Paul Morel's first love in D.H. Lawrence's autobiographical novel, *Sons and Lovers* (1913).

MITZI

A variant of Miriam, q.v.

MODESTA

Italian for Modesty, q.v.

MODESTIA

Spanish for Modesty, q.v.

MODESTINE

French for Modesty, q.v.

MODESTY

From the Latin, meaning 'modest'.

MOIRA

The anglicised version of the Irish name Maire, or Mary, used generally since the early twentieth century.

The French novelist Julien Green wrote *Moira* (1950).

MOIREEN

A variant of Maureen, q.v.

MOLLY

A pet-form of Mary, now independently used. Molly Mog (1699–1766) was an innkeeper's daughter and celebrated London beauty. The poet and playwright John Gay (1685–1732) wrote a ballad in her honour entitled *Fair Maid of the Inn.*

MONA
From the Irish, meaning 'noble'. The name has been used in Britain since the late nineteenth century, when Irish names became fashionable. (This is also the ancient name for the Isle of Man.)

MONICA
St. Monica (331–387) was the mother of St. Augustine of Hippo, whose early dissolute life caused her much distress.

Monica Dickens (1915–1992), great-granddaughter of Charles, wrote many popular books. Her very first, giving a servant's eye view of society and called *One Pair of Hands* (1937), made her a household name.

MONIQUE
French for Monica (q.v.), now generally used.

MORAG
From the Gaelic, meaning 'great'. It is considered an exclusively Scottish name.

MORENA
Spanish for Maureen, q.v.

MORGAN
From the Welsh, meaning 'sea-bright'. A surname, now used as a first name for both girls and boys.

The mysterious sorceress Morgan-le-Fay was sister to the legendary King Arthur. A fine picture entitled *Morgan-le-Fay,* painted by the Pre-Raphaelite artist Frederick Sandys (1829–1904), can be admired in the Birmingham City Museum and Art Gallery.

MORWENNA
From the Welsh, meaning 'maiden'. An obscure saint, patron of Morwenstow in Cornwall, bears the name. This has been increasing in popularity since the mid-twentieth century.

MOYA
A modern variation of Maria, taken from the Irish name Maire.

MOYNA
A variant of Myrna, q.v.

MURIEL

From the Celtic, meaning 'sea-bright'. The name was brought to England at the Norman Conquest and remained popular throughout the Middle Ages. It was revived in the latter half of the nineteenth century.

Muriel Spark is the author of *The Prime of Miss Jean Brodie* (1961), among other distinguished novels.

MYFANWY

From the Welsh, meaning 'my treasure'. Myfanwy Thomas, third child of the poet Edward Thomas (1878–1917), wrote about her father in *One of These Fine Days* (1982).

MYRA

This seems to have been invented by Sir Fulke Greville (1554–1628), English courtier, diplomat and Chancellor of the Exchequer as well as poet. He addressed many love poems to a lady of this name.

MYRNA

From the Gaelic, meaning 'gentle'.

MYRTLE

From the Greek, meaning 'like the myrtle'.

NADIA

From the Russian, meaning 'hope', used in Britain since the early twentieth century. The wife of Vladimir Ilyich Ulyanov, better known as the Russian Communist leader Lenin, was a bearer of the name.

NADINE
A variant of Nadia, q.v.

NAN
A variant of Ann, q.v.

NANA
A variant of Hannah, q.v.

NANCY
An eighteenth century pet-form of Ann, now considered an independent name.

The forthright American Nancy Astor (1879–1964) was the first woman to take her seat in the House of Commons in 1919. A blue plaque commemorating her has been placed on her home at 4 St. James's Square in London.

NANETTE
A pet-form of Nan, itself an early diminutive of Ann. It has been used in Britain since the early twentieth century.

No! No! Nanette! (1925), an operetta by Vincent Youman, was fabulously successful in England and Europe. The actress Nanette Newman is the best-known modern bearer of the name.

NAOMI
From the Hebrew, meaning 'pleasure'. The Old Testament Naomi was the beloved mother-in-law of Ruth, whose story is told in the *Book of Ruth*. This became a favourite with the Puritans of the seventeenth century and has been used since then.

The prolific novelist Naomi Jacob (1889–1964) is well-known.

NATALIA
A variant of Natalie, q.v. St. Natalia, a saint of the fourth century, instructed her husband St. Adrian in the faith and had to see him martyred for professing it. Her feast day is 1st December.

NATALIE
From the Latin, meaning 'birthday of the Lord'. It was often bestowed on girls born on Christmas Day.

The South African province of Natal was named by the Portuguese explorer Vasco da Gama, who landed at what is now the city of Durban on Christmas Day 1497, and dubbed it Terra Natalis.

NATASHA
The Russian pet-form of Natalia, now generally used. Natasha Rostova is the heroine of Count Leo Tolstoy's greatest novel, *War and Peace* (1864). After an unhappy love affair with Prince Andrei she makes a *happy* marriage with Pierre Bezukhov. (A literary rarity!)

NELL
A variant of Ellen (q.v.) and of Helen (q.v.).

NELLIE
A variant of Ellen (q.v.) and of Helen (q.v.).

NERISSA
From the Greek, meaning 'sea-nymph'. Shakespeare seems to have invented the name he gave to Portia's astute waiting-woman and confidante in *The Merchant of Venice* (1595).

NERYS
A modern Welsh name, meaning 'lady'. The actress Nerys Hughes (b.1941) has brought it to public attention.

NESSA
A variant of Nessie (q.v.) and of Agnes (q.v.).

NESSIE
A variant of Agnes, q.v. Nessie is also the name of the Loch Ness Monster!

NESTA
Welsh for Agnes, q.v.

NETTA
A variant of Henrietta, q.v.

NETTIE
A variant of Henrietta (q.v.) and of Annette (q.v.).

NICKY
A variant of Nicola (q.v.) and of Nicole.

NICOLA
The Italian feminine form of Nicholas (q.v.), now generally popular.

Nicola has been used in England since the twelfth century.

NICOLE
A French feminine form of Nicholas, q.v.

NICOLETTE
A French feminine form of Nicholas, q.v.
Aucassin and Nicolette is one of the best-known of all medieval romances. Nicolette, a king's daughter enslaved by the Saracens, falls in love with Aucassin, son of the Count of Beaucaire. After imprisonment, shipwreck and various disguises, all ends happily.

NIKKI
A variant of Nicola (q.v.) and of Nicole.

NINA
A Russian pet-form of Anne, used in England since the nineteenth century. (It can also be derived from the Spanish, meaning 'little girl'.)
In Babylonian myth Nina was a marine goddess prone to uttering dire predictions.
Anton Chekhov's play, *The Seagull* (1896), has a tragic heroine named Nina who compares herself to the dead bird of the title, destroyed by man's whim. (And the hero - you *knew* he would - commits suicide.)

NINETTE
A variant of Nina, q.v.

NISSA
From the Hebrew, meaning 'sign'. A modern name.

NITA
A pet-form of the Spanish name Juanita, now generally used.

NOELEEN
A variant of Noelle, q.v.

NOELLE
The French feminine form of Noël, meaning 'Christmas', an appropriate choice for girls born on that day.

NOLA
From the Gaelic, meaning 'famous'.

NONA
From the Latin, meaning the 'ninth child'.

NORA
A variant of Eleanora (q.v.) and Leonora (q.v.).

NOREEN
Irish for Nora, q.v.

NORMA
From the Latin, meaning 'precept'. *Norma* (1831), an opera by Vincenzo Bellini, appears to have brought the name to public attention. The eponymous heroine, a Druid priestess, is secretly married to a Roman pro-Consul. Naturally, it all ends in tears.

(Norma is also the name of a constellation in the southern Milky Way.)

NUALA
From the Irish name Fionnhuala, meaning 'white-shouldered'. The beautiful Fionnhuala of legend was transformed into a swan by her evil stepmother and wandered the lakes and rivers endlessly. She could not be released from the spell until Christianity came to Ireland.

OCTAVIA
From the Latin, meaning 'eighth'. In Roman history, two unhappy ladies with this name are memorable. The first was sister to the

Emperor Augustus and married Mark Antony, who promptly abandoned her on meeting Cleopatra.

The second (40–62) was a daughter of the Emperor Claudius and married to Nero. He divorced her in order to marry another (whom he later kicked to death), then had Octavia executed. Despite this, the name has been used in Britain since the eighteenth century.

A happier lady, who deserves our gratitude, was Octavia Hill (1838–1912), one of the three founders of the National Trust.

OCTAVIE
French for Octavia, q.v.

ODETTE
The French female diminutive of Odo, a medieval name meaning 'prosperity'. Its use in Britain began early in the twentieth century.

Odette de Crecy is an important character in Marcel Proust's epic novel, first published in sixteen volumes, *Remembrance of Things Past* (1913–1927).

Odette Sansom (later Hallowes) was the first woman to be awarded the George Cross for her bravery during World War II.

OENONE
In Greek mythology, a nymph from Mount Ida with the gifts of prophecy and healing. She was Paris' first wife. After he deserted her for Helen and was wounded, she refused to help him despite her promise to do so. On his death she committed suicide.

Alfred, Lord Tennyson's poems *Oenone* and *The Death of Oenone* made the name well-known to the Victorians. The name appears to be enjoying a revival.

OLGA
The Russian version of an Old Norse name, meaning 'holy'. St. Olga (879–969) was the wife of Igor, Prince of Kiev, and baptised at the age of eighty. Her grandson, St. Vladimir, introduced Christianity to Russia. The name has been used in Britain since the nineteenth century.

Grand Duchess Olga (1895–1918) was the first daughter of Tsar Nicholas II, murdered with all her family by the Bolsheviks in the cellar at Ekaterinburg.

OLIVE
The olive tree was sacred to the goddess Pallas Athene in Greek mythology. It signified peace and, when carried by new brides,

fecundity. The name has been used in England since the thirteenth century.

OLIVIA
The Italian version of Olive (q.v.), popularised by the rich countess in Shakespeare's play, *Twelfth Night*. It is also a 'romantic' name, bestowed upon a daughter of Dr. Primrose in Oliver Goldsmith's novel, *The Vicar of Wakefield* (1776).

OLWEN
From the Welsh, meaning 'white footprint'. Olwen was a giant's daughter in Welsh mythology; as she walked, white flowers sprang up beneath her feet.

OLWIN
A variant of Olwen, q.v.

ONA
A variant of Una, q.v.

OONA
A variant of Oonagh, the Irish for Una, q.v.

OONAGH
See under Una.

OPHELIA
From the Greek, meaning 'help'. Ophelia is the daughter of Polonius in Shakespeare's *Hamlet*. She becomes mad and drowns herself because her heart is broken. It was a favourite subject with the Pre-Raphaelite painters: the most famous example was painted by John Everett Millais in 1852. His *Ophelia* can be seen in the Tate Gallery, London.

OPHELIE
French for Ophelia, q.v.

ORIANA
From the Latin, meaning 'golden'.

ORIEL
Now a probable variation of Auriel, meaning 'golden'; but the Normans *did* bring Oriel to England at the Conquest and it may be a

revival.

Oriel College was founded by Edward II in 1326 and is the oldest royal foundation in Oxford. Sir Walter Raleigh was one of its famous members.

ORSOLA
Italian for Ursula, q.v.

ORTENSIA
Italian for Hortense, q.v.

OTTAVIA
Italian for Octavia, q.v.

OTTILIE
From the Old German, meaning 'fatherland', a feminine version of Otto.

St. Ottilia (d.720), who was reputedly born blind and regained her sight, is the patroness of Alsace and invoked by those afflicted with diseases of the eyes.

PAIGE
An occupational surname, meaning 'page'; now a modern first name for girls. In the Middle Ages, a boy who wished to become a knight had to serve an apprenticeship as a page in a royal household or nobleman's castle, waiting upon the family.

PAM
A variant of Pamela, q.v.

PAMELA
Supposedly coined by Sir Philip Sidney in his pastoral romance *Arcadia* (1590), the name became a favourite after the publication of *Pamela* (1740) by Samuel Richardson. The unsophisticated heroine, Pamela Andrews, convinces the son of her wealthy employer to marry her after rejecting his dishonourable attentions.

PANDORA
From the Greek, meaning 'all gifts'. In Greek mythology Pandora was the first woman, created by Zeus. Out of curiosity, she opened the box containing diseases and sorrow and all the woes now rife in the world. Only hope, slower than the rest, remained to give comfort.

PASCALE
The French feminine form of Pascal (q.v.), used in Britain since the 1960s.

PAT
A variant of Patricia, q.v.

PATIENCE
One of the Christian virtues, made a favourite by the Puritans of the seventeenth century. Sir Thomas Crewe, Speaker of the House of Commons from 1624 to 1625, had four daughters named Patience, Temperance, Silence and Prudence. Patience is the hero of the comic opera by Gilbert and Sullivan in which Oscar Wilde is caricatured, entitled *Patience or Bunthorne's Bride* (1881).

PATRICIA
The feminine form of Patrick, meaning 'noble'. Victoria Patricia Helena Elizabeth of Connaught (1886–1974), known as Princess Patricia, granddaughter of Queen Victoria and a painter, made the name a favourite.

PATRIZIA
Italian for Patricia, q.v.

PATSY
A pet-form of Patricia (q.v.), now used independently. (It is also American slang for someone who has been tricked!)

PATTIE
A variant of Patricia, q.v.

PAULA

The German feminine form of Paul (q.v.), used in Britain since the early twentieth century. The Roman St. Paula (347–404) was noted for her tact: as a friend and helper of the bad-tempered St. Jerome it was much needed. She built a hospice for pilgrims in Bethlehem.

Paula is the eponymous heroine of Arthur Wing Pinero's best-known play, *The Second Mrs Tanqueray* (1893). She has a lurid past and an unhappy present, becoming yet another literary suicide.

PAULETTE

French for Paula, q.v.

PAULINA

Spanish for Paula, q.v.

PAULINE

The French feminine form of Paul (q.v.), now generally used. Pauline Bonaparte (1780–1825) was the second and favourite sister of Napoleon I; she married Prince Camillo Borghese and lived a rather flamboyant life!

PEARL

A jewel name, which came into use in the late nineteenth century along with many others. Pearls have always been a royal favourite and remain so today. Queen Alexandra (1844–1925) once delayed the State Opening of Parliament because her string of pearls snapped. Everything came to a halt while they were being retrieved.

The American writer Pearl Buck (1892–1973) received a Pulitzer Prize for her novel *The Good Earth* (1931), and the Nobel Prize for Literature in 1938.

PEG

A variant of Margaret, q.v.

PEGGY

A variant of Margaret, q.v.

PENELOPE

From the Greek, meaning 'weaver'. In Greek mythology, Penelope was the wife of Odysseus. While he was wandering the globe she was besieged by suitors. Penelope promised to choose one to replace her vanished husband when her incessant weaving was done. As she unpicked the day's work every night, this was impossible. (Odysseus returned in time to slay all the suitors, who were becoming a trifle angry.) The name has been used in England since the sixteenth century.

PENNY
A variant of Penelope, q.v.

PERDITA
From the Latin, meaning 'lost'. Perdita, the heroine of Shakespeare's play, *The Winter's Tale,* is abandoned on a deserted shore and raised by a shepherd. As she is *really* a princess, everything ends happily. Shakespeare appears to have invented the name.

PERSEPHONE
From the Greek, meaning 'dazzlingly bright'. In Greek mythology, she was the daughter of Zeus and Demeter. While picking flowers in Sicily, she was kidnapped by Hades, god of the Underworld. Her mother rescued her, on the understanding that she had eaten nothing while abducted. Unfortunately, Persephone had devoured six pomegranate seeds and so had to remain in the Underworld for six months of each year. And that is why we have winter!

PETRA
From the Latin, meaning 'rock'. A modern feminine version of Peter. Petra, the ruined Jordanian city immortalised by the well-known line, 'a rose-red city half as old as time', was rediscovered by the Swiss explorer Johann Burckhardt in 1812. (It is now in peril from too many tourists.)

PETRINA
A feminine form of Peter, q.v.

PETRONELLA
The name of an early Christian martyr, it has been used in England since the twelfth century. Medieval legend decided that Petronella was the daughter of the apostle Peter and she was invoked by those suffering from fever.

PETRONILLE
German for Petra, q.v.

PHIL
A diminutive of Philippa, q.v.

PHILIPINE
German for Philippa, q.v.

PHILIPPA
The feminine version of Philip, meaning 'fond of horses'. Queen Philippa of Hainault (1314–1369), wife of Edward III, was responsible for introducing the herb rosemary into England. She later led the English army against the invading Scots. It was also the name of Geoffrey Chaucer's wife.

Philippa Garrett Fawcett (1868–1948) made history in 1890 when she was classed 'above Senior Wrangler' in the Mathematical Tripos at Cambridge. Being a woman, she was denied the title, but her college celebrated with fireworks and singing all the same. This prompted a *Punch* cartoon; showing her sitting alone in a railway carriage, with the title 'First Class. Ladies Only'.

PHILOMENA
From the Greek, meaning 'moon lover'.

PHOEBE
From the Greek, meaning 'bright'. In Greek mythology, Phoebe was a Titaness, one of the many children of Uranus and Gaia. The New Testament Phoebe carried St. Paul's letter to the Church in Rome from her home in Corinth. The name became popular in England after the Reformation.

Phoebe Tozer is the ebullient heroine of Mrs Oliphant's novel, *Phoebe Junior* (1880).

PHYLLIDA
From the Greek, meaning 'leafy'. The Phyllida of Greek mythology hanged herself because her lover did not return to marry her as he had promised. The poor girl was transformed into an almond tree.

An anonymous Elizabethan poet wrote *Phillada Flouts Me*: the name appears to have been used in Britain since the seventeenth century.

PHYLLIS
From the Greek, meaning 'leafy'. The name of a Thracian princess in Greek mythology, classical poets considered it a suitable name for beautiful country maidens. John Milton included 'neat-handed Phyllis' in his poem *L'Allegro*.

It was particularly popular in England in the eighteenth century.

PIA
From the Latin, meaning 'dutiful, godly'. This pretty Italian name is a modern favourite in Britain.

PIERETTE
French for Petra, q.v.

PIPPA
A pet-form of Philippa (q.v.), now used independently. Robert Browning made the name a favourite with his long poetic drama, *Pippa Passes* (1841). Pippa works at the silk mills in Asolo in Italy; her songs affect the lives of all who hear her. She it is who sings the well-known lines:
> 'The lark's on the wing;
> The snail's on the thorn;
> God's in his heaven –
> All's right with the world!'

PLEASANCE
From the Old French, meaning 'to please'. This was brought to England by the Normans.

POLLY
A venerable pet-form of Mary, via Molly; its age is demonstrated by various nursery rhyme characters.

The lovely Polly Peachum marries Captain Macheath in *The Beggar's Opera* by John Gay, first performed in 1728. A sequel to this, called *Polly*, was not popular with the government of the day who took umbrage at Gay's satire.

POLLYANNA
This name was made a favourite by the American writer Eleanor Hodgman Porter (1868–1920), who bestowed it upon the cheerful eponymous heroine of her best-known novel *Pollyanna* (1913).

POPPY
Another of the flower names which first became popular in the late nineteenth century.

The flower was established in Britain by the Bronze Age. It is most famously associated with the Royal British Legion and its November Poppy Appeal, which assists ex-service men and women and their families.

The Canadian soldier-poet John McCrae (d.1918) inspired the use of the flower when his poem *In Flanders Fields* was published in *Punch* in 1915.

'We shall not sleep, though poppies grow
   In Flanders fields.'

PORTIA
From the Latin, meaning 'hog'. The name of an ancient Roman family, it was given by Shakespeare to the heroine of his play, *The Merchant of Venice*. Portia, disguised as a lawyer, prevents Shylock from claiming his pound of flesh from Antonio. It is she who speaks the famous lines:

'The quality of mercy is not strained,
   It droppeth as the gentle rain from heaven'.

POSY
This seems to have become popular in the 1920s, perhaps a logical progression from the Victorian love for flower names.

Posy is the ballet-obsessed youngest of the three Fossil sisters in the classic children's story, *Ballet Shoes* (1936), by Noel Streatfield.

PRIMROSE
A flower name, popular since the late nineteenth century. It is also a surname, most notably of the earls of Rosebery. The Primrose League was founded in 1833 to promote the principles of the Conservative Party.

PRIMULA
A botanical name, used as a first name since the late nineteenth century. Cowslips, oxlips and polyanthus are just three of the flowers which belong to the primula family.

PRISCILLA
From the Latin, meaning 'ancient'. The New Testament Priscilla and her husband, Aquila, were close friends with St. Paul and involved in the tent-making business of Corinth, as he was. The name became popular with the Puritans of the seventeenth century.

PRISSIE
A variant of Priscilla, q.v.

PRUDENCE
From the Latin, meaning 'discretion'. Although used in the Middle Ages, the Puritans of the seventeenth century took up the name and

made it a favourite.

PRUE
A diminutive of Prudence, q.v.

PRUNELLA
From the Latin, meaning 'little plum'. This is another of the botanical names favoured by the Victorians. (It is also a smooth, woollen fabric much used in the eighteenth century for clerical and academic garb.)

The actress Prunella Scales, always remembered as the long-suffering Sybil Fawlty in the manic television series *Fawlty Towers*, is the best-known modern bearer of the name.

PURDIE
A variant of Perdita, q.v.

QUEENIE
From the Anglo-Saxon, meaning 'like a queen'.

QUINTA
From the Latin, meaning 'fifth'. The feminine form of Quintin and much used in Ancient Rome. Quintana is a modern variation.

(And if you didn't already know, the 'via quintana' was the place for exercise in a Roman soldiers' camp and Quintana Roo is a state in Mexico!)

QUINTANA
A variant of Quinta, q.v.

RACHEL
From the Hebrew, meaning 'ewe'. The Old Testament Rachel was the beautiful second wife of Jacob. Her tomb, which stands just outside Bethlehem, is venerated by Christians, Jews and Moslems alike. The name came into general use in Britain after the Reformation.

Rachel was the stage name of Elizabeth Felix (1820–1858), the French tragic actress renowned worldwide.

RACHELE
Italian for Rachel, q.v.

RACHELLE
French for Rachel, q.v.

RAE
A variant of Rachel, q.v.

RAHEL
German for Rachel, q.v.

RAMONA
From the Spanish, meaning the 'wise one'.

RANEE
From the Hindi, meaning a 'queen'.

RANI
A variant of Ranee, q.v.

RAQUEL
Spanish for Rachel, q.v.

RAY
A variant of Rachel, q.v.

REBECA
Spanish for Rebecca, q.v.

REBECCA
From the Hebrew, meaning 'heifer'. The Old Testament Rebecca, a Syrian, was the wife of Isaac and mother of Jacob and Esau. The name came into general use in Britain after the Reformation.

Ten-year-old Rebecca Randall, heroine of Kate Douglas Wiggin's best-seller, *Rebecca of Sunnybrook Farm* (1903), made the name a favourite.

REBEKKA
Swedish and German for Rebecca, q.v.

REGAN
A variant of Regina, q.v. Shakespeare gave the name to one of King Lear's unpleasant daughters!

REGINA
From the Latin, meaning 'queen'. This was originally bestowed upon girls in the Middle Ages, referring to the Blessed Virgin under her title 'Queen of Heaven'. It was revived in the nineteenth century.

Regina is the capital of the Canadian province of Saskatchewan, named in honour of Queen Victoria.

REINA
Spanish for 'queen'.

REINE
French for 'queen'.

RENATA
From the Latin, meaning 'reborn'.

RENATE
German for Renata, q.v.

RENE
A diminutive of Irene, q.v.

RENÉE
A French feminine name, meaning 'reborn', now generally used. This was derived from the Latin Renatus, popular with the early Christians. St. René Goupil (d. 1642) was martyred by North American Indians for making the sign of the cross.

RHIAN
From the Welsh, meaning 'maiden'. A modern name.

RHIANNON
From the Welsh, meaning 'nymph' or 'goddess'. In Celtic mythology the wife of Prince Pwyll, falsely accused of murdering her kidnapped baby son. After seven years her innocence was proved when the boy returned.

RHODA
From the Greek, meaning 'rose'. In the New Testament, she was the servant girl who was too excited to let St. Peter into the house after he had been miraculously released from prison in Jerusalem by an angel. The name came into use in Britain after the Reformation.

Rhoda Fleming (1845), a novel by George Meredith, concerns the efforts of the eponymous heroine to help her sister, Dahlia.

RHONA
A Scottish place name, used as a first name since the late nineteenth century.

RHONDA
A twentieth-century name derived from two Welsh rivers, Rhondda Fawr and Rhondda Fach.

The American film star Rhonda Fleming (b.1922) made the name known in the 1940s and 1950s.

RICHENDA
An eighteenth century feminine form of Richard, q.v.

RILLA
From the German, meaning 'brook'.

RITA
A pet-form of Margarita, used independently. St. Rita of Cascia (1381-1457) married at the behest of her parents a man who was ill-tempered and profligate. After his violent death, she became an

Augustinian nun and many miracles were attributed to her.

The film star Rita Hayworth, best remembered for her appearance in *Gilda* (1946), made the name a favourite.

ROBERTA
The feminine form of Robert (q.v.), used since the mid-nineteenth century. Roberta (together with her sister Phyllis and her brother Peter) is one of the heroines of Edith Nesbit's famous book, *The Railway Children*, first published in 1905.

ROBINA
A variant of Robyn, q.v. Oliver Cromwell, Lord Protector of England after the execution of Charles I, had a sister named Robina.

ROBINE
French for Roberta, q.v.

ROBYN
A feminine form of Robin, itself once considered a pet-form of Robert, now used independently.

Robyn is a character in the Coventry Mystery Play of the fifteenth century.

RODERICA
The feminine form of Roderick, q.v.

ROLANDA
The feminine form of Roland, q.v.

ROLANDE
French for Rolanda, the feminine form of Roland, q.v.

ROMA
From the city, used as a first name in this century. The goddess Roma had a temple built in her honour in Rome by the Emperor Hadrian (76–138), and her cult spread throughout Greece and Asia Minor.

ROMAINE
A French feminine name, meaning 'Roman', now generally used.

ROMAYNE
A variant of Romaine, q.v.

RONA
A variant of Rhona, q.v.

ROSA
From the Latin, meaning 'like a rose'. Spanish, Italian, Danish, Swedish and Dutch for Rose, q.v.

ROSABEL
This name, which is a combination of Rose and Belle, means a 'beautiful rose'.

ROSALIE
The French feminine form of Rosalia, now generally used. Rosalia was the name given to the yearly ceremony of hanging garlands of roses on the tombs of the dead in ancient Rome. The twelfth century St. Rosalia is the patron saint of Palermo.

ROSALIND
Brought to England at the Norman Conquest, the name was made popular by Shakespeare when he bestowed it upon the courageous and witty heroine of his play *As You Like It.*

The English poet and physician Thomas Lodge (1558–1625) wrote *Rosalind's Madrigal.*

ROSALINDA
From the Spanish, meaning 'like a beautiful rose'.

ROSALINE
A variant of Rosalind, q.v.

ROSAMOND/ROSAMUND
The name was brought to England by the Normans and has remained in use since then.

'Fair Rosamund' Clifford (d. 1176) was the mistress of Henry II. She lived at Woodstock Palace, Oxfordshire; reputedly at the heart of a maze to prevent discovery by the outraged wife, Eleanor of Aquitaine. (The site is now enclosed in the grounds of Blenheim Palace.)

Algernon Charles Swinburne wrote a poem about her, *Rosamond* (1860).

ROSANNA
A conjunction of Rose and Anna, first used in the eighteenth century

and now very popular.

ROSE
From the Old German, meaning 'horse', but now considered purely a floral name. It was brought to England by the Normans, and has always been the most popular of all the flower names. St. Rose of Lima (1586–1617) was the first person in the Americas to be canonised.

A mural containing a pink rose was painted before 1450 B.C. at Knossos, in Crete: the Imperial Chinese had over six hundred books about them before 500 B.C. and the Romans loved them, encircling the heads of newborn babies, statues, tombs and themselves with rose garlands.

Dame Rose Macaulay (1881–1958), the English novelist, is a famous bearer of the name.

ROSEMARY
From the Latin, meaning 'sea dew'. Another of the botanical names which became popular at the end of the nineteenth century.

The plant is the symbol of the Sue Ryder Homes for the sick, founded by Lady Ryder of Warsaw, C.M.G., O.B.E., prompted by the following lines from Shakespeare's *Hamlet*:

'There's rosemary; that's for remembrance;
Pray, love, remember. . .'

ROSEMONDE
French for Rosamond, q.v.

ROSETTA
A variant of Rose, q.v.

ROSETTE
French for Rose, q.v.

ROSIE
A variant of Rose, q.v.

ROSINA
A variant of Rose, q.v.

ROSITA
Spanish for Rose, q.v.

ROSMUNDA
Italian for Rosamund, q.v.

ROWENA
From the Celtic, meaning 'fair'. The name was made popular by Sir Walter Scott in his novel *Ivanhoe* (1819). Wilfred, knight of Ivanhoe, loves Rowena, his father's ward: he finally marries her after rejecting the far more interesting Rebecca.

ROXANA
From the Persian, meaning 'dawn'. Roxana was the Persian wife of Alexander the Great, remembered for stabbing a rival in a fit of violent jealousy.

ROXANE/ROXANNE
Variants of Roxana, q.v.
Roxane is the heroine of *Cyrano de Bergerac*, a play by Edmond Rostand (1868–1918).

ROXIE
A variant of Roxana, q.v., and of Roxanne.

ROZAMUND
Dutch for Rosamond, q.v.

RUBY
From the precious stone, first used by the Victorians in the late nineteenth century. Fine quality rubies are the costliest of all gems, found particularly in Burma.
One of the most renowned jewels owned by the Crown is the Timur ruby, once the property of Tamerlane, conqueror of Afghanistan, India and Persia. It was presented to Queen Victoria after being displayed at the Great Exhibition of 1851.

RUTH
From the Hebrew, meaning 'beloved'. The Old Testament *Book of Ruth* tells the story of its eponymous heroine, daughter-in-law to Naomi and great-grandmother to King David. The name came into use in Britain after the Reformation.
The Pre-Raphaelite painter, Thomas Matthews Rooke (1842–1942), painted *The Story of Ruth* and this can be admired at the Tate Gallery in London.

SABINA
From the Latin, meaning a 'Sabine woman'.

SABINE
German, Dutch and French for Sabina, q.v.

SABRINA
The Latin name for the River Severn. In legend, the daughter of King Locrine and his mistress Estrildis, who was drowned by the jealous Queen Gwendolen.

Sabrina is the nymph who helps the heroine to escape the attentions of Comus in the masque of the same name by John Milton, first performed in Ludlow Castle in 1634.

SADIE
A pet-form of Sarah (q.v.), used as an independent name since the late nineteenth century.

Sadie Thompson is the eponymous flamboyant 'heroine' of a short story by William Somerset Maugham (1874–1965), later successfully dramatised as *Rain.*

SAFFRON
A modern name, taken from the flower or spice. Saffron is the most expensive spice in the world. It takes approximately four thousand flowers to produce a mere 28 grams of it, and all have to be picked by hand.

The Essex town of Saffron Walden once specialised in the growing of saffron crocuses.

SAL
A diminutive of Sally, q.v.

SALLIE
A variant of Sally, q.v.

SALLY
A pet-form of Sarah, used as an independent name since the eighteenth century. The English poet and composer Henry Carey (1687–1743) is remembered for his lengthy ballad, *Sally in Our Alley*:
    'Of all the girls that are so smart
    There's none like pretty Sally;
    She is the darling of my heart,
    And she lives in our alley'.

SAM
A diminutive of Samantha, q.v.

SAMANTHA
A feminine version of Samuel, coined in America in the eighteenth century. The American composer Cole Porter (1893–1964) had a hit with the song *I Love You, Samantha* in the 1950s; while the nose-wriggling witch in the television series *Bewitched* also bore the name. The English actress Samantha Eggar (b. 1939) is well-known.

SANDI
A variant of Sandy, q.v.

SANDIE
A variant of Sandy, q.v.

SANDRA
A diminutive of the Italian Alessandra or Alexandra, now generally used.

SANDY
A pet-form of Sandra, now used independently. The American actress Sandy Dennis (1937–1991) won an Oscar for Best Supporting Actress in the film *Who's Afraid of Virginia Woolf?* in 1966.

SARA
German, French, Italian and Spanish for Sarah, q.v. Now also an

English variant of Sarah. Sara Teasdale (1884–1933), the American lyric-poet, received the Pulitzer Prize for *Love Songs* (1917).

SARAH

From the Hebrew, meaning 'princess'. In the Old Testament she was the wife of Abraham, who gave birth to her son Isaac at the age of ninety and lived to the ripe old age of one hundred and twenty-seven. The Puritans of the seventeenth century made the name a favourite, but it has been used in England since the Middle Ages.

Mrs Sarah Siddons (1755–1831) was the greatest tragic actress of her generation, famous for playing Lady Macbeth and Zara in Congreve's *The Mourning Bride*.

SARI

A variant of Sarah, q.v.

SARITA

A Spanish diminutive of Sarah, now generally used.

SASHA

A Russian pet-form of Alexander, used increasingly for girls in the last few years.

SASKIA

A Dutch name, popular in Britain for the last twenty years. This was the name of the wife of the Dutch painter, Harmensz Rembrandt (1606–1669). Married in 1634, Saskia was his favourite model until her death in 1642: *Self-Portrait with Saskia* (1635), which can be seen in Dresden, is the finest example of this.

SCARLETT

From the vivid red colour, made popular by the heroine of Margaret Mitchell's best-selling (and only) novel *Gone With The Wind* (1936). Vivien Leigh played the beautiful and selfish Scarlett O'Hara in the equally famous film.

SCILLA

A variant of Priscilla, q.v.

SELENA

A variant of Selina, q.v.

SELENE
A variant of Selina, q.v.

SELINA
From the Greek, meaning 'moon', or from the Latin, meaning 'heaven'. In Greek mythology, she was the goddess of the moon who bore two daughters by Zeus, Herse ('dew') and Pandia. Her brother was Helios, the god of the sun. The name has been used in England since the seventeenth century.

Selina, Countess of Huntingdon (1707–1791), devoted all her time and energy to religion and good works after being converted to Methodism in the 1730s.

SELINDA
A variant of Selina, q.v.

SERAPHINA
From the Hebrew, meaning 'ardent'.

SERAPHINE
A variant of Seraphina, q.v.

SERENA
From the Latin, meaning 'calm'. Two early saints bore this name, and it has been used in England since the thirteenth century.

William Hayley (1745–1820), the English poet and biographer, chose Serena as the heroine of his lengthy poem, *The Triumph of Temper.*

SHARI
A variant of Sharon, q.v.

SHARON
A Hebrew place name, meaning 'a plain', which stretches from Jaffa to Caesarea Philippi on the coast of Israel. The Biblical 'Rose of Sharon' is now considered to have been a narcissus. It has been used as a first name in Britain since the mid-twentieth century.

SHEELAH
From the Hebrew, meaning 'petition'.

SHEENA
The anglicised version of the Gaelic name Sine, the Scottish form of

Jane, used generally since the 1950s.

The singer Sheena Easton is a well-known bearer of the name.

SHEILA
The English version of the Irish name Sile, itself a form of Cecilia.

SHELAGH
A variant of Sheila. Shelagh Delaney (b. 1936), the English playwright, had a success with her very first play, *A Taste of Honey*, later made into a film.

SHELLEY
An Old English place name, meaning 'clearing on a plateau', and surname, now used as a first name.

Exclusively masculine in the nineteenth century, it is now bestowed on girls. Perhaps this was prompted by the American film star Shelley Winters who won an Oscar as the best supporting actress in *The Diary of Anne Frank* (1959).

SHEREE
A variant of Charlotte, q.v.

SHERYL
A variant of Shirley, q.v.

SHEVAUN
A variant of Siobhan, q.v.

SHIRL
A diminutive of Shirley, q.v.

SHIRLEY
An Old English place name, meaning 'bright wood', and aristocratic surname, used as a first name since the nineteenth century. It is the surname of the earls Ferrers.

Shirley Keeldar is the heroine of Charlotte Brontë's novel *Shirley* (1849), set in Yorkshire at the end of the Napoleonic Wars.

Shirley Temple (b.1929), the American child star, made the name very popular indeed after her debut in the film *Red Haired Alibi* at the grand old age of three.

SHONA
The anglicised version of the Gaelic name Seonaid, a form of Joan,

used in England since the mid-twentieth century.

SIAN
The Welsh form of Jane, now generally used. The actress Sian Phillips (b.1934) has made the name known.

SIBBY
A variant of Sibyl, q.v.

SIBELLA
A variant of Sibyl, q.v.

SIBYL
From the Greek, meaning 'prophetess'. The ancient world had many sibyls, in Babylonia, Italy, Greece and Egypt. The Sibyl of Cumae sold three books of oracles to Tarquin Superbus, the last king of Rome, which were consulted by the Senate in times of danger. These were destroyed in the great fire which swept Rome during the reign of the tyrant, Nero.

St. Augustine included a sibyl in his great work, *The City of God*, which made it acceptable as a Christian name.

Robert, Duke of Normandy, a son of William the Conqueror, married Sibylla and she introduced the name to England. Dame Sybil Thorndike (1882–1976), the English actress, remains the best-known modern bearer of the name.

SIBYLLA
Dutch for Sibyl, q.v.

SIBYLLE
German and French for Sibyl, q.v.

SIENA
From the Italian city, used as a first name since the nineteenth century. The ancient, originally Etruscan, city is famous for its magnificent collection of art treasures and its famous 'Palio', held in August. The citizens parade in medieval costume and compete in a horse race through the narrow winding streets.

SILVANA
A variant of Sylvia (q.v.) and Silvia.

SILVIA
A variant of Sylvia, q.v.

SILVIE
French for Sylvia, q.v.

SIMONA
A variant of Simone, q.v.

SIMONE
The French feminine form of Simon, meaning 'snub-nosed'. The French character actress Simone Signoret, who won an Oscar for best actress in the film *Room at the Top* (1958), made the name known world-wide.

SINEAD
The Gaelic form of Janet, now increasing in popularity generally.

SIOBHAN
A Gaelic name, an Irish version of Joan, widely favoured in recent years.

SIS
A variant of Cecilia, q.v.

SOFIE
French, Dutch and Danish for Sophie, q.v., now widely used in the U.K.

SONIA
The Russian pet-form of Sophia, used in Britain since the early twentieth century.

SONJA
Russian and Scandinavian for Sophie, a variant of Sophia (q.v.).

SONYA
A variant of Sonia, q.v.

Sonya Marmeladova is the heroine of Dostoyevski's masterpiece, *Crime and Punishment* (1866). Forced into crime to support her father, stepmother and their small children, she urges Raskolnikov to confess to the murder he has committed and accompanies him when he is sentenced to exile in Siberia.

SOPHIA
From the Greek, meaning 'wisdom'. The name of a number of early Christian martyrs, the great church in Istanbul called St. Sophia is dedicated to Holy Wisdom. The name has been used in Britain since the seventeenth century. There is a touching monument to Princess Sophia, who was born the youngest daughter of James I in 1607 and lived for only one day, in Westminster Abbey. The baby is sculpted asleep in her cradle.

Countess Sophia Chotek married Archduke Franz Ferdinand of Austria in 1900. Their assassination in 1914 precipitated the First World War.

SOPHIE
A variant of Sophia, q.v.

STACEY
A modern pet-form of Anastasia (q.v.), used since the 1970s.

STASIA
A variant of Anastasia, q.v.

STEFFI
A variant of Stephanie, q.v.

STEFFIE
A variant of Stephanie, q.v.

STELLA
From the Latin, meaning 'star'. Sir Philip Sidney loved Lady Penelope Devereux and celebrated her under the name of Stella in his sonnet series *Astrophel and Stella* (1591). The name has been used in Britain since the Middle Ages, originally in honour of the Blessed Virgin under her title 'Stella Maris' (Star of the Sea).

STEPHANIE
The French feminine form of Stephen (q.v.), used in Britain since the early twentieth century.

STEVIE
A modern feminine version of Steven. The English poet Stevie Smith (1902–1971), whose real name was Florence Margaret Smith, is best remembered for her poem *Not Waving But Drowning*.

STORM

From the term for a wind force of 10 on the Beaufort scale, used in the twentieth century as a first name.

The novelist Storm Jameson, who often set her stories in Yorkshire, is well-known.

SUE

A variant of Susan, Susanna (q.v.), Susannah and Suzanne.

SUKEY

An old name for Susan, variant of Susanna (q.v.).

SUSAN

A variant of Susanna, q.v.

SUSANNA

From the Hebrew, meaning 'lily'. Mentioned in the New Testament as one of the women who gave assistance to the disciples, it is best known through the Apocryphal Susanna who was surprised by the Elders as she was bathing and falsely accused of adultery. The name has been used in England since the thirteenth century. Shakespeare gave the name to his eldest daughter, born in 1583.

SUSANNAH

A variant of Susanna, q.v.

SUSANNE

German and French for Susan, variant of Susanna (q.v.).

SUZANNE

A variant of Susanna, q.v.

SUZIE

A variant of Susanna, q.v.

SYBIL

A variant of Sibyl, q.v.

SYLVIA

From the Latin, meaning 'wood'. Rhea Silvia was the mother of Romulus and Remus, the founders of Rome in 753 B.C.

In Shakespeare's play *Two Gentlemen of Verona*, Silvia is the beautiful daughter of the Duke of Milan, who finally marries

Valentine. The use of the name in Britain appears to have stemmed from this. (A picture entitled *Valentine Rescuing Sylvia from Proteus* (1851) by William Holman Hunt hangs in the Birmingham City Art Gallery.)

If you are a ballet fan you will think of Delibes's *Sylvia* (1876), the heroine of which is beloved by Amynta.

SYLVIE
A variant of Sylvia, q.v.

SYRIE
A feminine form of Cyril, from the Greek meaning 'lord'. It is best remembered as the name of the wife of the writer William Somerset Maugham. She swept away the fussiness of décor in the twenties and thirties and began the craze for white paint and austere furnishings. The name is now enjoying a revival.

TABITHA
From the Aramaic, meaning 'gazelle'. In the New Testament, Tabitha was a woman full of good works who became ill and died. The Christians of Lydda sent for St. Peter who, after prayer to God, raised her to life. (Dorcas is the Greek equivalent of the name.) The Puritans of the seventeenth century began its use in Britain.

On a less rarified level, Beatrix Potter created Tabitha Twitchit, the long-suffering mother of the naughty Tom Kitten.

TALIA
A variant of Thalia, q.v.

TALLULAH

From the American Indian place name, meaning 'running water'. Tallulah Falls is a notable beauty spot in the American state of Georgia.

The name was brought to prominence by the actress Tallulah Bankhead (1903–1968), who was named after her grandmother.

TAMARA

The Russian version of an Old Testament name 'Tamar', meaning 'palm tree'; the granddaughter of King David, she was noted for her beauty. It has been used in Britain since the 1950s.

The Russian composer Mily Balakirev (1837–1910), inspired by Lermentov's poem, wrote a piece of music entitled *Tamara*. This dealt with a beautiful Caucasian princess who lured her victims to a violent death. It later became a ballet.

Tamara Karsavina (1885–1978), the legendary Russian ballerina and teacher, a member of Diaghilev's Ballet Russe, married an Englishman and settled in England. A commemorative blue plaque has been placed on her home at 108 Frognal, London NW3.

TAMMIE

A diminutive of Tamara, q.v.

TAMMY

A diminutive of Tamara, q.v.

TAMSIN

The Cornish pet-form of the medieval Thomasin, a now obsolete feminine form of Thomas.

Tasmin is a modern variation. The violinist Tasmin Little has brought the name to public attention.

TANIA

A variant of Tatiana, q.v.

TANSY

From the flower, derived from the Greek 'athanasia', meaning 'immortality'. The pretty yellow, button-like flowers and aromatic leaves were used in the sixteenth century as a medicinal herb, or strewn upon the floor to scent the air. It became popular as a first name in the twentieth century.

TANYA
A variant of Tatiana, q.v.

TARA
An Irish place name, used as a first name since the late nineteenth century. The kings, princes and bards of Ireland met at a castle on the hill of Tara, in Co. Meath, to decide on matters of public importance. Thomas Moore (1779–1852) included the song *The Harp That Once Through Tara's Halls* in his *Irish Melodies*. (It is also the name of Scarlett O'Hara's home and estate in *Gone With The Wind*.)

TASHA
A variant of Natasha, q.v.

TASMIN
A variant of Tamsin, q.v.

TATIANA
A Russian name, used as a first name in Britain since the early twentieth century. St. Tatiana was martyred in Rome c.288.
Grand Duchess Tatiana (1897–1918), second daughter of Tsar Nicholas II, was murdered by Bolsheviks in the cellar at Ekaterinburg, together with all her family.

TAYLOR
An occupational surname, now used as a first name by both girls and boys. The English-born American novelist Taylor Caldwell is best remembered for *Dear and Glorious Physician* (1959).

TERESA
From the Greek, meaning 'to reap'. St. Teresa of Avila (1515–1582), reformer of the Carmelites and mystic, and St. Theresa of Lisieux (1873–1897), who became a saint by doing ordinary things extraordinarily well, made the name very popular. It has been used in England since the eighteenth century. A modern bearer of the name was Mother Teresa of Calcutta (1910–1997), the Albanian foundress of the Missionaries of Charity.

TERI
A variant of Teresa, q.v.

TERRY
A variant of Teresa, q.v.

TESS

A variant of Tessa (variant of Teresa, q.v.).

TESSA

A variant of Teresa, q.v.

THALIA

In Greek mythology one of the nine Muses, daughters of Zeus and Mnemosyne. Thalia is the muse of comedy, represented in art as holding a comic mask and a shepherd's crook.

THEA

A variant of Theodora (q.v.) and of Althea (q.v.).

THELMA

This was invented by the best-selling writer Marie Corelli (1855–1924), for the Norwegian heroine of *Thelma: a society novel* (1887).

THEODORA

From the Greek, meaning 'divine gift', the feminine form of Theodore. Theodora (500–548), the beautiful wife of the Byzantine Emperor Justinian I, was notorious before her marriage as an actress and dancer. She became empress in 527. The name came into use in Britain in the seventeenth century.

THERESA

A variant of Teresa, q.v.

THOMASINA

The medieval feminine form of Thomas (q.v.), revived in the mid-nineteenth century.

THORA

This name is derived from Thor, the Norse god of thunder.

TIFFANY

From the Greek, meaning 'manifestation of God'. The name was originally given to girls born on the 6th January, the feast of the Epiphany, when the three Kings brought their gifts to the Infant Jesus. The film *Breakfast at Tiffany's* (1961), starring Audrey Hepburn, made the name very popular and was a good advertisement for the eponymous New York jeweller's shop.

(It was also the name of a material. The first hot-air balloon, made by Monsieur Testu, rose up from Paris in 1786. It was made of glazed tiffany and sported wings.)

TILLY
A variant of Matilda, q.v.

TINA
The modern pet-form of Christina, now used independently. The American singer Tina Turner (born Annie Mae Bullock) is well-known for the songs *River Deep Mountain High* and *What's Love Got To Do With It?*

TONI
A variant of Antonia, q.v.

TONIA
A variant of Antonia, q.v.

TONYA
A variant of Antonia, q.v.

TRACEY
A variant of Tracy, q.v.

TRACY
The French place name and surname, used as a first name since the beginning of the nineteenth century.

It was originally bestowed on boys, but is now considered exclusively feminine. The film *High Society* (1956), in which Grace Kelly starred as the heiress Tracy Samantha Lord, was responsible for its great popularity.

TRIXIE
A variant of Beatrice, q.v.

TRUDIE
A variant of Trudy, q.v.

TRUDY
A pet-form of Gertrude (q.v.), now used independently.

ULRICA
A feminine form of Ulric, meaning 'wolf's ruler'.

UNA
From the Latin, meaning 'one' or an anglicised version of the Irish name Oonagh. Una is the heroine of the first part of Edmund Spenser's allegorical epic poem, *The Faerie Queene* (1596). After interminable misfortunes, including a rampaging dragon, she is married to the Red Cross Knight.

The actress and television personality Una Stubbs (b. 1937) is a well-known bearer of the name.

URSOLA
Spanish for Ursula, q.v.

URSULA
From the Latin, meaning 'she-bear'. This has been used in England since the Middle Ages, prompted by devotion to St. Ursula. She was reputedly the daughter of a British king, martyred with her eleven thousand companions by Huns at Cologne.

Ursula March is the heroine of Mrs Craik's classic novel *John Halifax, Gentleman* (1856).

URSULE
French for Ursula, q.v.

VAL
A diminutive of Valerie, q.v.

VALDA
From the Scandinavian, meaning a 'ruler'.

VALENTIA
A variant of Valentina, q.v.

VALENTINA
From the Latin, meaning 'strong'.

VALERIA
Italian for Valerie, q.v.

VALERIE
The feminine form of Valerius, derived from the Latin 'strong', the name of an ancient Roman family. It came to Britain from France in the late nineteenth century.

VANESSA
This was invented by the clergyman, satirist and poet Jonathan Swift (1667–1745), being a partial anagram of the name of his friend, Esther Vanhomrigh. She is the heroine of his poem *Cadenus and Vanessa* (1713).

The actress Vanessa Redgrave is a well-known bearer of the name.

VANGIE
A variant of Evangeline, q.v.

VANIA
A variant of Vanessa, q.v.

VASHTI
From the Persian, meaning 'beautiful'. In the Bible Queen Vashti was the wife of King Asaheurus.

VELDA
A variant of Valda, q.v.

VENETIA
The Latin form of the city of Venice, used as a first name since the sixteenth century. The noted beauty Venetia Stanley married Sir Kenelm Digby in 1625. She was reputed to drink viper wine to preserve her looks; perhaps that is why she died at the early age of thirty-three. Her husband never shaved again, which is an unusual way to express grief, while Ben Jonson and many other poets mourned her in verse.

VERA
From the Russian, meaning 'faith'. The name was popularised by its use in several novels published in the nineteenth century, notably *Moths* (1880) by the sensational English novelist Ouida (Marie Louise de la Ramée).

Dame Vera Lynn, the singer notable as 'The Forces' Sweetheart' in the Second World War, must always spring to mind.

VERITY
From the abstract noun meaning 'truth', first used by the Puritans of the seventeenth century.

VERONICA
From the Latin, meaning 'true image'. St. Veronica was reputed to have wiped the face of Christ with a cloth as he suffered on the way to crucifixion. An image of his features remained on the material.

The name has been popular in Scotland since the seventeenth century, but was not used in England until the nineteenth.

VICKIE
A variant of Victoria, q.v.

VICKY
A variant of Victoria, q.v.

VICTORIA
From the Latin, meaning 'victory'. Queen Victoria (1819–1901), christened Alexandrina Victoria, was solely responsible for bringing the name into favour. Her influence was incalculable; she gave her name among other things to cities, railway stations, fruit and a military medal, while her outlook characterised most of the nineteenth century. She was survived by six of her nine children, forty grandchildren and thirty great-grandchildren. Her statue in Kensington Gardens was the work of her daughter, Princess Louise.

VIDA
The pet-form of Davida, used independently since the mid-nineteenth century. (It is also the Spanish for 'life'.)

VIKKY
A variant of Victoria, q.v.

VILHELMINA
Swedish for Wilhelmina, q.v.

VILMA
A variant of Wilhelmina, q.v.

VIOLA
From the Latin, meaning 'violet'. Shakespeare bestowed the name on the heroine of his play, *Twelfth Night.* She disguises herself as a boy and becomes a page to Duke Orsino, whom she later marries. This character made the name a favourite.

Viola is the title of the last, unfinished opera of the Czech composer Bedrich Smetana (1824–1884).

VIOLANTE
Spanish for Violet, q.v.

VIOLE
French for Violet, q.v.

VIOLET
From the flower name, used in Britain since the Middle Ages.

VIOLETTA
Italian for Violet, q.v.

VIOLETTE
French for Violet, also used in the U.K.

The Londoner Violette Szabo (née Bushell) (1921-1945) worked as a secret agent in France during the Second World War. Captured, tortured and executed, she was posthumously awarded the George Cross for bravery. Virginia McKenna portrayed her in the film *Carve Her Name With Pride* (1958).

VIRGINIA
From the Latin feminine form of Virginius, the name of an ancient Roman family. The French novel by Bernardin de Saint-Pierre, entitled *Paul et Virginie* (1787), made the name a favourite.

The first English child born in America in August 1587 was named Virginia Dare but she vanished mysteriously, together with the remainder of her colony. The reason has never been established.

VIRGINIE
Dutch and French for Virginia, q.v.

VITORIA
Spanish for Victoria, q.v.

VITTORIA
Italian for Victoria, q.v.

VIV
A variant of Vivien, q.v.

VIVIANA
A variant of Vivien, q.v.

VIVIEN
The feminine form of Vivian, made popular by Alfred, Lord Tennyson in his poem *Vivien and Merlin* (1859). The magician Merlin fell in love with the beautiful Vivien, Lady of the Lake. She turned his magic against him and imprisoned him in a castle of air, from which he could not escape.

VIVIENNE
A variant of Vivien, q.v.

WANDA
From the Old German, meaning 'a young shoot'. A novel entitled *Wanda* (1883) by Ouida brought the name to public attention.

WENDY
The name was invented by the writer J.M. Barrie. He had a young friend named Margaret Henley, who called him 'friendy' and then 'friendy-wendy'. Margaret died very young, and Barrie called the heroine of *Peter Pan* (1904), his most famous play, 'Wendy' in her memory.

(Incidentally, Margaret's one-legged father was the model for Long John Silver in *Treasure Island* by R.L. Stevenson. Surely a unique literary father and daughter!)

WHITNEY
From the Old English, meaning 'white island'. A place name and sur-name, now used as a first name.

The American singer Whitney Houston (b.1964) is well-known. Mount Whitney, in Southern California, is the highest mountain in the U.S.A.

WILHELMINA
From the Teutonic, meaning 'bold protector'.

WILHELMINE
Danish for Wilhelmina, q.v.

WILLA
A pet-form of the German name Wilhelmina, now used independently. Willa Cather (1873–1947), the American writer, is best

remembered for *Youth and the Bright Medusa* and *Death Comes For the Archbishop*.

WILMA
A variant of Wilhelmina, q.v.

WINIFRED
From the Welsh, meaning 'blessed reconciliation'. The seventh century St. Winifred was beheaded by Prince Caradoc for refusing to marry him. Restored to life by St. Beuno, a spring of water appeared where her head had fallen. She lived the rest of her life as a nun in Denbighshire. Pilgrimages to St. Winifred's Well, Clywd, still take place today.

Winifred Ashton was the real name of the English playwright and novelist Clemence Dane (1888–1965).

WINNIE
A variant of Winifred, q.v.

WYNN
From the Welsh, meaning 'fair'. Used as a first name since the mid-twentieth century.

XANTHE
From the Greek, meaning 'yellow', so it is particularly suitable for a child with fair hair.

XENIA
From the Greek, meaning 'hospitality' or 'stranger'. In Greek mythology a Sicilian cowherd named Daphnis, son of a nymph and the inventor of pastoral poetry, wasted away with unrequited love for a princess named Xenia.

YASMIN
A variant of Jasmine, q.v.

YOLANDE
A medieval French name, from the Greek meaning 'violet flower', used in Britain since the early twentieth century.

YOLANTHE
A variant of Yolande, q.v.

YOUNICE
A variant of Eunice, q.v.

YSABEL
Spanish for Elizabeth, q.v.

YSEULT
From the Welsh, meaning 'one who is fair'.

YSOBEL
A variant of Isobel (variant of Isabella, q.v.).

YVETTE
The French feminine form of Ivo (q.v.), brought to England at the Norman Conquest.

YVONNE
Another French feminine form of Ivo (q.v.), meaning 'yew wood'. This has been used in Britain since the twentieth century; perhaps prompted by the Canadian actress Yvonne de Carlo (born Peggy Middleton), who is best-remembered as Lily in *The Munsters*.

ZANDRA
A variant of Sandra, q.v. The British dress designer Zandra Rhodes (b.1940), whose clothes and character are larger than life, keeps the name in the public eye.

ZARA
From the Arabic, meaning 'brightness of the dawn'. The Yorkshire-born dramatist William Congreve (1670–1729) included an African queen with this name in his tragedy, *The Mourning Bride* (1697).

The Princess Royal helped to make this a modern favourite when she bestowed it on her daughter, born in 1981.

ZELDA
A modern pet-form of Griselda, now independently used. Zelda Fitzgerald (1899–1948), wife of the American writer F. Scott Fitzgerald, whose tragic life reads like one of his novels, is well-known.

ZELIE
A French name, meaning 'ardent', now generally used.

ZELMA
This name comes from the Old Norse Anselm.

ZENA
A variation of Xenia (q.v.), used regularly in Britain. Zena Dare (1887–1975) was a notable British beauty and actress.

ZETA
The sixth letter of the Greek alphabet, but probably a variation of Zita

(q.v.). The Welsh actress Catherine Zeta Jones has brought the name to public notice.

ZILLA
A variant of Zillah, q.v.

ZILLAH
From the Hebrew, meaning 'shadow'. The Old Testament Zillah was married to Lamech, a descendant of Cain, and was the mother of Tubal-Cain. The name came into use in England after the Reformation, when non-Biblical names were abandoned.

ZILPAH
From the Hebrew, meaning 'sprinkling'. The Old Testament Zilpah was Leah's maid. When Leah believed herself to be past childbearing age, she gave Zilpah to her husband, Jacob, as a concubine. Two sons, Gad and Asher, were born of their union. The name came into use after the Reformation.

ZILPHA
A variant of Zilpah, q.v.

ZITA
From the Greek, meaning 'to seek'. St. Zita (1218–1278) was a servant in one household from the age of twelve. Her lavish gifts of food to the poor and punctiliousness in her work did not endear her to her fellow workers, but she is the patron saint of domestic servants. The name has been used in Britain since the late nineteenth century.

Zita (d. 1989) is remembered as the last Hapsburg Empress. She and her husband, Emperor Charles, abdicated on 11th November 1918.

ZOË
A Greek translation of Eve, meaning 'life'. It was popular with the early Christians and the name of a martyr of the third century. Not used in Britain until the nineteenth century, it has become a favourite.

ZORA
From the Arabic, meaning 'dawn'.

ZSA-ZSA
Hungarian for Susan (variant of Susanna, q.v.).

BIBLIOGRAPHY

Friedman, Bill. *Casino Management.* New York: Lyle Stuart, 1979.

———— *Designing Casinos to Dominate the Competition: The Friedman International Standards of Casino Design.* Reno: Institute for the Study of Gambling & Commercial Gaming, University of Nevada, 2000.

Fussell, Paul. *Class: A Guide Through the American Status System.* New York: Summit, 1983.

Goldberg, David A. *Stupidity and Slot Machine Players in Las Vegas.* Frederick, Md.: PublishAmerican, 2006.

Peterson, Ivars. *The Jungles of Randomness: A Mathematical Safari.* New York: John Wiley & Sons, 1998.

Wolfram, Stephen. *A New Kind of Science.* Champaign, Ill.:, Wolfram Media, Inc., 2002.

Michael Forrest

When Fortune smiles.
Model: Lynne Stetson.